Sport, Leisure and Culture In Twentieth-Century Britain

Sport, Leisure and Culture In Twentieth-Century Britain

JEFFREY HILL

palgrave

First published 2002 by
PALGRAVE
Houndmills, Basingstoke, Hampshire RG21 6XS and
175 Fifth Avenue, New York, N.Y. 10010
Companies and representatives throughout the world

PALGRAVE is the new global academic imprint of
St. Martin's Press LLC Scholarly and Reference Division and
Palgrave Publishers Ltd (formerly Macmillan Press Ltd).

ISBN 0–333–72686–3 hardback
ISBN 0–333–72687–1 paperback

This book is printed on paper suitable for recycling and
made from fully managed and sustained forest sources.

A catalogue record for this book is available
from the British Library.

Library of Congress cataloging-in-Publication Data

Hill, Jeff, 1943–
    Sport, leisure, and culture in twentieth-century Britain /
Jeffrey Hill.
        p.   cm.
    Includes bibliographical references and index.
    ISBN 0–333–72686–3 (cloth)
    1. Sports—Social aspects—Great Britain—History—20th
century.   2. Leisure—Social aspects—Great Britain—History—
20th century.   3. Great Britain—Social life and customs—
20th century.   I. Title.
GV706.5   .H55   2001
306.4'812–dc21

Transferred to digital printing 2003

Printed and bound in Great Britain by
Antony Rowe Ltd, Chippenham and Eastbourne

For Mary

Contents

Acknowledgements

This book was written over the course of three springs and two summers between 1999 and 2001. Its gestation, however, has stretched over a much longer period. During this time, which goes back to the early 1990s, I have benefited from advice, discussion and support from a number of sources: colleagues and students at Nottingham Trent University, especially those involved in one way or another in the modules *Popular Culture and Society in Europe, 1900–1950, Sport and Leisure in Britain Since 1945* and *Society, Culture, Economy: Britain Since 1940*; friends and associates of the MA Sport seminar at De Montfort University, Leicester, whom I thank for several invitations to attend their stimulating group; members and friends of the British Society of Sports History and North American Society for Sport History, whose advice and comments on my work have often been incisive and always constructive; and, once the draft chapters of this book began to appear, a group of historians and friends who have kindly read sections and given me the benefit of their knowledge and judgement – Mike Cronin, Tina Parratt, Nick Hayes and Gary Moses. Ian and Lesley Inkster were most generous with their hospitality in London; and, finally, my Dean, Stephen Chan, provided in ways of which he probably isn't fully aware the encouragement I needed to keep going in the midst of other cares.

In spite of its title this is not a comprehensive history of sport and leisure in twentieth-century Britain. So vast a topic, even with a publisher's liberal wordage, would be impossible to encompass in a single volume. What follows is an attempt to deal with some of what I see as the more important aspects of sport and leisure during this period. With such an approach there will inevitably be much subjectivity over what is 'important', and, equally inevitably, there will be many who claim that what has been left out is more significant than what has been included. All books which adopt a broad topic in a long sweep run this risk. Richard Holt, whose magisterial *Sport and the British* has been an inspiriation to me as to many others, recognized this when he said, quite simply, 'it is impossible to give each sport the space it deserves . . .'. The best an author can do is to construct a framework that tries to cover some of the main themes. Topics of varying importance thus fail to appear. I apologize to Gary Moses that carp keeping, about which he informed me in some detail during a stroll around Amsterdam, does not get a mention. Its time will come, unfortunately. Not much is said about the more significant activity of shopping as a leisure pastime, and I can only plead that the subject is treated better than I could ever hope to do by John Benson in *The Rise of Consumer Society* and Bill Lancaster in *The Department Store*.

Thanks, too, are due to Terka Bagley and all the people involved in the production process at the publisher (which I must now learn to call 'Palgrave'), especially the anonymous reader whose comments were most instructive. And to the librarians of the British Library, Nottingham University Library, and to those of Library and Information Services at Nottingham Trent University, where most of the work was done, especially Karen Roberts of the inter-library loans service. Finally, thanks to Tim Hill for helping to compile a bibliography from which the final section of the book is composed.

Nottingham, May 2001.

chapter 1

Introduction: 'Free Time' in the Twentieth Century

A common justification for writing a new book is that it covers a 'neglected' field. This could scarcely be said of a book on sport and leisure. Over the past couple of decades in Britain there has been an immense outpouring of work on sport alone, so much so that there is now a strong case for regarding the study of sport as a distinct sub-branch of the discipline of history.[1] Leisure has likewise attracted much attention, and from a wider range of disciplines. Social surveys of the late twentieth century constantly reveal an increasing though unevenly spread involvement of the population in leisure activities.[2] Phrases such as 'leisure society' and the more dramatic 'leisure revolution' are uttered time and again. Yet for all this, there is a sense in which the subjects still exist on the margins of academic discourse. Many historians have been unwilling to bring them into the mainstream.[3] Work on sport and leisure finds little space in the major journals[4], and few general histories accord them a prime place. They have either been spatchcocked into a final chapter, or relegated to a subsidiary theme. Thus, even the former football-playing Arthur Marwick paid scant regard to sport in his authoritative *British Society Since 1945*, though he did give rather more attention to the larger field of leisure.[5] No doubt such an emphasis is pragmatically forced on authors by publishers' constraints, but it none the less suggests an order of priority in which the turn of sport and leisure comes only when the more important aspects of society – the 'proper' history – have been dealt with. The emergence of the undeniably vigorous and extensive historiography of sport and leisure has tended, paradoxically, to reinforce this process. The existence of detailed work has absolved those historians who do not have a specialist interest in the field of the need to incorporate the subjects into the mainstream.[6] A division of labour has therefore resulted, the choice often being between social history with the sport left out, or sports history with the politics, society and economy left out.[7]

Whichever variant is chosen, a common tendency is observed. This is to regard sport and leisure as processes 'shaped', or even 'determined', by economic, political, demographic, intellectual and other forces. Sport and leisure emerge in this way as social activities which have their existence only as by-products of other, *prior* developments. A clear example of this is the study of the influences that account for the emergence during the second half of the nineteenth century of association football as the 'people's game'. Several studies of this process have now established beyond any doubt that it was a combination of changes in work patterns, transport, business organization and the communications media that enabled association football to take the form it did. Such an approach is helpful, enabling us to understand how the process of modernization affected sport, but it stops short of according any autonomous agency to sport itself. The history of sport becomes a 'window' through which to study developments in other areas of society.[8]

The present volume attempts to strike out in a new direction; or at least to point a different path that future historians might take in traversing these fields. The book's 'big idea' is that sport and leisure are processes which themselves have a determining influence over people's lives. Far from being marginal, things which at most have only 'entertainment' value, they have a pervasive influence which students of society ignore to their disadvantage. The practices and texts of sport and leisure exist not simply as something shaped by other forces, but as cultural agencies with a power to work on their participants and consumers ideologically. In other words, they are processes from which we derive *meaning*. In their manifold activities are inscribed and structured habits of thought and behaviour which contribute to our ways of seeing ourselves and others, to a making sense of our social relationships, and to the piecing together of some notion of what we call 'society'. Features as diverse as gender, nationalism, hero-worship, bodily exercise and commercialism are all produced and re-produced through, among other things, sport and leisure. Such an approach is not new, though it has been applied more readily in the area of leisure studies than in that of sports history. Thorstein Veblen's *Theory of the Leisure Class*, published at the very end of the nineteenth century, first drew attention to the idea that leisure had a symbolic value, that the importance of leisure activity lay as much in how it was seen to be conducted as in what constituted it, and that the reproducing of power relations was closely connected to this process.[9] It is this last point that has sustained leisure studies through many manifestations since Veblen, whose notion of conspicuous leisure consumption and its symbolic significance finds echoes in the work of several contemporary (and mainly French) theorists. Roland Barthes, Pierre Bourdieu, Jacques Derrida and Jean Baudrillard have each in their own distinctive way formed a connection between leisure and social meaning, producing a hermeneutical analysis which 'reads' the texts and practices of leisure and sport activities to discern the ideological significance (the 'meaning') they communicate in society generally.[10]

It is a method also to be found in the cultural anthropology of the American Clifford Geertz, whose work connects with much of the 'postmodern' methodology from which some of the perspectives in the present book take their cue.[11] Though they differ in several ways, this quintet of writers none the less shares a belief in the importance of 'signification'. Geertz has, perhaps, expressed this the most eloquently: 'the concept of culture I espouse . . . is essentially a semiotic one. Believing, with Max Weber, that man is an animal suspended in webs of significance he himself has spun, I take culture to be those webs, and the analysis of it to be therefore not an experimental science in search of law, but an interpretive one in search of meaning.'[12] In the postmodern paradigm to which each of these writers subscribes, the certainties about 'knowing' the world and achieving a purchase on 'objective' reality, certainties that characterised the 'modernist' epistemology which developed out of the scientific revolution of the seventeenth century, have dissolved into a less determinate world, in which the relationship between subject and object is blurred and in which meanings shift and change: a world of 'signs about signs', where language plays a constitutive role in giving us the capacity for thought. Rather than being something which *expresses* our thoughts, language, both written and visual, actually shapes our understanding of the world, and the languages of sport and leisure are especially significant because they reach so many.[13] In the last analysis, sport and leisure are important not simply because they give pleasure to millions (though anything that achieves this status in social life should willy-nilly be the concern of the social historian), but because they contribute crucially to this process of 'knowing' the world, in so far as it is possible to know it at all.

To this eclectic ensemble of philosophical postmodernism should be added a sixth intellectual influence, that of Antonio Gramsci. Gramscian theory has exercised such a profound hold on British cultural studies that it is almost impossible to ignore it when considering any processes that form part of the 'cultural', and sport and leisure certainly do that.[14] In Gramsci's work there are many variations and subtleties, stemming in part from the coded vocabulary of a thinker and activist of the left whose major writing was mostly done in a fascist prison. But two over-riding features help to inform the present volume. One is Gramsci's idea of civil society, that constellation of voluntary associations and organizations separate from the state through which so much of social life is organized.[15] Civil society is a major site of sport and leisure activity and ranges from the most local and amateur forms to the most commercialized and professional, taking in the various agencies that disseminate ideas of sport and leisure. Added to this is Gramsci's emphasis on power and power relations. It is, I feel, sometimes not emphasized sufficiently that Gramsci was peculiarly interested in styles of political leadership – how power and leadership were exercised, and how these styles changed according to changing historical circumstances.[16] The importance of sport in this respect has been clearly articulated by John Hargreaves, and the present volume simply underlines Hargreaves' insistence on treating sport (and leisure) as processes that contribute to relations of power.[17] The emphasis here, however, falls rather more than it does in Hargreaves's work on the ideological processes in sport and leisure that are present in civil society; where Hargreaves casts ideology as 'misrepresentation' (a variant of the old Marxist notion of 'false consciousness') I regard it less conspiratorially as 'knowledge formation', a process of 'knowing' and 'understanding' in which sport and leisure are intimately implicated. Thus Gramsci, writing long before 'postmodernism' was invented, none the less takes his place as a postmodernist *avant la lettre*. Ultimately, he seems to be saying, if modern democratic societies are to be changed (and this is a process that will only happen if human beings decide it should happen), what needs first of all to be challenged in a long-term 'war of position' are the meanings and understanding of life and power constructed in civil society. If we want to change society, we need therefore to engage culturally as well as politically with the status quo.[18]

In terms of its range, the present book attempts to mark out a big field. In this respect it does take on a neglected area. It picks up and extends themes already explored in previous work. Martin Polley, for example, has covered a broad span of sporting activity in relation to the second half of the twentieth century, though his study does not address itself specifically to the problem of leisure. Richard Holt's history of sport in Britain, like those of Birley, Brailsford and Wigglesworth, begins in the eighteenth century and carries the analysis almost to the end of the twentieth.[19] It is the best history of this subject, and is likely to remain so for some time to come.[20] But like Polley, neither Holt nor the others include the wider aspects of leisure. It is a gap the present book seeks to bridge, if not to fill.

Such an objective calls for a particular form of organization. None can claim to be all-inclusive. What is needed is a method that captures the main processes through which sport and leisure operate. Both are activities of a very wide ranging nature affected by a number of changing chronological contexts, social pressures and geographical variations. Some features, however, remain constant, and it is these constants that provide the basis of the following chapters. A thematic structure, organized around analytical tools that have become the stock-in-trade of social historians – class, gender, race, ethnicity, age – has some attractions. But such an approach was rejected because, in spite of its many virtues, it tends to offer an over-classified format which militates against the interactions and totality of sport and leisure. Instead, an approach was adopted which, I felt, better enabled the primary focus on sport and leisure to be integrated with wider social history. This is a similarly thematic approach, but one which directs attention to the various agencies through which sport and leisure activities are created and developed. The principal ones, which constitute the main sections of this book, are the *commercial* sector, in which leisure provision is created for sale in a business/market context to leisure-users who are 'consumers'; the *voluntary* sector, characterized by the fashioning by people themselves of their own leisure activities, though not always in conditions of their own making; and the *state* sector, where national or local state agencies take an interest or responsibility for leisure, either because of concern over the general well-being of the population or for more 'political' reasons.

For this framework the book owes something to Gramsci's notions of 'civil society' and 'state', and much to the work of Stephen G. Jones, a historian whose achievement and promise in the realm of sport and leisure during the 1980s was cut short by a tragically early death. Jones, who arrived at sport from a background in economic history, first drew attention to the main 'sectors' (as he described them) through which sport and leisure provision becomes available.[21] His model has a functional simplicity. In seeing leisure as a 'provision' it identifies those channels through which the provision is made. But instead of seeing the provision as simply an economic 'good', whose existence is regarded virtually as pre-ordained, the operation of the model by Jones himself allowed for the interplay of various energies and interests. The multifarious aspects of sport and leisure in the twentieth century are handled in a way that incorporates the tensions and negotitions that arise when the social historian's key explanatory tools are applied.

As with all models there are limitations. Influences such as private patronage and company paternalism, important in some instances in twentieth-century Britain, are missing as independent 'sectors', their exclusion defended only by reasons of space and the fact that, by comparison with the main sectors of provision, their place has been a relatively peripheral one.[22] The model is also limited in its universality. It applies best to the twentieth century, and is less readily transposable either to earlier periods, or to other countries. But the most important limitation is the model's mechanistic nature. The 'reality' of the situation the model is designed to analyse is one in which there is no clear-cut distinction between commercial, voluntary and state sectors; in fact, there is a great deal of overlap between them in the form of an endless circularity of influences in all directions. But in spite of this, the model offers an analytical framework which distinguishes the main pathways of sport and leisure development. Providing it is not slavishly applied it will afford a useful frame of reference for what follows. In all this I follow Marwick's lead in his work on war and social change. Having elaborated his by-now famous four-tier model of the relationship between war and social change Marwick plans his escape route: 'though I see the model as playing a central organising and explanatory role, I leave the exact shape of each chapter to be determined by the historical reality as I perceive it'.[23]

DEFINING TERMS: 'LEISURE'

Some of the most problematical themes of the present discussion are contained in the title: 'sport', 'leisure', 'culture', 'Britain' and 'twentieth century'. As an introduction to what follows, a consideration of these themes will form the remainder of this chapter.

'Leisure', within which the more finite concept of sport can be placed, provides a good point at which to begin. Leisure covers a multiplicity of activities, from sitting at home watching television to circumnavigating the globe in a small boat. To render down this vast range of pursuits to a manageable concept, it has been customary to attribute to them a single common feature: they can all be defined as having no 'use' value. In other words, leisure equates with activities that provide personal satisfaction and pleasure, rather than things done for use. Thus, for example, the various hobbies involving collecting – stamps, coins, football programmes, knitting patterns – are 'leisure' to the extent that they remain activities which in themselves give pleasure; beyond that, when the items collected begin to have a further use – collecting buttons, for example, in order to build up a stock for clothes repair – the activity ceases to be leisure and assumes an economic purpose.[24] This common-sense and valuable understanding of leisure leads on to the most common of the binary oppositions employed in academic writing about leisure. Leisure is defined as the opposite of work.[25] The refrain of the Eight Hours movement of the late nineteenth and early twentieth century, familiar to many thousands of trade unionists at the time, points up the chief idea:

> Eight hours work, eight hours play;
> Eight hours rest, eight 'bob' a day.

It has been a major characteristic of much of the founding work in leisure studies that 'leisure' thus becomes that which is 'non-work'.[26] It is a way of understanding which implies a number of other oppositions. The most critical of these is the conception of leisure as a period of measured time that is separable from working time, resulting perhaps in the further notion of leisure being something that is 'earned' through work. This implies that leisure is a 'surplus' that comes about as a consequence of the productivity of work, and the implication therefore tends to prioritize work as a social activity and relegate leisure to a secondary role, an ordering which might not always give to leisure the emphasis it deserves as a *creative* social activity.[27] Further, there is assumed to exist a qualitative, indeed spiritual, difference between these opposed times. If work involves regulated and bought time, leisure is 'free' or 'spare' time, when the individual may choose what s/he might do. Leisure therefore represents freedom, time in which individuals can 'be themselves', when they reveal their authentic nature as autonomous human beings. The activities pursued in work, it is implied, cannot achieve this, since they happen in someone else's time, the purposes of which are determined by those who are paying for the labour power.

The tendency to see work/leisure in this way is not only a feature of recent sociological and historical writing. It has been historically deep-rooted in British society, and explains many of the enduring concerns that have made leisure into more than a subject of academic discourse. It has been a focal issue in contemporary class and gender relations, and the academic analysis of leisure has become inseparable from the consideration of it as a social 'problem'. Quite apart from the concerns over how people physically spend their leisure time – concerns expressed mainly by those in authority – there has been since at least the mid-nineteenth century a preoccupation with the qualitative aspects of leisure. This has usually been (not to put too fine a point on it) a matter for middle-class intellectuals. At the stage when leisure time ceased to be the monopoly of what Veblen called, with some distaste, 'the leisure class', the non-work activities of the masses became the focus of keen scrutiny. The Spanish conservative José Ortega y Gasset spoke for many when he expressed in 1930 his anxieties over what he called 'plenitude' – too many people doing what previously had been confined to the few:

> Towns are full of people, houses full of tenants, hotels full of guests, trains full of travellers, cafés full of customers, parks full of promenaders, consulting rooms of famous doctors full of patients, theatres full of spectators, and beaches full of bathers. What previously was, in general, no problem, now begins to be an every-day one, namely, to find room.[28]

In more general terms, however, the discourse centred upon the question of whether all these people, many of whom were of the working class, were spending their leisure time wisely. Since Matthew Arnold's concern with the political dimensions of this in the 1860s[29] a great deal of intellectual energy was expended at all points along the political spectrum to ensure that leisure time was genuinely 'improving'. All too often, it seemed, the new commercial leisure pursuits of music hall, sport and popular literature were offering up a hedonism that contrasted starkly with the Victorian ideal of 'recreation': the concert hall contrasted with the music hall to provide a clear class contrast in leisure habits.[30] In other words, instead of acting to reinvigorate the mind after the hours of work, making it ready for new challenges in labour, leisure was becoming for many a sensuous and preferable alternative. Work was drudgery, leisure the pinnacle of living. This might be all very well, but as the market researcher Henry Durant pointed out in the late 1930s, the commercialization of leisure resulted in enjoyment being dependent on money. What happens if the pinnacle of people's existence is found to be beyond their means? Many of these questions were taken up by the popular writer and broadcaster J. B. Priestley in his contribution to the famous 'reconstruction' edition of *Picture Post* of January 1941. Priestley was looking forward to a world after the war in which life would be better, both materially and spiritually; a reduction in the hours of labour would, he felt, benefit all, but what would fill the new 'leisure' time thus achieved?

> Not, I hope, an orgy of silliness and passive mechanical enjoyment. We do not want greyhound racing and dirt track performances to be given at all hours of the day and night, pin table establishments doing a roaring trade from dawn to midnight, and idiotic films being shown down every street. We do not want a terrifying extension of that 'Why Move From Your Armchair?' spirit, which persuades the average citizen that he is really an invalid in one of the final stages of heart disease. If we are all to be freed from hours of work simply in order to lie back and be mildly tickled, then I cannot see that much will be gained.[31]

Priestley did not himself subscribe to a particularly elitist view of culture, but he did believe that people should fashion their own spare-time activities. He was part of a tradition which, though it went back into the previous century, had certainly not exhausted itself by the mid-twentieth. It continued to show much vitality into the second half of the century, as leisure continued to be a problem in the age of 'affluence'.

Such a discourse has served to reinforce the idea we began with, namely the separation of work and leisure. It contains, however, some problems. For one thing, it fails to capture the experience of those people for whom work and leisure are fused. Priestley would no doubt have considered himself to be one of them, a group of people which J. K. Galbraith was later to describe as the 'new class'.[32] For another, it cannot adequately explain the existence of non-work time which is neither 'free' nor 'leisure', as for the many millions of unemployed in the British labour force at various times in the twentieth century. Unemployment, as enforced leisure, remains one of the great uncharted territories of the social historian. Both of these problems are acknowledged in a new perspective on leisure that has emerged during the past twenty or so years, and which is itself part of the broader paradigm of 'postmodernity' influential in recent sociological debate. The idea of 'postmodern' (sometimes 'post-Fordist') society describes a world in which fundamental changes in organization and behaviour, as profound in their way as those which marked the passage from 'traditional' to 'modern', call forth new conceptual approaches from those analysing society. Among the changes that have been perceived are the diminution of the power of the nation state within a globalized polity in which international media organizations exercise extensive influence. Alongside these developments are changes in the centrality of production and employment, with the emergence of a more consumption-based economy with discontinuous employment experiences for those able to find work. Having a settled job for life is becoming, it is claimed, a thing of the past; instead, people are likely to pass through several different employment experiences in the course of a working life which might be shorter and which might involve several different work locations – a lifetime, almost, of 'hot-desking'. In all this, leisure takes on a new role. No longer is it secondary to work, defined in oppostion to it as 'non-work', but a central feature of life and production existing in a complex inter-relationship with work.

These new perspectives have wrought important effects on the understanding of the relationship between leisure and gender. Deeply inscribed in the conventional 'common-sense' understanding of leisure was an implicit *male* orientation. It described, indeed sprang from, an experience of the labour market that was confined largely to waged working men, for whom leisure existed because of the domestic labour of their wives and, to a lesser degree, their daughters. In this sense, then, 'leisure' became something appropriated by men at the expense of women. It was, therefore, only fully understandable in the power relations of gender, although rarely was this fact recognized. The conventional understanding of leisure has quite properly been challenged by feminist historians. Not only can it no longer be judged an adequate analytical approach to the leisure experience, but it might also be seen as an ideological obstacle to the attempts by women to make sport and leisure more accessible. It is this that explains why so much feminist writing on sport and leisure seeks not only to explain that particular world, but also to change it.[33]

In *Women's Leisure, What Leisure?*, a publication which exemplifies much of the best in recent feminist scholarship, the authors present an indictment of this conventional wisdom.[34] The familiar trinity of the male historian – that leisure is defined by time, money and energy[35] – is given a new critical slant by these feminist historians. They show that women, particularly married women, experienced leisure in different ways from men. In the course of a detailed survey of women in Sheffield in the 1980s, it emerged that many respondents did not use the term 'leisure' at all, 'seeing it as a vague and amorphous concept'. Instead of fixed periods of time, women preferred to think of those moments which produced a 'special state of mind or quality of experience'. Opportunities to be 'free', to 'be yourself', to 'do nothing' if the fancy so takes you, to rest, relax, or gossip, all these were experiences treasured by the women interviewed.[36] In many cases they were brief moments. This is a feature of women's leisure confirmed by historical studies. Catriona Parratt, for example, has shown that women were disadvantaged by comparison with men in the leisure climacteric that occurred in the late nineteenth and early twentieth centuries. The gains made in leisure as a consequence of improving material standards – rising real wages, shorter working hours and improved health – were gains that chiefly accrued to men. For women of the working class, whether they worked for wages or carried out a domestic role in the home, 'relatively few . . . had the means or time that made much leisure possible'.[37] Constraints of both social class and gender therefore shaped the experience of these women. Similarly, the research of Ellen Ross has highlighted the sexual division of leisure that occurred in poor neighbourhoods, where the general working-class culture was constituted by a constellation of different, but overlapping 'spaces' and subcultures. Women dealt with the constant threat of poverty through a robust and intimate system of neighbourhood sharing, helping each other out with money, domestic utensils, food and child care, gathering as and when they could to gossip and drink; Mondays, when goods redeemed from the pawnshop for the weekend were pawned once again for the much-needed weekly cash, provided the opportunity for a brief meeting at a local pub: a leisure break timetabled into the endless round of making ends meet. And a time for specifically female conviviality. For most families there was a fairly rigid gender division – 'London husbands and wives lived in quite separate worlds' – and so links between women were often stronger than those between men and women.[38]

Research of this kind has opened up important new dimensions in our understanding of social history. Though on occasions it can produce rather 'Whiggish' interpretations, as in the case of Nicky Hart's castigating of men for a selfish hedonism which placed intolerable burdens on their families,[39] the research generally has served to establish gender as a tool of historical enquiry alongside class. But even feminist scholars have not always penetrated the experience of those women for whom class and gender relationships have been overlain by those of race.

While historians of sport are gradually coming to terms with the diversity of experience that exists among women, relatively little has so far been achieved in the sensitive area of racial experiences.[40] Western perspectives, even among feminist writers, have been an obstacle to the understanding of, for example, Muslim women's involvement in sport. In an important study based on interviews with Muslim schoolgirls and young women in London, Hasina Zaman has attempted to expose some of the misunderstandings that accompany this subject, especially the notion that Muslim women are the victims of a conservative and patriarchal culture, symbolized in its gendered codes of dress.[41] Zaman shows that the women themselves are often anxious to retain an Islamic philosophy about exercise and the female body, and consequently find Western-style changing provisions in schools and leisure centres offensive to their sensibilities. Religious teaching causes them to regard sport and fitness not as a secular pursuit of fitness and health for its own physiological sake, which is equated with vanity, but as an extension of their faith, a way of praising god. Zaman's interviewees were all keen to participate in sport but found western attiudes about it difficult to circumvent from the point of view of their religion. The problem was summed up by one woman who went along to what she thought would be a women-only swimming session at her local baths:

> I don't think that being a Muslim woman should prevent you from doing sports. I go to 'women-only' . . . because you know that my religion says that I shouldn't expose my body to men, but you know that when I went to women's night, I assumed that it will be all women and even lifeguards or the safety people would be women and I was shocked that it was men. But I tried to get into the pool as soon as I could, that is the only thing that ruined my swimming apart from that I like swimming.[42]

Zaman's work helps to explain some of the difficulties faced by women from this religious culture, and might also begin to explain why participation in sport and other leisure activities is so uneven across the range. In fact, there are some similarities between the milieu described by Zaman and that investigated by feminist historians like Parratt and Ross. Gender inequalities in leisure, as in work, exist in part because women themselves are, so to speak, complicit in their creation. What seems like oppression to historians, such as Hart looking back into the past, was not experienced in that way by women at the time. Nor are religious precepts necessarily something that 'hold back' women.

DEFINING TERMS: 'SPORT' AND 'CULTURE'

'Sport' is perhaps a less problematical concept than leisure. It seems more finite, though Tony Mason's definition – a helpful one – gives it a broad horizon: 'a more or less physically strenuous, competitive, recreational activity . . . usually . . . in the open air and [which] might involve team against

team, athlete against athlete or athlete against nature, or the clock.'[43] Of course
the concept has changed as historical circumstances have changed. The
'sportsman' of 1850 – hunting, shooting and fishing – would be very different from the sportsman of 1950, whose main interest would perhaps have
been watching football played by others. And the sportsperson of 2000 might
have reverted to a more active form of sport, though in a more individual-
ized capacity: jogging, fitness-training in a gym, doing aerobics, or length-
swimming. There are two axes to all these activities that provide two broad
distinctions: participation and spectating; and elite and mass performance.
Generally, sports history has produced more work on the participation–elite
axis. Popular writing on sport, as seen in the extensive range of books and
magazines available in high street newsagents and booksellers, notably produces a fixation with the elite sportspeople, a process also evident in the
reports of sporting contests to be found in the popular press and television.
The reporter's technique here has changed over the course of the twentieth
century. Instead of a 'balanced' account of the ebb and flow of the play, there
developed at some point in the inter-war period a clear focus on the personalities in the drama. By the end of the century the standard approach of all
sporting journalism, whether in the press or the electronic media, was to build
a story around a character, preferably a well-known one who was also a man.[44]
Academic writing has been less inclined to follow this example. Historians
influenced by the emphasis on 'history from below', which developed in both
British and American social history from the 1960s onwards, have produced
some noteworthy contributions to our understanding of the sporting process.
Nevertheless, there is still a marked leaning towards the commercial-
professional aspects of sport, and even in this context relatively little on those
who only stand and watch. Thus academic histories of association football in
Britain, the sport most intensively studied so far, have said little about
amateur-recreational football (although this is the form the vast majority of
footballers play); and whilst football hooligans have received more than their
share of attention the 'ordinary' spectator has been virtually overlooked.[45]

It might be possible to set limits on 'sport' as a physical activity, but culturally it is experienced in a mutitude of different ways. In Britain these cultural experiences of sport have been bound up with social position. If leisure
studies have been beset by a particular gender orientation towards the idea
of leisure, sports history has developed under the shadow of social class. This
is not simply a case of an undue emphasis on working-class sport, a preoccupation recently pointed out by Mike Huggins.[46] The 'history from below'
paradigm has probably shifted the perspective too much towards the working
class, and Huggins is right to attempt to trim the balance. But sport in Britain
has long been a marker of social class and therefore an agent in those complex
processes that produce social relations and status. Men and women were
judged socially by the games they played. Gentlemen did not play rugby
league or professional soccer, indeed they did not play anything for wages;
and if, as with cricket, the game was played by all sorts and conditions of men
(though by a more limited social range of women), then strict status distinctions would be enforced within the game.

From its class nexus sport has acquired a meaning that has become deeply entrenched in British mentalities. It is regarded, especially in its participant forms, as (in the language of *1066 And All That*) 'a good thing'. The importance accorded to games in the curriculum of the British public schools and their imperial replicas[47] in the late nineteenth century sprang from a belief in the character-building properties of athletic exercise and contest.[48] These had individual and collective relevance, starting with the benefits bestowed by sport on the person participating, which included respect for rules, playing fair and carrying one's triumphs modestly, and led on to the social bonding and qualities of teamwork that helped create loyalties to class, nation and empire. Through educational practice and through representations of school-life in popular literature this set of beliefs was perpetuated into the twentieth century. In the course of time the mystique of sport as a character-building process lost some of its power, especially as the behaviour of many leading sportspeople seemed so completely to disprove the notion. In its more recent manifestations the idea of sport as a 'good thing' has passed into the leisure industry, and is to be found as an underpinning philosophy for the many programmes in sports science and leisure studies that became popular in higher education in the 1980s. Physically, it is most readily seen in the sport and leisure centres that sprouted in Britain during the preceding decade. Their attempt, however, to reach out to the whole of the population through the 'Sport For All' campaign launched by the Sports Council has not been especially successful. The relative failure to promote the idea of sport in this way has many explanations, some relating to the different ways of understanding sport that we observed in talking about women's leisure and race. Similarly, social class perspectives on sport have varied. Richard Holt has made it clear that conceptions of masculinity in sport differed according to the social class position of those involved: the giving and taking of 'hard knocks' in the rugger scrum was not the same as 'being hard' on the football pitch.[49] For many working-class men and women, 'sport' is not about physical fitness or moral behaviour; it is to do with reading about sporting activity in the newspapers, talking about it with one's friends, watching the racing on the television, studying 'form', and maybe having a bet or doing the pools.

In this sense, sport becomes part of a broader social process which we might want to describe as 'culture'. Culture absorbs everything covered in this book. That, of course, is one of the problems with the concept. It can be so all-embracing as to mean everything. In speaking about sport and leisure as culture, then, it is important to outline exactly how these processes are cultural. The approach adopted here is, first, to delineate the two basic components of culture – 'practices' and 'texts'. 'Practices' are those activities such as going on holiday, visiting the cinema, watching the television, or simply meeting friends at a café, which are part of everyday life. 'Texts' are the representation of cultural activity in the form, say, of holiday brochures, films, television programmes, or reviews of them, and even a café menu. What binds these different forms together, and constitutes them into 'culture'? This brings us to the second aspect of our approach. It follows the path marked out by Francis Mulhearn, and followed in the Open University's seminal work on popular culture, in pursuing culture as a process to do with *meaning*. Cultural practices and texts, though they might also have their economic, political, and social aspects are seen essentially as having a *signifying* purpose; as Mulhearn puts it, they 'produce sense'.[50]

THE TWENTIETH CENTURY

The period covered by this book presents its own problems, at many different levels. For one thing, the author's own lifetime covers a good half of it. As Eric Hobsbawm has pointed out: '[N]obody can write the history of the twentieth century like that of any other era, if only because nobody can write about his or her lifetime as one can (and must) write about a period known only from the outside.'[51] For another, there are the ingrained assumptions of others to confront. The historian of sport and leisure has to contend with what is commonly perceived as being a century of immense change, if not 'revolution'. This is doubtless a fair assumption, to a degree. Quite apart from the statistical information which shows the increased personal involvement in and financial outlay on sport and leisure,[52] there are the many measurements of times, heights, numbers and money generated that commemorate something beyond mere change. They imply improvement. This idea is reinforced every time a great sportsperson dies. Two themes prevailed in the praises sung when Stanley Matthews passed away on 23 February 2000. First, he was universally acclaimed for his sportsmanship, a quality evident among his successors mainly by its absence; second, there were many who noted that in contemporary football, his delicate, precise, skilful style of play would have been brutally erased.[53] *Sic transit gloria mundi*: the game has 'moved on'. The meaning is clear. To 'move on' is to 'progress'. And this is the historian's real problem; countering the tendency to assume that change is improvement, that more leisure is better leisure, and that sporting skill and achievement advances by qualitative leaps from one generation to the next. Sport has a peculiar capacity for generating this kind of 'onwards and upwards' thinking. We do well to remember the many continuities alongside the changes. One very simple aspect of this, as Tony Mason has reminded us, is that the sports 'played and watched in Britain in the 1990s showed a stubborn similarity to the 1890s'.[54]

SPORT, IDENTITY AND BRITAIN

'Britain' is a slippery concept. Those who live outside the British Isles have difficulty in grasping it, largely because, as Linda Colley has pointed out, it has been a typically English habit to make 'Britain' and 'England' synonymous terms.[55] Where four nations conjoin in one state it is perhaps understandable, if not excusable, that the most populous and economically powerful should attempt to embrace the other three. Moreover, for at least part of this period, English/British hegemony extended to large areas of the overseas world through the system of colonialism. In political life the identity of Wales, Scotland, Ireland and many other places has been subsumed into that of an English-based polity. To varying degrees national identity within the British/English umbrella has been preserved within the official structures of the legal, religious and educational systems. These have allowed the Scots, with a distinctive system in all three, a reasonable degree of identity, strengthened by the creation in 1999 of the Scottish Parliament. But the Welsh, on the other hand, until the arrival of the Welsh Assembly (not Parliament), have had to content themselves with a set of institutional symbols (museum, university, dual language) created with English acquiescence, and since 1964 a Secretary of State for Wales who has not always been Welsh. In Ireland and other colonial areas the issue is so complex that some have taken up arms to proclaim their national identity. In this context the cultural marker of nationalism has, not surprisingly, often been provided by sport.

Sport, indeed, has been responsible for maintaining some sense of Britishness, though by stressing the 'unity in diversity' of the British Isles rather than any commonality. Apart from athletics, which sponsors a team representing Great Britain in the Olympics, few sports have moved beyond a limited national field as the basis of their organization. Association football typifies this, with separate associations for each country. The result is fierce competition between them. Sport's capacity to express an anti-English feeling is unsurpassed. In Wales, the vehicle has been rugby, the sport housed for 30 years after 1970 in the National Stadium in Cardiff, contradictorily the most cosmopolitan of Welsh cities where the contiguous university and civic centre, with its statue of Lloyd George – all ostensibly icons of Welshness – actually serve as a continuing reminder of English hegemony. The National Museum of Wales was opened in 1927 by King George V, who came down from London to perform the ceremony and thus confirm the subordinate position of Wales within a British state. The Museum formed the last part of an urban development, begun in the late nineteenth century, based on outside capital, masterminded by a Scottish nobleman, and dependent upon imported English labour. Rugby, however, has unambiguously articulated the populist pride of Wales, through its heroes from Arthur Gould to Barry John, and through its victories, the sweetest of which historically was the celebrated triumph of 1905 over the mighty All Blacks.[56]

A similar landmark came in 1999. Playing a 'home' match at Wembley, because the National Stadium was being reconstructed as the Millennium Stadium, Wales defeated their arch-rivals England with a score in the last minute to win the Triple Crown and, equally important, come out of a long trough of rugby adversity. Welsh rugby, as its leading historians show, had been an intrinsic element of Welsh nationalism since the 'golden age' that followed the burgeoning of the South Wales coalfield in the late nineteenth century, its fortunes closely linked to the changing economic fortunes of the country.[57] Alongside rugby players were the world-renowned boxers of Wales – Freddie Welsh, Jimmy Wilde, Jim Driscoll, Tommy Farr and more recently, Howard Winstone – whose triumphs 'continued to seize the imagination of its working class'.[58] During the Depression of the 1930s clubs declined with the economy, players migrating to safer havens such as Torquay or Weston-super-Mare, or, if they were very good, like Jim Sullivan and Gus Risman and a host of others, to the rugby league clubs of the North – 'the road to Wigan Pier' as Gareth Williams has spendidly described this process.[59] The most sustained period of rugby success, associated with John, Edwards, Dawes, Williams, Bennett and other illustrious folk heroes, came in the 1960s and 1970s, a time when the rugby world in Wales was revitalized by a new affluence and modernization similar to that of the earlier 'golden age'. Rugby helped Welsh people at this time to identify themselves as a nation, perhaps more than they were able to through politics. In 1979, after all, devolution was rejected by a large majority.

Rugby exercised its hold because of the place it occupied in Welsh male society, a place the same game never captured in England. On the other hand, soccer, in spite of occasional pulsations, failed to claim the popular mood in Wales to anything like the same extent that it did in Scotland, where it has articulated class and nation more than any other popular cultural form. In a country where, since the Act of Union of 1707, there have been ever-present fears of economic subordination in an Anglicized empire, the development of soccer in the late nineteenth century provided in itself evidence of this English dominance. The extensive work of H. F. Moorhouse, among others, has made it clear that Scottish soccer existed in a neo-colonial relationship to its English neighbour, being financially dependent upon transfers to England for its clubs' continuing existence.[60] It has been this subordination that has accounted for the different soccer culture of Scotland, which creates a particular kind of 'repressed nationalism' exhibited in a number of forms: in, for example, a hostility to England that results in Scottish supporters siding with anyone playing against England; in a longstanding if idealized desire to see a Scottish national side which does not include 'Anglos' (i.e. Scottish players from English clubs); and in a sense of superiority that springs from the view that, in spite of exporting so much talent to England, Scotland still manages to keep its own leagues afloat and to produce good football.

The mark of this last point was a belief in the existence of a certain Scottish 'style' of play – clever football played on the ground to players who switched positions intelligently. The myth, for such it often was, depended on an accompanying belief in a cruder English 'other', depending on muscle, speed and aerial brawn – 'kick and rush'. The results of Scotland-England international matches sometimes supported these views, most frequently in the inter-war years and never more so than in the encounter at Wembley in 1928 when Scotland's 'wee blue devils' ran five goals through a stately English defence. There were periodic repeats of this lesson, the last major one being at Wembley in 1967 when Scotland again defeated England – now World Champions – with a display that was held to epitomize Scottish soccer panache ('gallus') in the form of players such as Law, Baxter and Johnstone.[61] Such events and ideas expressed a certain kind of Scottishness, but one which since the 1980s, with the discontinuance of the annual match against England and Scotland's relative failure in international competition, it has been difficult to perpetuate through soccer. Scotland's two big clubs, Rangers and Celtic, have, like their English counterparts and for the same reasons, become increasingly cosmopolitan since the early 1990s with the importation of foreign players.[62] Scotland's peculiarly indigenous soccer culture is now something of a memory, of a time in the 1930s when the massed terraces of working-class males from the shipyards set British attendance records at the Hampden and Ibrox stadiums. Soccer might now carry less emotional weight for Scots than it once did, but it is difficult to see any other sport matching it for national significance, even after the successes of the rugby team in the early 1990s. But whatever the code, sport plays a key part in Scottish national identity. So much so that in 1992, shortly after the general election, the Nationalist politician Jim Sillars was led to despair of Scots as 'ninety-minute patriots', unable to extend into the political arena the sense of nationalism they displayed at Murrayfield or Hampden.[63]

In Ireland, the relationship between sport and politics has operated along quite different axes. To begin with the context was different; the sense of nation, and of being a *colony*, was stronger. The location was also different. Whereas in Wales and Scotland popular sport was largely concentrated in the industrialized, working-class regions of the country, in Ireland this was true only of parts of Ulster, and Dublin. Elsewhere the country was agricultural and unmodernized, but at the same time dominated to an extent unknown in the rest of Britain by a single institution – the Catholic Church. Social elites, which in England had often championed the cult of sport among the masses, were in Ireland far less dynamic. The early life of the playwright Samuel Beckett, scion of an Anglicized Protestant bourgeois family from Dublin, illustrates this feature very well; at schools and later at Trinity College, Dublin, Sam played cricket, the English game, among a restricted circle of like-minded Anglo-Irish schoolboys and students, often touring England to do so. He is still the only Nobel prize-winner to be cited in the pages of *Wisden*, the cricketer's almanac.[64]

The popular sports of Ireland, Gaelic games (principally hurling), were established in the late nineteenth century by promoters such as Michael Cusack and Maurice Davin, using, as Michael Cronin's work has stressed, English models of sporting codification.[65] The contradiction in this stems from the political purpose of Irish popular sport. As inspired by the Gaelic Athletics Association (GAA) since the 1880s, sport has been a weapon in the struggle against British domination in Ireland, a vehicle for the articulation of Irish national feeling very much in the same way that sport and leisure fulfilled a propaganda role for European socialist movements in their battle against industrial capitalism. The GAA went one step farther than the socialists, however, in insisting that their sport not only generated a nationalist sociability and consciousness; it did so by being a *different* sport from that of the enemy. The GAA's nationalist mission was plain for all to see, most evident, as Cronin has also shown, in the unique naming of its sports grounds after martyrs to the cause. Of the grounds – Croke Park, Pairc Mhic Dhiarmada, Casement Park, Davitt Park and many others – Cronin notes: 'their very names celebrate the shared history and identity of the Irish as a whole, not solely those attending the ground.'[66] But sport can never entirely encompass a nation. Just as Scottish soccer has its rivalry between Rangers and Celtic, which plays upon pre-existing religious and political traditions of the Orange and the Green, so in Ireland itself the inclusive effect of the GAA and Gaelic Games must be set against the competing attractions of other sports and the interest they arouse. Soccer, as the demythologizing novels of Roddy Doyle indicate, is immensely popular in both the Republic and in Northern Ireland, yet serves to divide as much as to unite. In the North it is organized along largely sectarian lines, thus helping to maintain conflicts.[67] In the South, the success of Ireland's international team under the managership of Jack Charlton in the early 1990s produced contradictory effects. The national side enjoyed a longer period of success and support than it had ever known, but it was produced by a manager who was English and a team of talented players whose Irish lineage was often spurious. Their achievements were as much a reminder of the globalizing forces that were shaping society and soccer at this time as of any intrinsic Irishness.

The Irish example, however, has a uniqueness in the British context; it shows a political connection between sport and nation of colonial dimensions, which makes it closer in some respects to that of overseas areas of the former British Empire than to the mainland examples. The role of the GAA reveals, albeit in somewhat sharper form, a resort to sport as an instrument of colonial liberation that has been evident in varying forms in other places. Cricket, originally a means of bonding the Empire, as often as not became the means of prising it apart. Success at cricket helped Australians to throw off the inferior status assigned to them by the English, and the rows generated by the 'Bodyline Tour' of 1932–33 had to do with much more than the pros and cons of fast leg-theory bowling and fair play. They signified tensions of both a political and economic nature between the industrialized metropolitan core and its primary-producing periphery at a time of falling world agricultural prices. In this context Australia produced its first truly national hero, the respectable, petty-bourgeois Don Bradman, whose extraordinary exploits on the field provided the inhabitants of Australia with a focal point of unity to over-ride the ethnic and religious conflicts that beset the country's white immigrant society.[68] At a rather later stage, by the 1970s and 1980s in fact, cricket became the agent for the assertion of national pride in Pakistan, especially once the game there had shed the elitist configurations inherited from colonial days.[69] But it was in the Caribbean that cricket became most closely associated with colonial nationalism. Cricket exercised an important symbolic meaning in this part of the world, where national identity was fragmented and black people subordinated. For them, as the Trinidadian radical C. L. R. James observed, cricketers filled 'a huge gap in their consciousness and in their needs'. In its club organization cricket in the Caribbean developed a subtle hierarchy of race and class status.[70] Until well after the Second World War, however, although its leading performers were black men such as George Headley, Learie Constantine and the three 'Ws' – Weekes, Worrell and Walcott – the representative team of the West Indies was firmly controlled by white captains like the patrician H. B. G. Austin and the autocratic J. D. Goddard.

In fact, the captaincy of the team became itself a symbol of power. In the 1930s Constantine had begun to hint at the unfairness of this system,[71] but it was not until the 1950s that any significant changes occurred. The triumphant West Indies team in England in 1950 was still led by the white Goddard. His mantle passed to a succession of light-skinned men during the course of the decade, when not only were there far better and more experienced black cricketers to choose from, but anti-colonial sentiments were gathering strength in the Caribbean. Black national consciousness brought to prominence, and in some cases to political power, leaders of the stamp of Cheddi Jagan, Forbes Burnham, Norman Manley and Eric Williams. Two tours of the region by the English national team – in 1953–54 and 1959–60 – were affected by demonstrations which, while sparked by incidents on the cricket field, revealed tensions in society over decolonization issues. Following a campaign in Trinidad by C. L. R. James in *The Nation*, the newspaper of Eric Williams's People's National Movement, a black captain – Frank Worrell – was eventually selected.[72] The decision marked more than a recognition by the West Indies cricket establishment of Worrell's sagacity as a tactician. It was an acceptance that the balance of power in the Caribbean was shifting, that cricket had played its part in that shift, and that white supremacy in cricket, as in society generally, could no longer be sustained.[73]

The end of empire placed Britain in a changed international position. Adapting Arnold Toynbee's verdict on Europe after the Second World War, we might say of Britain that it became a centre on which external international influences converged rather than, as it once had been, a centre from which influences radiated to the outside world.[74] This change was particularly acute in sport, which the British liked to think they had invented and exported to others. The impact in the 1950s of defeats by apparently 'lesser' countries – the West Indies (1950) and Pakistan (1954) at cricket, and most dramatically by Eire (1949), the USA (1950) and the Hungarians (1953 and 1954) at football – underlined the fact that sporting excellence was diffused throughout the world, and that there was much the British could learn by lifting their gaze and looking abroad. In doing so it became apparent that neither 'Britain' nor the national sub-units within it were any longer quite as distinct an entity as they once had been. In fact, the whole process produced something of an identity crisis. Just as the rise of multi-national corporations and the European Union has thrown the idea of a national sovereign identity into confusion, so in sport it was no longer possible to cling to old certainties. The English cricket team, for example, was not the lodestar of nationality that it had been in the inter-war years.[75] Changes in both the team and the country it represents have undermined the site of morality and nationality on which the cricket team was once firmly based. It has not been composed entirely of English players for some 20 years past, it has certainly not lived up to its old position as one of the 'masters' of the game, and it cannot necessarily count on the natural support of many English people. Multi-culturalism has produced conflicting loyalties, so that for many residents of Britain it might seem more natural to follow the fortunes of the West Indies, India, Sri Lanka or Pakistan in international cricket.

Key Reading ●

Cox, R., Jarvie, G., and Vamplew, W. *Encyclopedia of British Sport*. Oxford: ABC-Clio, 2000.

Green, E., Hebron, S., and Woodward, D. *Women's Leisure, What Leisure?* Basingstoke: Macmillan – now Palgrave, 1990.

Guttman, A. *From Ritual to Record: The Nature of Modern Sports*. New York: Columbia University Press, 1978.

Hargreaves, Jennifer, ed., *Sport, Culture and Ideology*. London: Routledge and Kegan Paul, 1982.

Holt, R. *Sport and the British*. Oxford: Oxford University Press, 1990 edn.

Jones, S. G. *Workers at Play: A Social and Economic History of Leisure, 1918–1939*. London: Routledge and Kegan Paul, 1986.

part one

Commercial sport and leisure

chapter 2

The 'Peculiar Economics' of the People's Games

Throughout the twentieth century there has been a connection between the popular and the commercial in sport. But it has never been a straightforward relationship, let alone an unproblematical one. This was illustrated at the very end of the century by the association football club Manchester United. Its supporters had four reasons to feel happy at this time. Three of them were to do with their club having uniquely triumphed in the major competitions of the 1998–99 season: the Premier League, the FA Cup, and the European Champions' League. Such a feat was unprecedented, and gave just cause for much celebration. The fourth reason, however, related to events off, rather than on, the field of play. In April 1999 the Monopolies Commission had blocked a move by Rupert Murdoch's media company BSkyB to buy the club. The decision was applauded by those supporters who had lobbied to prevent 'their' club being swallowed by a global corporation. It slowed down, if it did not halt, an aspect of commercialism which had been evident for the previous 20 years, especially in football. In the same way that it used to be said that sport sold newspapers, so businessmen like Murdoch had come to realize that sport, and especially a world game like football, could give access through television to huge audiences of consumers. Immense opportunities therefore existed for those who controlled the airwaves and the clubs to sell advertising time. A club like Manchester United, with its own television channel, a global base of supporters, and with its already strong reputation enhanced by recent victories, was a great prize. The decision of the Monopolies Commission notwithstanding, those who had campaigned against this process realised the dilemma that faced them. The more their club won, and the more its games dominated television sports coverage, the keener would be the quest of media moguls to control the club.[1]

ASSOCIATION FOOTBALL: PROFIT MAXIMIZATION?

Some 90 years earlier, in Arnold Bennett's fictitious Bursley, these links between sport and commerce were being forged. Councillor Barlow, 'fifty and iron-grey, with whiskers but no moustache; short, stoutish, raspish', was telling the supporters of ailing Bursley F. C. straight:

> He said he had given his services as Chairman . . . for thirteen years; that he had taken up £2000 worth of shares in the Company; and that as at that moment the Company's liabilities would exactly absorb its assets, his £2000 was worth exactly nothing. 'You may say', he said, 'I've lost that £2000 in thirteen years. That is, it's the same as if I'd been steadily paying three pun' a week out of my own pocket to provide football matches that you chaps wouldn't take the trouble to go and see. That's the straight of it! What have I got for my pains? Nothing but worries and these!' (He pointed to his grey hairs).[2]

He was not to know that the arch-operator 'Denry' Machin, a small-town Rupert Murdoch if ever there was one, would rescue Bursley with a star centre-forward, put the club back on the map, and himself in the Mayor's seat. Denry, too, understood the links between sport and commerce, and knew that they also extended to politics.

Between the two cases is a century of change, but also some continuities. For most of the time, sport as big business was a rarity. Councillor Barlow's early-century version of *noblesse oblige* represented better, and for longer, the commercial side of sport than does Murdoch's pursuit of mega-bucks. It is undeniable that since the late nineteenth century many of Britain's most popular sports have existed in a commercial form: as commodities provided at a cost by business people for spectators/consumers. But often this provision has not come in a 'normal' business relationship. For one thing, language has transmuted commerce. Sports businesses are 'clubs', a term which implies membership and belonging. Consumers are 'supporters' or 'fans'. It is difficult to imagine even the most loyal customers of Marks and Spencer being described in such a way. Nor would Marks and Spencer have any compunction about moving their stores around to meet changing consumer styles, location and demand. By the end of the century the retail trade was doing this with a vengeance, often in the face of customer protest. Marks and Spencer's leaving of downtown Dudley in the West Midlands, for example, for the new retail park at Merry Hill provoked anger and dismay from local people who feared the decay of their town centre, but the move went ahead none the less. It made sound business sense. Few sports businesses, by contrast, have operated quite in this way in Britain. They have proved to be remarkably loyal to their supporters, and therefore conservative in their business approach. Until the changes of the late twentieth century, few of the major popular sports have undergone significant commercial changes. The most obvious example of this has been the refusal to consider moving their business to a more economically propitious area. Charles P. Korr has reminded us that baseball teams in the USA are not at all averse to the idea, as the example of the Brooklyn (later Los Angeles) Dodgers reveals.[3] In Britain, even in the flurry of soccer ground rebuilding of the 1990s, shifts of such proportions are unknown. Arsenal Football Club, whose commercial development in inter-war Britain represented the *avant-garde* of the sporting world, was the first and only business to engage in a major re-siting of its operations when it moved across London from Plumstead to Highbury just before the First World War.[4] Only its name remained to remind people of its origins as a club of south London artisans. This exception points up the rule; namely, that in sport commercial relationships, and perhaps even a commercial ethos, are of a particularly muted nature. As Richard Holt has noted of soccer clubs, their supporters are as much 'members' of the business as they are 'customers'.[5] A moral obligation exists on both sides – owners and consumers – which ensures that sport is not simply a money-making process.

Wray Vamplew, whose work on the theme of sport and commerce in Britain is seminal, has summed up this central issue in terms of a choice between profit and utility maximization.[6] Is sport, on the one hand, a pursuit of profits? Or, on the other, is it a commercial undertaking which nevertheless places a premium on winning matches and thereby providing *pleasure* for its many followers? Though the overall picture is a complex one, with many variations between different sports, Vamplew tends to come down in favour of sport as a process in which 'normal' methods of business analysis do not always apply, and where at the very least a considerable degree of 'peculiar economics' prevailed.[7] The experience of Councillor Barlow might not, therefore, be all that exceptional in considering the commercial development of popular sport in the twentieth century.

There was ample opportunity for the real-life counterparts of Councillor Barlow to take a hand in the development of popular games. At some point in the third quarter of the nineteenth century, conditions began to crystallize which allowed a largely localized and fragmented sporting culture to be transformed into a national leisure market with patterned regularities in its financing, organization and morality. Briefly summarized these conditions were: the concentration of an increasing proportion of an increasing population into urban settlements, with a growing civic culture and identity (which sport contributed to as well as benefited from); the general rise in the real and therefore disposable incomes of most of the population, though important regional, class and gender variations persisted; the general reduction in hours of work, making spare time on Saturdays possible for men; improvements in transport, both within and between towns, which allowed for the existence of organized league fixtures such as those in cricket and football, as well as the large-scale movement of bloodstock, people and equipment for a national calendar of horse-racing events;[8] and, of crucial importance, the developments in printing, telegraphy and distribution which enabled information to be transmitted quickly: the Saturday evening 'Pink 'Un' was in many ways the archetypal symbol of this communications revolution in sport. Clearly such conditions did not apply universally. Some areas gave themselves more readily to commercialized sport than others. London and the North West were the two leading examples. Lancashire was possibly the paradigm: the world's first industrial region and also the cradle of its commercial sport. Nor, when the conditions did apply, were all people necessarily drawn into the market that was created. Women, for example, were scarcely part of the 'people's games'. This was in part, as historians of women's leisure have shown,[9] because of differential economic opportunities in the sexual division of leisure. But it also had to do with ideologies of gender communicated through the leisure pursuits themselves. There is no *a priori* economic reason why sport should have been regarded as a male pursuit while the cinema, by contrast, often repelled (older) men because it was seen as the 'woman's sphere'. In other words, there are explanations for these differences to be pursued outside the realm of the economic.[10] Even in the world of men, there were notable exclusions from commercial sports – age, class and status being important determinants. Thus, for example, rugby union (except in South Wales, Devon and Cornwall, and parts of the Scottish borders) worked to preserve a middle-class clientele, and harboured a hostility towards commercialism in sport which explains its hatred for rugby league, where the open payment of players occurred.[11] Soccer spectating seemed to be the pastime of the skilled working-class male and few others until the 1990s when, it has been asserted, the game became 'embourgoiseified'.[12] Cricket had the capacity to draw in all under its umbrella, though not all together: county cricket and regionalized league cricket were in many respects quite different versions of the game, with different followings and codes.[13]

Given, as Neil Tranter has observed, the immense *enjoyment* derived by so many people from watching sports performed,[14] the prospects in sport for business success might well have seemed rosy. The sport which appeared most to lend itself to commercialism, and certainly the one to which most historians of sport have directed their attention, was football (or, to give it its formal name, Association football). The research of Mason is of paramount importance here. He it was who first directed serious study to that key period between the foundation of the Football Association (FA) in 1863 and the First World War which saw the 'modern' form of the game established. Mason's interpretation (still in many ways the orthodoxy) presents a 'top-downwards' process of diffusion, in which the public-school version of soccer was transmitted by former pupils as schoolteachers, businessmen and ministers of religion to the masses in the provinces. The movement was orchestrated by the FA and its county bodies which oversaw a standardization of the whole game at various levels of competence. But it was the initiative of elite clubs like Sheffield United and Notts County, sporting associations of 'respectable' middle-class men, which propelled soccer into a commercial ambience as a result of the desire to achieve high-quality play and success in competition.[15] In the history of Notts County, for example, there is a seemingly inexorable drive towards the enclosing of the ground, the charging of 'gate' money to spectators, the paying of players, and the creation of that combination of capital formation and legal protection enshrined in limited liability status.[16] Similar landmarks occurred in the development of many other clubs. The two characteristic features of twentieth-century commercial football – limited liability and professional players – came about almost hand-in-hand during the 1880s and 1890s, and were epitomized in the formation in 1888 of the first football league – the Football League – whose headquarters were a front parlour in Stoke-on-Trent until moved in 1902 to slightly grander premises in only marginally more fashionable Preston. The geographical axis was not accidental. It was here that the most favourable conditions for spectator sport at this time existed. The League's clubs were financed by the issue of shares which provided for the necessary capital outlay on grounds, equipment and wages. Under the provisions of parliamentary legislation the directors of limited liability companies were protected against actions for debt in the event of a bankruptcy of the company. The basis for sound business appeared to be secured.

Who ran these clubs, and how did they run them? Judging from various studies at both the macro- and micro-levels it becomes clear that we should approach the idea of the 'people's game' – a term increasingly being appled to football in the early years of the century – with some caution. As with other forms of popular culture, the involvement of 'the people' in soccer was limited. To begin with, control was not always in the hands of the many. Vamplew's work, in which he seeks to relate the acquisition of shares to occupation and, by association, social class, reveals some important features in the financial control of clubs.[17] In spite of the opaqueness of some of the evidence, it seems that a broad distinction of social type can be drawn between ordinary shareholders and those who became directors of clubs. Among the former was usually a fair representation of working people before the First World War, though there were important differences between Scotland and England. In both countries shareholders before the First World War were men (not women) of the particular locality served by the soccer club. Local identity and pride seems to have been a factor in buying shares. In Scotland, the proportion of these people who came from the working class appears to have been greater than in England, where higher share prices not surprisingly tended to discourage those on lower incomes. An ordinary share in Sheffield United, for example, cost £20 in 1899.[18] Darwen and Woolwich Arsenal were two clubs which, exceptionally, could be described as working class in view both of the nature of their origins and their financial support.[19] Though in both countries the absolute numbers of working-class shareholders was significant, most of them had small holdings, often a consequence of having been club members previously and having taken out a few shares at incorporation as a mark both of support for the club and the few advantages shareholding brought. As Vamplew notes of such people in Scotland: 'dividends were less important than a cheap season ticket and voting rights at the annual general meeting'.[20] Among directors of clubs there was in Scotland a consistent representation of the manual working class at this time of just under a third overall, whereas in England, where shareholding qualificationas for board membership were higher, the proportion was lower. As may be imagined, directors in England were drawn predominantly from the middle classes, often with a strong presence of businessmen in the drink trade. There were some direct advantages to joining a board; for example, in Scotland (though not in England) clubs could pay board members a fee for their services, and the club could be a source of contracts for the member's firm. In England, where the Football Association placed a 5 per cent limit on dividends in 1896, where profits made by big clubs were usually ploughed back into ground improvements, and where fees for board membership were not allowed, club directors looked to indirect economic spin-offs or, in the Denry Machin mould, social prestige and political influence as the benefit of their involvement. Many of these trends are illustrated by the history of the east London club, West Ham United, which had begun life in 1895 as Thames Ironworks Football Club. Under the auspices of A. F. Hills, the proprietor of the Ironworks, it was incorporated in 1900 with a capital of £2000 in 4000 shares at a 10 shillings (50 pence) face value. Some 1700 had been bought within two years by 92 people, only 21 of whom held more than ten shares and were therefore eligible to sit on the board. Hills possessed the vast majority of shares, though did not sit on the board. Thus, in this most working class of London suburbs the local team, strongly supported by the populace to the extent that, after early losses, it regularly made a profit before the First World war, was never controlled by the working people. Their participation, as Charles Korr notes, 'was limited to work either as players or as supporters'.[21]

Such patterns of ownership and control characterized British football clubs for a remarkably long period of time. Not until the 1960s did significant changes begin to occur, intensifying in the last two decades of the century. Why was it left until this time before profit maximization of the kind represented by Rupert Murdoch and the Manchester United case of 1998–99 intruded into the economics of the sport? The answer is provided if we examine two aspects of the business: its labour force, and its support.

What must be accounted, by most standards of British male employment, a draconian system of industrial relations, explains a control over the labour force that made possible the continuation for so long of Vamplew's 'peculiar economics'. Two aspects need emphasis. In 1901–02, in order to place a check on what were seen as escalating wage costs, the FA instituted a ceiling on earnings – the 'maximum wage'. Though periodically increased in the light of price inflation, and frequently subverted by richer clubs anxious to placate good players (it was, says Mason, 'honoured more in the breach than in the observance'[22]), the control nevertheless prevented a free market in wages. It was linked to a second and possibly more effective aspect of labour relations: the 'retain and transfer' system. This restricted the player's freedom of movement to the extent that, once his contract of employment (usually of 12 months duration) had expired, he was still unable to move to another employer in football without the agreement of his present club, which held his registration as a player. This arrangement allowed the club to capitalize on it by selling the player on the transfer market to another club. No other worker experienced such a restriction. Given that most players were drawn from the ranks of the working class, there was a social tension between directors and players which resulted in an employer attitude which was, at best, enlightened paternalism and, at its worst, downright implacable. The experiences of Wilf Mannion, a brilliant inside-forward for Middlesbrough and a member of the successful England team of the late 1940s, throw into sharp focus those shared by many a lesser-known player under this regime. When, in 1948, Mannion sought to challenge his club over the retain and transfer rules and refused to sign a new contract, he was met with a flat refusal to co-operate from Middlesbrough. The club simply asserted its interest in retaining the player, though handsome transfer offers from other clubs had been submitted. Mannion, out of contract though still tied to his club, embarked on a personal strike. The struggle availed naught. After six months, and with his wife expecting their first child, Mannion returned to his club where he remained for the rest of his career. Not all players were treated so strictly, and perhaps even Mannion might have secured his transfer had he himself been less obdurate, but the case revealed the residual power that clubs could draw upon if they so wished.[23]

Both the maximum wage and the retain and transfer system could have been challenged by a combination of legal argument and, more appropriately, trade union action. That they were not testifies to the absence of a collective will for change in the labour force. Soccer presented many obstacles to trade unionism. In spite of occasional bursts of energy, such as that led by the Manchester United player Charlie Roberts before the First World War,[24] the professional players posed little threat to the power of the clubs. Whilst playing, their wages placed them comfortably-off in relation even to skilled working men. The paternalist atmosphere of the club and the dressing-room meant that little initiative or responsibility was required from the player, and as a consequence a culture of control developed over players, who one recent journalist has likened to 'overgrown schoolboys'.[25] Directors, moreover, were adept at individualizing the workforce, playing on petty jealousies to set one employee off against another (which explains why Mannion received no support from his fellow players at Middlesbrough), and, when necessary, remorselessly victimizing the employee.

If the labour force provided no pressure for change, what of the supporters or, reverting to the language of business, the consumers? As a general rule it would be fair to say that, until the 1950s, soccer supporters were numerous, well-behaved and loyal. Though clearly important in any discussion of the soccer business, supporters have proved a difficult entity for historians to grapple with.[26] One feature of them that we can describe with some certainty is their numbers. From the beginning of the century attandance figures at football matches show a steady upward trend which reached a peak in the 1948–49 season of over 41 million spectators. The 1890s seems to have been the time when attendances began to scale new heights, with the first 50 000 Cup Final crowd at the Crystal Palace, and 'gates' at some of the bigger grounds in excess of 30 000. In the inter-war years many clubs set their ground records for attendances, Glasgow Rangers leading the way with 118 567 at their Ibrox

Stadium in 1939. Admission charges were suffciently low (a shilling [5p] in the 1920s–1930s) to draw in a wide range of people, though research on Salford at this time suggests that for the poor and the unemployed the cost of attending League fixtures was prohibitive.[27] There is some conjecture in the remarks that historians have made about the composition of soccer crowds, but it seems likely that working men and their sons made up the vast majority of them, with a sprinkling of (probably unmarried) younger women and middle-class men.[28] Historians have also argued about their behaviour. There is plenty of evidence of disorderliness at soccer grounds from the very beginning, but whether this should be interpreted as early manifestations of the 'hooliganism' that appeared from the 1960s onwards is open to debate. Some have explained scenes such as that exemplified in the riot that occurred in the match between Newcastle and Sunderland in 1901 as 'situation-specific' (related to particular incidents in the match itself) rather than as an extension of general social misbehaviour into the soccer stadium.[29] Whatever the explanation, it is worth bearing in mind that clubs considered their support worth investing in. In spite of their poor public relations, the often despicable treatment they meted out to their supporters' clubs, whose efforts on the clubs' behalf were unrequited,[30] and the bad press clubs have received for the state of their grounds, many soccer businesses did divert much of their profit into stadium rebuilding, an endeavour amply illustrated in the excellent research by Simon Inglis on the architecture and development of British soccer grounds.[31]

Not until the 1950s did the labour relations that had prevailed in soccer since the early years of the century begin to change. Even then, as the Mannion case showed, clubs could still be obdurate. But as a result of general economic and social changes in British society, which brought about what has often been termed the 'affluent society', there developed among soccer players a greater determination, accompanied by a keener sense of solidarity, to do something about their position. By the end of the decade the Players' Union, renamed in 1958 the Professional Footballers' Association (PFA), had formulated a clear strategy for removing simultaneously the two pillars on which the clubs' strength had rested: the maximum wage and the retain and transfer system. Led by a new chairman, the Fulham player Jimmy Hill, who adroitly used the press and television to publicize their case, the PFA, after a threat of industrial action, secured the agreement of the League early in 1961 to end the maximum wage system. Retain and transfer, however, proved less amenable to industrial action. It took a legal battle in the case of the Newcastle player George Eastham before the court eventually ruled in 1963 that the system was in restraint of trade. In the following year the Football League agreed to the creation of new contractual relations between players and clubs. They fell short of complete freedom of contract (which did not come until the late 1970s) but the new system meant that the overbearing power previously exercised by clubs over individual players no longer operated. If a player wanted to leave, the club found it much less easy to stand in his way.[32]

These decisions inaugurated a period of unprecedented change in British football which, for some clubs, brought to an end the 'peculiar economics' of the previous half century. Paradoxically, the immediate aftermath of the Eastham case saw a decline in football. A combination of factors – boring play, increasing admission charges, crowd troubles, the relative decline internationally of the England team after winning the World Cup in 1966, and the counter-attractions of other forms of entertainment – all brought about a steady decline in attendances which placed soccer in a serious financial plight. The attendance levels of the late 1940s had virtually halved 30 years later. By the early 1980s, as the Chester Report revealed, many clubs had sunk desperately into debt and were only kept going through the good grace of their bankers. The general financial situation of professional football was, the Report claimed, worse than the previous Chester Committee had found it in the late 1960s.[33] Only a few clubs were able to climb out of this morass. In the main they were those which formed in 1992, under the auspices of the Football Association, the new Premier League. Their financial salvation came from selling to large media companies like BSkyB the rights to televise their matches – 'a Faustian pact with television' in the words of sports journalist Brian Glanville.[34] The deal struck with this company in 1997 gave the Premier League £670 million over four years. Television exposure triggered other forms of sponsorship, and enabled the 20 clubs that made up the 'Premiership' to invest in a host of overseas players,[35] whose availability was now made certain by the easing of work restrictions by the European Union. The Bosman Ruling (so called) of the European Court in 1996 permitted players to move without even the requirement of a transfer fee, thus prompting smaller clubs to claim that without the proceeds from transfers, the gap between them and the elite would widen still further. Thus, in a short space of time, while most soccer clubs continued to find existence a struggle, a few entered a land of riches that their predecessors could scarcely have dreamed about.[36]

The creation of this new plutocracy has, it is claimed, produced new social relations in soccer. The 'working man's game' has disappeared and soccer has become embourgeoised. By the 1990s there was much talk about the 'middle-class revolution' in soccer.[37] To be sure, there are various signs to suggest that this might be true. Admission prices for Premier League matches, which often vary according to the quality of the opposition, have soared. The introduction of foreign players has brought a new cosmopolitanism to the game, reinforced by the increased dominance of clubs from the big conurbations, traditionally powerful but now threatening to erase altogether the localism which had always been a part of the game, especially in the FA Cup.[38] Increasingly, too, the leading players have acquired a cult status as *nouveau riche* icons whom the press lauds for their lifestyle and conspicuous spending. It was a trend that began with the idolization of George Best in the 1960s.[39] In company with this came a new, literary interest in soccer, prompted largely by the success of Nick Hornby's autobiographical memoir *Fever Pitch*[40] and attractive magazines such as *When Saturday Comes* and *Four Four Two*, which managed to balance a serious approach to the game with an interesting format. In their wake a succession of books and magazines, often written by celebrity fans or, in some cases, players themselves, combined to give soccer a fashionable, quasi-intellectual image as a subject for lively debate and comment among a readership of relatively prosperous, young-ish males.[41] It contrasted with the stale sensational tabloid reportage and 'ghosted' auto-biographies that had been the stock-in-trade accompaniment of the game for many years.

Much of this was happening in a changed political culture. It was inspired by a brand of Conservatism that purported to be reviving and modernizing British society around a set of values derived from the principles of the free market, sometimes traced historically to the Victorian bourgeosie, and an authoritarian use of state power on a very selective basis. Football had a curious part to play in this politics.[42] Mainly because of the behaviour of some supporters – the 'hooligans' – the game had come to be seen as a 'problem', reflective of wider social ills engendered in the 'dependency culture' of the welfare state and requiring coercive and containing measures to control it. This discourse was conducted mainly at a rhetorical level as a means of generalizing views about 'what had gone wrong' in Britain – with the working class (and especially its organized elements) being held in part responsible – and what needed to be done to put things right. Apart from Margaret Thatcher's own preference for an identity card scheme as a solution to crowd problems, a scheme which few agreed with, the government had no particular policy on football to bring to the discussion. The Thatcher government's stance was that of middle-class people with a notion that the game could be improved through rational reforms but with little feeling for football's traditions, and in many cases little knowledge of, or interest in, the game. A similar view was inscribed in the Taylor Report, sponsored by the Home Office to inquire into the causes of the disaster in 1989 when 96 soccer supporters lost their lives as a result of overcrowding at the Hillsborough ground in Sheffield.[43] The report produced a series of practical recommendations to improve safety standards at football grounds, the chief one being the removal of the perimeter fences that had been installed at all leading grounds to prevent invasions of the pitch by unruly spectators. In other respects, however, Taylor's tone and assumptions were those of the modernizer who regarded the football stadium as a rational business enterprise which should be presented as such. In the matter of catering, for example:

The refreshments available to supporters are often limited and of indifferent quality. They are sold in surrounding streets from mobile carts and inside many grounds from other carts or from shoddy sheds. Fans eat their hamburgers or chips standing outside in all weathers. There is a prevailing stench of stewed onions. Adequate numbers of bins for rubbish are often not available; so wrappings, containers and detritus are simply dropped. This inhospitable scene tends to breed bad manners and poor behaviour. The atmosphere does not encourage pride in the ground or consideration for others. I accept that many fans are quite content to eat on the hoof when visiting a match, but there is no reason why the fare available should not be wholesome, varied and decently served from clean and attractive outlets. Fast food establishments meeting these requirements are readily to be found at railway stations and on high streets; why not at football grounds?[44]

Such thinking provoked derision from those fans who saw football grounds as being different from multiplex cinemas and supermarkets. They actually *liked* (or at least claimed they did) the very ambience that Taylor was condemning. In resisting the sanitizing of football grounds with all-seating arrangements and wholesome food 'outlets', the opponents of Taylor were rejecting a vision in which the soccer club became a rational business and the fan a 'customer'. It was a vision that lacked the atmosphere of the crowd, especially its male sociability, and which did, indeed, appear to have as its principal aim the casting out of the troublesome working-class fan who was giving soccer its bad name: 'a slum sport played in slum stadiums' as the *Sunday Times* described it in 1985.[45] The idea of soccer with the spectators left out is not entirely fanciful, at least when the Italian club Juventus were reported as considering building a new stadium in Turin to hold only 32 000 spectators. The 'real' audience was out there in televisionland.

Whether all these new commercial and political pressures did effect a transformation of bourgeois proportions on the elite soccer clubs, let alone the lesser ones, is uncertain. There was certainly no shortage of comment on this at the close of the 1990s, when Manchester United achieved its remarkable treble. But even at this most commercial of all British sports clubs there seemed to be plenty of fans prepared to campaign for a retention of the old ways.

COMMERCIALISM IN OTHER SPORTS

How far were the patterns seen in football displayed in other sports? At the beginning of the twentieth century, there were actually few that combined the same degree of popular interest and commercial orientation to be found in football. But by the 1930s a range of sports – some old-established, others quite new, some distinctly 'popular', others retaining a definite social exclusivity – developed a commercial side. Cricket was the sport that rivalled soccer in its widespread appeal, and continued to be known by many as the 'national game'. In some respects its commercialization came very early. In the 1850s and 1860s the proselytizing of the game had been done by touring teams of paid players organized by cricketer-entrepreneurs like William Clarke of Nottinghamshire, who took advantage of the railways to send his elevens across the country to play 'twenty-two' in various districts. The eventual failure of English cricket to adopt this highly commercialized format, somewhat akin to the style introduced by Kerry Packer in Australia in the 1970s, and to take up instead an amateur-led form based upon county clubs is an interesting case of historical development.[46] As Simon Rae has shown in his excellent biography of the game's great champion of the 1870s – W. G. Grace – the two forms coexisted for a time, and it was probably the decision of Grace himself, by far the outstanding performer of his day, to throw in his lot with the counties that caused the demise of the professional touring circuses.[47] Thereafter, the professionals, always an important part of the game, were subordinated socially in the rule of the county clubs, dominated by a middle- and upper middle-class leadership who saw in cricket a repository of certain English values of sportsmanship. Such clubs remained voluntary associations of private individuals. Scarcely any interest was expressed in adapting the game for capital maximization. As Vamplew and Sandiford have revealed in their examination of the 'peculiar economics' of English cricket, various avenues of business exploitation were unexplored so that 'English cricket decidedly was not profit-oriented'.[48]

What also needs to be stressed about cricket, and which has perhaps been under-investigated by historians, is the strong sense of the game's 'aesthetic': of a game which enshrined features of athletic skill, style and strategy that evolved over the course of a lengthy period of play, and which were contained within a set of social relationships publicly displayed on the field and commemorated in the game's extensive literature. Cricket was the very haven of amateur control. No county team was captained, except in emergencies, by a professional, and the England XI had only one professional captain (Len Hutton, 1952–55) between Arthur Shrewsbury (who captained a tour to Australia in the 1880s) and the ending of the amateur/professional distinction in 1963. In the inter-war years, as Jack Williams's work has clearly brought out, this form of cricket not only succeeded in remaining insulated from commercialism, but stood itself as a beacon of that distinctive English upper-class ethos that affected distaste for trade and money making and which, according to historians such as Martin Wiener and Perry Anderson, helps to explain a curious absence of 'modernization' in twentieth-century British society.[49] Cricket took its place alongside a number of other conservative institutions and practices that set their face against the 'age of the masses' and everything that notion implied about popular participation and democracy. 'First-class' cricket, as this form described itself, undoubtedly had a popular following, as attendances for county matches, especially at holiday times, and at almost all international fixtures, testify. But such popularity was not courted. The strained relationship between first-class cricket and the masses is summed up in the words of a northern working man: 'Tha's got to be a man o' means to watch first-class cricket . . . and besides, tha's expected to wear a collar and tie when tha goes to Old Trafford.'[50]

The league cricket that developed in the North and Midlands, and to a lesser extent in South Wales, Scotland and north-east England, during the course of the early-twentieth century was far more populist in its forms and general attitudes. As amateur, club-based cricket, it evolved a distinctive style which marked it out from the club cricket played in the south of England, and also from the recreational cricket universally popular among enthusiastic but untalented players at the very local level.[51] League cricket adhered strictly to the principle of the 'league table', the placing of teams in a hierarchy of positions according to points achieved from matches won, so that something was at stake in each match. Keen attention was paid to time-keeping, so that each game began and ended according to an agreed schedule. A good standard of ground and pitch maintenance was expected in order to ensure decent levels of skill. Spectating was encouraged, and grounds equipped to handle it, often by charging for admission. And, perhaps most important, though the league clubs were always captained by amateur members, they depended heavily on the services of paid players. Such players, often former county professionals but increasingly in the bigger leagues by the inter-war period international stars, became local heroes and the focus of identity and pride. In the Lancashire League from the 1920s until the 1960s many of the leading test cricketers of Australia, the West Indies and India could be found playing as professionals for local clubs. The Trinidadian Learie Constantine was thus employed at Nelson from 1929 until 1937, during which time he brought the club great success and himself much esteeem and financial reward. He was said to have been one of the highest-paid sports performers at this time, certainly earning more from his basic wages and frequent 'collections' from the crowds for outstanding performances than did his contemporaries in the soccer world. League cricket, especially in Lancashire, was thus far more attuned to the local community than its first-class counterpart ever was, and in some ways was more commercialized. Although it did not exist essentially to make profits for its clubs, and thus remained 'utility maximizing', it was not resistant to the idea of linking a popular form of entertainment to the securuing of revenues from crowds, and the hiring of stars on the basis of such a strategy. It thus had a little more in common with other forms of popular entertainment such as music hall and cinema. One reason why it has for long been 'hidden from history' – for the literature of cricket has said little about the activities of the leagues – might be to do with the threat it represented to the 'aesthetic' of the game as defined by the county establishment.[52]

Cricket occupied a unique place in that its appeal was too widespread for it ever to have been consigned rigidly to being a 'middle-class' sport. Golf, athletics and tennis could more readily be so classified, at least for most of the century. Golf had strong associations in the popular mind with suburbia, though in fact its expansion as a sport had occurred in many other settings. But many features of the game affirmed its middle-class nature: the expense of golf, for example, in terms of the equipment needed, the fashion to be followed, and the cost of subscribing to a club. The socially-exclusive nature of many clubs also distanced the sport from the masses. The threat of the penetration of mass society into golf usually provoked a *frisson*. John Lowerson has aptly brought this to our attention in the form of *Golf Illustrated*'s anguished outburst in 1929, when a suggestion had been made to open a totalizator at a tournament at Frinton-on-Sea: 'Do we want our golf courses crowded with a set of raucous-voiced thugs whose ideas on sportmanship are as far removed from the ideals as the earth is from the moon?.'[53] But golf had always had its popular heroes, presented to the public through newspapers like the *News of the World*, which since 1903 had sponsored the Professional Golfers' Association (PGA) World Match Play tournament. With the coverage of golf on television from the 1950s (the sport, says Lowerson, is 'singularly telegenic'[54]) it began to enjoy a profile which stimulated a proliferation of both public and private course building in the 1970s, as well as a significant increase in commercial sponsorship of the major tournaments. As a result, golf has become rather more of a 'people's game' than its origins might suggest. Moreover, it is one whose domestic context has been reconfigured on to an international scale, not only through the long-standing domination of golf tournaments by overseas (mainly American) players, but in the way that even for quite ordinary practitioners, the playing of golf overseas has become possible through packaged holidays.

The two other sports with a close affinity to the middle class – tennis and athletics – similarly experienced a late blossoming into commercialism. Lawn tennis was invented in an upper-class milieu in the 1870s and for a long time remained within this sphere. The popular saying, 'anyone for tennis?', instantly connoted social privilege and a leisured life-style. Like golf, it was expensive to play, and tennis clubs were not noted for their proletarian image. Only after the Second World War were attempts made to extend the sport widely. Yet tennis produced one of Britain's greatest sporting heroes of the inter-war period, Fred Perry, who won the Wimbledon men's singles championship three times in succession between 1934 and 1936, before turning professional and emigrating to America. Perry, as the son of a Labour MP, was hardly from an underprivileged background, but he lacked the social status needed for complete acceptance at Wimbledon, and his desire to make money through his talents (which he did in abundance) was not considered sporting. He played 30 years too soon. By the 1960s much had changed, notably the acceptance by Wimbledon and other leading tournaments of professionalism, which had hitherto been confined to separate, American-based organizations and circuits. The explanation lay in Wimbledon's need to continue attracting the world's best players in order to maintain its status as a premier event, and competition from rivals and the importance of television fees ensured that even Wimbledon had to move with the times.[55]

Athletics acquired its upper-class characteristics in the 1860s, when the more plebeian variants of running, which had become associated with betting, race fixing and professionalism, were taken over and cleaned up by university men from Oxbridge. Though professional athletics continued to exist it was pushed to the margins, with the mainstream activity shaped and controlled by the Amateur Athletics Association (AAA) after 1880. It permitted no professionalism, nor even, until 1899, the payment of expenses for athletes attending meetings. Pocket money for athletes representing the AAA was not allowed until 1956. The amateur ethos was firmly entrenched by the early years of the century, with the 1920s representing 'the high point of the cult of the gentleman amateur'[56] embodied in Oxbridge figures such as Harold Abrahams, Eric Liddell, Douglas Lowe and Lord Burghley, all commemorated in Hugh Hudson's 1981 award-winning film *Chariots of Fire*. But like golf and tennis, the major athletics meetings aroused deep popular interest, and leading athletes such as Gordon Pirie and Roger Bannister in the 1950s were widely admired. Television similarly helped to sustain and gradually expand this interest, and the opportunities it offered for commercial sponsorship introduced a financial element into athletics which athletes themselves sought to exploit and which undermined the amateur traditions. As Jeremy Crump has observed, in the 1960s and 1970s 'the status of athletes was transformed'.[57] Under pressure from athletes, and sensitive to the poor international performances of British teams in the 1970s, the athletics authorities recognized that an elite squad, effectively financed, was needed. By 1982 the trust-fund principle of placing income from appearances and from commercial sponsorship and contracts into a fund to provide for athletes' training and subsistence, as well as for income in later life, had become an established feature of remuneration in athletics. The champion athletes – Linford Christie, Daley Thompson, Denise Lewis, Jonathan Edwards and others – were earning sums similar to those of top sportspeople in other fields, and much more than most practitioners in their own field.[58]

Another group of sports developed commercialism much earlier and had strong support from the working class. Of these, speedway is one of the most interesting (though under-researched) since it was not an indigenous growth. It arrived from Australia in the late 1920s in the care of impresarios Johnny Hoskins and A. J. Hunting. Speedway was quickly taken up by owners of greyhound stadiums who saw it compensating for a feared decline in interest in the dogs. From the outset it was, says Jack Williams, 'almost totally commercialized'.[59] There was virtually no amateur speedway racing. The better riders could expect earnings of around £40 a week in the 1930s, though at a price: overheads (mainly bikes and their repair) were high, the risk of injury was great, riders had to make frequent appearances to rack up their earnings, and the long-term prospects for the sport were uncertain. The life of many a speedway club was short, and there was a rapid turnover of business ventures and the venues associated with them. Only Wembley, West Ham, Wimbledon and Belle Vue (Manchester) enjoyed any permanence. By the late 1930s most of the activity was concentrated in London. For some it was an exciting entertainment with a unique 'modernist' aesthetic in which, unlike most other sports, nature was erased in favour of the machine. Even the rider was masked. This could create an excitement which brought large crowds. *Speedway News* reported an attendance of 93 000 at Wembley in 1938 for the final of the world championship, but that was exceptional and the unreliability of spectator support made speedway an unpredictable business in most venues. Though it still endured in Britain as a minority sport at the end of the century, its most successful period was that between its foundation and the outbreak of the Second World War, when the growth of the motor-cycle industry and the popularity of motor bikes with working-class men provided an important context and stimulus.[60]

Far more durable, because it emerged from the social relations of real communities rather than being imposed from the outside, was rugby league. Its very origins were intimately connected with commercialism, and the desire of northern rugby clubs to pay their working-men members for time lost from work – 'broken time' payments. It was this issue that provoked the 'great schism' of 1895, when a group of clubs from Yorkshire and Lancashire broke away from the Rugby Football Union to form the Northern Union (which in 1922 adopted the Australian name Rugby League). The important research of Tony Collins reveals both class and regional tensions in the breakaway.[61] Many of the northern rugby clubs, which by the 1890s were powerful forces in the English game, had a strong working-class membership and following which contested the amateur ethos expounded by the Rugby Football Union. Covert payments to amateur players were, as in cricket, an established feature of the game, and in seeking to regularize 'broken time' payments the northern clubs wanted to introduce a degree of openness about pay without going the whole way towards a soccer-style professionalism. In addition to having this different perspective on payment, many clubs of the Northern Union had a distinctive social character, being run by men from that borderland between the working and the middle class, where publicans, shop-owners, teachers and skilled working men commingled. Collins suggests, perhaps not unfancifully, that within this social bracket, there was a desire among its members to assert themselves in the face of what was seen as the power and privilege exercised by those above. Carrying forward some of the old radical tradition of 'Jack is as good as his master', there was a natural inclination towards liberalism and the Liberal Party, and political affiliation might have been a factor in determining initial responses to the formation of the Northern Union in 1895. In Manchester, for example, Broughton Rangers (Liberal) joined, while Salford (Conservative) stayed with the RFU. More important than this, however, was the way the Northern Union was seen, by both its adherents and its opponents, as having a special affinity with the working class, and as expressing, perhaps better than any other sport, a particular idea of 'the North'. This remained a feature of the game for many years, being exploited and transmuted by the BBC in the 1960s,[62] and then diluted in the 1990s by the BSkyB presentation of the sport, which re-emphasized the international community of rugby league that had existed since the beginning of the century.

GAMBLING

It is impossible to conclude this discussion of commerce and sport without a consideration of horse-racing: or more precisely, the culture of betting that surrounded horse-racing. Though nationally organized, and enjoying high social esteeem as a consequence of its associations with royalty, horse-racing is much less a *sport* than the other activities so far examined. For the many who show an interest in horse-racing the attraction is simply explained. As Vamplew has put it: 'To racegoers, almost as much as to the betting shop *habitués*, the horse is an agency for gambling.'[63] It was the most important of a whole series of sporting activities in which betting had become a chief interest for the spectator, and sometimes for the participant. Greyhound-racing, football, pigeon-racing, crown-green bowling in the north of England, professional athletics, angling, boxing, knur and spell, and some forms of cricket were all the subject of passionate betting. 'For some', McKibbin has observed, 'the bet was more important than the sport'.[64] Most of these sports had a strong working-class following; some, like greyhound-racing or crown-green bowling (especially the professional form known in Lancashire as 'Panel' bowling), were almost exclusively working class in character. They reveal the remarkable degree of betting at this social level, carried out through an intricate web of small-capitalist neighbourhood bookmakers and their 'runners', whose operations were mostly illegal. For although credit betting 'off course' was permissible, as was 'on course' betting for cash, betting for cash in the street, pub or the illicit betting shops that abounded, especially in the north of England, was against the law, and subjected to frequent raids by the police.

The effects of the Street Betting Act of 1906, the principal piece of legislation to encapsulate these reglations, thus fell most heavily on working people. Middle-class punters could place their bets on credit. Only betting by coupon on soccer matches – the 'pools' – which began in earnest with the Moores brothers in Manchester in the 1920s and quickly developed into one of the great institutions of British life, escaped the stigma of being outside the law. Not that its illegality, nor the moral opprobrium directed at it by members of higher social groups, deterred working-class men and women from indulging in a 'flutter'. And that, mostly, is what it was. In spite of the fears of politicians and religious leaders, who regarded betting by working people as an irrational and feckless pursuit liable to lead to poverty, gambling seems to have been a modest, if pervasive, social pastime which, according to the leading social historians of gambling, was kept under control by its practitioners.[65] The allure of betting was not only in the excitement it offered in the prospect of a win – Orwell's 'cheapest of luxuries' – but in the way it provided a means of controlling chance (and thus one's life) by working out a 'system' to beat the bookies. Though much betting was whimsical, particularly on the pools or the popular sweepstakes organized on the Grand National steeplechase, for many people the bet was placed instrumentally, after careful consideration of form, to gain a windfall that would secure a material possession. McKibbin has described this as English betting's 'markedly intellectual character'.[66] The whole culture of betting, which was frowned upon not only by moral observers, but by the leaders of most of the sports around which betting occurred – in the 1930s, for example, the Football League unsuccessfully attempted to ban the pools – shows very clearly how popular commercial entertainments could be adapted to meet the tastes and interests of popular society.

CONCLUSION

The link between sport and commerce has been present throughout the twentieth century. Few sports have been unaffected in one way or another by commercial considerations. This is true even of sport played at the recreational level, a dimension usually disregarded by historians interested in the economics of sport. But, as every member of an amateur sports club knows, the raising of funds by selling raffle tickets, organizing social events, and seeking sponsorship from local businesses and grants from local government is an essential part of raising the money to keep voluntary associations afloat. But in the higher reaches of spectator sport, such concerns have long assumed a major place. Britain was well ahead of other European countries in developing commercial sport, closer perhaps to the United States than to countries like France and Germany until the inter-war years. What is interesting in this respect, however, is the relative lack of American influence on the development of British sport. Not only did few American sports succeed in penetrating the British sporting culture (and this was not for the want of trying by American entrepreneurs such as A. G. Spalding, who sought to introduce baseball before the First World War), but American business models also seem to have exerted little influence. Compared with the hard-nosed capitalist attitudes displayed in sports like baseball, the main British sports retained a curious mixture of gentlemanly restraint, localism and loyalty to supporters. Clear links with distinctive communities were cultivated. Thus developed the 'peculiar economics' of many British sports. It was only late in the century that these traditions began to dissolve, and opportunities for commercial development that had lain dormant for many years were seized.

This was most clearly witnessed in the 1990s in the remarkable and sudden transformation that overtook rugby union, a game that had seemed for long the quintessence of amateurism. Faced with the competition of both rugby league and association football, and tempted by the money of television companies looking for dramatic sporting action, rugby union emerged by the end of the decade as a professional game with all the attendant media exposure that sports fans had come to expect from association football. Perhaps the most striking feature of all this was the way rugby restyled its form of play. A game that had often made for a rather scrappy spectacle because of the frequent stoppages for line-outs and scrums (albeit an enjoyable one to play) had its rules adjusted to allow for more continuous action and, it was assumed, excitement. It became, ironically, more like rugby league. And, also like rugby league, the sport's long-standing international associations, bred of empire, were developed into a new form of commercial sporting globalism.[67]

Rugby's experiences encapsulate many of the shifts in the commercial orientation of sport that were taking place at this time. The explanation for these shifts is to be found in forces present both inside and outside sport, but one profoundly influential process was what has become known as 'globalization'; namely the operation of economic and cultural interests and activities on a global rather than a national scale. For much of this century, although international sporting competition was commonplace, power in sport radiated for the most part from national and even sub-national sources. By the end of the century this was no longer the case. It was global influences that triggered the issue with which this chapter began. The attempt to gain control of Manchester United illustrates not only the extent to which the club itself had acquired an international standing through the success of its sporting exploits, but also the way in which it was felt that the club's name would further enhance the global interests of a company like BSkyB. Thus Manchester United had become a leading example of a sports business which had outgrown its national market and which had accumulated the capital and fashioned the brand image that enabled it to operate in a world context. Its operations were characterized by features shared by a number of other elite football clubs which increasingly drew their resources of players, television viewers, capital, and match competitions from an international pool. The process further emphasized the economic disparity that had always been present between clubs in commercial sport.

Key Reading

Benson, J. *The Rise of Consumer Society in Britain, 1880–1980*. London: Longman, 1994.

Mason, T. *Association Football and English Society, 1863–1915*. Brighton: Harvester Press, 1981 edn.

Mason, T. *Sport in Britain: A Social History*. Cambridge: Cambridge University Press, 1989.

Russell, D. *Football and the English: A Social History of Association Football in England, 1863–1995*. Preston: Carnegie Publishing, 1997.

Vamplew, W. *Pay up and Play the Game: Professional Sport in Britain, 1875–1914*. Cambridge: Cambridge University Press, 1988.

Chronology of Events

1870s Establishment of the County Championship in cricket, with professionalism well established.

1885 Acceptance by the Football Association (est. 1863) of professionalism; soon followed in late 1880s and early 1890s by the conversion of football clubs into limited liability companies.

1887 Establishment of the Talbot Handicap for professional bowling, staged at the Talbot Arms hotel, Blackpool; followed by the Waterloo Handicap in 1907, also staged at Blackpool.

1888–89 Inauguration of the Football League, with 12 clubs from the North and Midlands; extended with a second division in 1892–93, and two regional third divisions in 1920–21, by which time the number of League clubs had increased to 88.

1890 Formation of the Scottish Football League.

1895 Establishment of the Northern Rugby Union (renamed the Rugby Football League in 1922) after breaking away from the Rugby Football Union.

1896–c.1900 Series of measures introduced by the Football Association to prevent excessive commercialism: restriction of dividends paid to shareholders of clubs, maximum wage imposed on players, and harsh master–servant relationship between clubs and players encoded in the retain and transfer system.

1901 Formation of the Professional Golfers' Association (PGA).

1903 Establishment of the *News of the World* tournament in golf.

1906 Street Betting Act banned cash betting except on racecourses.

1913 Attendance of over 120 000 at the FA Cup Final, Crystal Palace, London.

1923 Football pools company established by John Moores in Manchester, later moved to Liverpool where Vernons was also set up in 1925.

1926 Introduction of commercial greyhound racing from the USA; first meeting held at Belle Vue, Manchester.

1927 Introduction into Britain from Australia of speedway racing; first meeting at Droylsden, Manchester; league formed 1929.

1928 Introduction of the 'Tote' (Totalizator) system of on-course betting in horse-racing, designed to direct gambling profits back into the sport.

1933–36 Fred Perry, after helping Great Britain to win the Davis Cup at Lawn Tennis on four successive occasions (1933–36), and having himself won the singles title at Wimbledon on three successive occasions (1934–36), turned professional, had his Wimbledon membership withdrawn and emigrated to the USA.

1961 Abolition of the maximum wage system in football.

1963 Court ruling in the case of *Eastham v. Newcastle Utd F.C.* found the old retain and transfer system in football to be 'in restraint of trade'.

1963 Abolition of the distinction in cricket between 'amateurs' and 'professionals'; institution of the Gillette limited overs knock-out cup competition (became the NatWest Trophy in 1980).

1968 First 'open' Wimbledon tennis championships, to which professional players were admitted.

1982 Establishment of trust funds for athletes.

1980s Extension of sponsorship by commercial organizations (especially beer, tobacco, financial services) into many sports; e.g. horse-racing, association football, snooker, rugby.

1987 Establishment of Rugby World Cup.

1992 Formation by the FA and the 22 clubs of the First Division of the Football League of the new FA Premier League (the 'Premiership'), sponsored by the beer firm Carling. It followed various indications over the previous few years that leading clubs wanted to break away from the League to take advantage of the money to be gained from selling television rights. A £304 million deal was then concluded between BSkyB and the Premier League for exclusive television coverage of live Premiership matches; bidding for exclusive rights had been permitted by the 1990 Broadcasting Act.

1995 Concluding of £550 million deal between SkyTV and rugby authorities in southern hemisphere professionalized the game in that part of the world; rapid professionalization of British rugby.

3

Sport and the Media

CONTENTS

There is a sense in which a discussion, as in the previous chapter, of those who ran, played and watched commercial sport is only half the story. And perhaps not the more important half. Many people (possibly even most) who possessed an interest in sport were not officials, practitioners or spectators. Their 'experience' of sport was an indirect one, communicated to them through a variety of forms of information. This process of mediation – carried out, of course, by 'the media' – through written, visual, oral and aural means was responsible for what many people understood sport to be. Within these media texts were inscribed many assumptions, preconceptions and 'common-sense' attitudes about sport and life that positioned readers, viewers and listeners in relation not only to sport, but to many other aspects of society. It is as a consequence of this that, as J. A. Mangan has pointed out, 'sport not only reflects culture: it shapes it.'[1]

Much of this is illustrated in the way we think about sporting heroes. In the years immediately after the Second World War, the cricketer-footballer Denis Compton was one of Britain's most popular sports stars, so well known that he became a household name. His exploits on the cricket field in the summers of 1947 and 1948 gave him a status which rivalled that of many a contemporary film star. Compton's dark good looks, his dashing style of play and his apparent boundless natural ability marked him out as an obvious national hero. At a time of post-war austerity, when the population generally was experiencing shortages and sports-lovers, in particular, were smarting from the lack of British achievement, Compton was one a very small band of sportspeople who could repay foreigners (especially Australians) in their own coin. In a glorious summer of sun in 1947, Compton reached a higher aggregate total of runs in an English county cricket season than anyone before or since, and seemed to symbolize in his rich vein of form everything the British people were deprived of in their daily lives. As the cricket writer Neville Cardus famously put it: 'there was no rationing in an innings of Compton'. Beaverbrook's Conservative-inclined *Daily Express*, given to attacking the contemporary Labour government's austerity measures, lauded Compton as the man of the people who put pride back into Britain: 'the Englishman, the Briton, the eternal athlete, the phenomenon . . . this scion of a lost race.'[2]

This image of Compton, strong at the time and fondly remembered in later years by middle-aged men who had been schoolboys in the 1940s, was largely a media creation.[3] The qualities perceived in Compton were those inscribed in the written and recorded reports and visual images of the period. They embellished the personal memory of those (a minority) who actually saw him play. But they went further than this, forming an assemblage of ideas about class, gender, ethnicity and place. The figure of Compton, a focus for hero worship, became also a text in which was elaborated a complex set of meanings about sport and the English at a time of post-war adjustment to the decline of Empire and the rise of the superpowers. Denis Compton conveyed more than just the pleasure of sport to the population of Britain at the time.

THE NEWSPAPER PRESS

There was, in fact, a 'discourse' of sport, which had the capacity to shape social attitudes. The principal agency in creating it was, and had been since the nineteenth century, the newspaper press. Until the rise of television, it was the principal medium for transmitting information and ideas about sport. All sections – the national dailies, the Sundays, the local newspapers and the specialist sports papers and magazines – reported it, and to extensive readerships. It was estimated, for example, that just after the Second World War each of the most popular dailies was read by over 20 million people. The Sundays had even higher readerships, with that of the *News of the World*, its coverage spiced by divorce cases and sex scandals, reaching possibly 46 million people.[4] In their various ways all operated on a long-held assumption that sport sold newspapers. Since the later years of the nineteenth century a strong specialist sporting press had been in existence, establishing codes of sportswriting either on a focused area, like *Sporting Life* which concentrated on the turf, or, like the Manchester-based *Athletic News*, on a range of sports. Their style, in company with that of most of the late-Victorian and Edwardian press, tended to be heavy and detailed. J. A. H. Catton, who edited the *Athletic News* in its later days, was a distinguished sports journalist whose classically inspired byelines ('Ubique' and 'Tityrus') say something about the man and his prose.[5] Detailed narratives were the style of the local press too. When Bury won the

FA Cup twice within the space of three years at the beginning of the century, the *Bury Times* first recorded the club's achievement in four columns of tightly packed reporting, and on the second occasion (a 6–0 Cup Final record) with a full six-column page, illustrated only by small vignettes of players and officials.[6] Things were beginning to change with the foundation in 1896 of the first mass-circulation daily, the *Daily Mail*, and in 1903 of the *Daily Mirror*, initially a paper aimed at middle-class women with plenty of pictures and advertisements for expensive shops. They departed from the dense layout of the established press to introduce a more readable page on which pictures increasingly conveyed much of the story. By the inter-war years the specialist sporting press had lost some of its appeal to the national 'tabloid' dailies and Sunday newspapers, with their characteristic sports pages placed at the back of the paper and covering some 10–15 per cent, and in the case of the *People* just after the Second World War 20 per cent, of its entire content. In contrast with the classical pseudonyms and factual style adopted by Catton, or the continuing anonymity of sports reporters of *The Times*, writers were emerging by the 1930s as media personalities in their own right. In the manner of the American journalist Grantland Rice, credited with the invention of the 'gee whiz' school of sportswriting, they forsook the prosaic for the imaginative, the human drama, and the 'behind the scenes' story: in short, sensationalism.[7] The sports editor of the *Daily Express* in the 1930s, Trevor Wignall, was one of the pioneers of this new style in Britain, alongside such journalists as Henry Rose, also of the *Express*, Peter Wilson, himself the son of a *Daily Mirror* writer, and Alan Hoby of the *Sunday Express*. The last two were proclaimed by their papers as 'The Man They Can't Gag' (Wilson) and 'The Man Who Knows' (Hoby, re-interpreted by his more sceptical readers as 'The Man Who Knows —— All').[8]

The style of the popular press served to position its readers to sport in a number of distinctive ways. First, sport for the most part was cast in terms of popular sports. Horse-racing, because of its betting appeal, soccer, boxing and cricket made up the vast majority of the sports pages. Other sports were covered only when they possessed a well-loved national event such as the Boat Race, or when a British competitor had achieved success, as with Fred Perry's triumphs at Wimbledon in the mid-1930s. Otherwise minority sports were felt to have little intrinsic appeal to readers, especially in the 1930s, a time of competition for circulation when the newspaper market was overstocked with popular titles. Second, such a focus emphasized male interests. Though some of these sports, cricket and soccer for example, were played by women, female contributions to them were almost wholly neglected, except when they had a 'novelty' value, as in the brief flurry of women's soccer during and just after the First World War. There was no sense in which the popular newspaper press felt that it had any obligation to inform and educate its younger female readers, which in some cases made up a considerable proportion of the readership, about the possibilities open to them in sport. If readers wanted to know about women's cricket, for example, they would usually need to consult a specialist publication like *Women's Cricket*.[9] The press therefore conformed to a conventional wisdom that sport was a male preserve, and thereby helped to reinforce popular attitudes about the sexual division of leisure.

Third, there was a markedly insular approach to sports coverage which ensured that readers viewed the sporting world from a British perspective. In fact, that world was largely coterminous with Britain, or even localities within it. The local press continued to be an important part of sports coverage and a major force in stimulating local partisanship. One section of it in particular became a regular and well-loved feature of local life. This was the football special – often printed on coloured paper and known as the *Pink 'Un* or the *Green 'Un*. Before radio started to broadcast soccer results at 5 o'clock on Saturdays after the Second World War, the football specials, which were on the streets by 6 o'clock, were first with the results and often with extensive match reports. At the national level developments in sport were well covered by all the major dailies by the inter-war years, but developments in other countries were less prominent. They came into the reckoning only when British competitors and teams were contesting a sport with foreigners. Thus the early soccer World Cup competitions of the 1930s, in which no British teams took part, were ignored. The fourth World Cup of 1950, held in Brazil, was contested by England, though without success as the team was eliminated at an early stage. At this point, as if to emphasize their insularity, the entire British press corps took the plane back to London. This astonished the cosmopolitan journalist Willy Meisl, who could scarcely believe that British reporters would want to miss 'watching and studying the cream of the world's foremost soccer nations'.[10]

Three years later, when the England team lost a home match for the first time against foreign opposition – the famous 3–6 defeat by Hungary – the popular press suddenly discovered that things had been going on abroad of which it, and its readers, were quite ignorant. The Wolfenden Report of 1960, *Sport and the Community*, sponsored by the Central Council of Physical Recreation (CCPR) to look into the apparently backward state of British sport, rounded on the press. 'It was remarked with some justice', concluded the Report, 'that the outlook of our sporting Press is often as insular as the attitude of some Governing Bodies. Britain's position and problems in international sport are not generally understood because the public are rarely made aware of developments abroad until they are taken by surprise by the results.'[11] It was a fair point, but it made little difference to the basic approach of the popular press. By the closing decade of the century the sports content of the popular press was little different in tone from what it had been in the inter-war years. More international competition in many sports brought an apparently more cosmopolitan outlook, though the near-racist way in which this was handled when reporting cricket matches against Pakistan in the 1980s and 1990s showed that some of the old traits were still present.[12]

What used to be called the 'quality' press – mainly the *Times*, the *Daily Telegraph*, the *Guardian* and the *Scotsman* – did not always share these characteristics. For many years the *Daily Telegraph*, which in 1937 had absorbed the *Morning Post*, has been able to claim the most comprehensive sports coverage of the dailies, spanning both the popular and the minority, the amateur and the professional sports. As a paper of the aspiring middle classes of the Home Counties it was especially sound on rugby football, and was unique in maintaining a full reporting of private school sports. The *Times*, as Mason has noted, 'generally looked down its aristocratic nose at sports with large spectator followings'.[13] It did cover the Cup Final regularly, mainly because it was a national event whose significance transcended football. This became apparent to the paper in 1914 when the monarch attended the match for the first time. The reports of the *Times* correspondent on this event were an interesting mixture of court news and contemporary politics, with some football observations (of a quite perceptive nature, to be sure) thrown in. None the less, because of the Kings's presence the paper was moved to pronounce that 'professional football of the best kind is no longer regarded as a spectacle suitable only for the proletariat'.[14] For the most part, however, the *Times* showed as much interest in amateur sports as professional ones. It reserved a special place for cricket, a game which kept its professionals firmly in their place. Cricket earned the *Guardian* (when still the *Manchester Guardian*) a reputation for literary style. Its main writer on this sport was Neville Cardus, who significantly doubled as music critic. His reports and essays were considered to have elevated sportswriting – not generally regarded in Britain as a high art – to a level and quality more usually associated with American authors such as Ring Lardner and Ernest Hemingway. Spanning the worlds of sport and literature in this way was exceptional, and Cardus's achievement was matched by few others: Henry Longhurst, Hugh McIlvanney and Brian Glanville were notable later examples. Glanville, indeed, has claim to have written the only serious novel on association football, *The Rise of Gerry Logan*.[15]

RADIO AND TELEVISION BROADCASTING

The influence of the newspaper press was strong in other areas of sports presentation. One of these was broadcasting, which has always drawn heavily in both technique and personnel from the newspaper office. Between 1922 and 1955 broadcasting in Britain was a monopoly of the British Broadcasting Corporation (BBC), and it was during these years that a particular 'style' was developed, initially in radio and then transported into television by both the BBC and its commercial rivals.[16] The BBC imbibed a range of influences from all sections of the press and moulded them into a unique cultural product of its own. The history of the BBC, especially during its monopoly phase, is often interpreted in terms of the influence of its first Director General, the redoubtable Scot John Reith, who left the Corporation in 1937. Reith's rather austere vision of public broadcasting as an essentially educational service purveyed in a dignified, respectable manner (typified in the wearing by male radio announcers of black tie when at the microphone in the evening) is often parodied. In fact, it was consistent with a philosophy enunciated by the Sykes Committee of 1923 which, in its inquiry into broadcasting, had regarded the airwaves as 'a valuable form of public property' entrusted to the broadcasting authority, which was charged with administering it responsibly.[17]

In this context the broadcasting of sport was given a number of distinctive inflexions. To begin with, and to be expected, there was a notably upper-class, public-school manner of presentation. This was illustrated in the accents and demeanour of a succession of radio and television sports presenters. Starting with the commentator at the first broadcast Cup Final in 1927 – George Allison, the later manager of Arsenal F.C. – there is a clear lineage through Raymond Glendenning and Peter Dimmock, Head of Outside Broadcast and presenter of television's *Sportsview* in the 1950s, to Brian Johnston ('Johnners'), a television and later radio commentator on cricket who invested the popular 'Test Match Special' commentaries in the 1970s and 1980s with the culture of the preparatory school. Not surprisingly, there was maintained in the BBC's approach to sport a keen amateur ethic. Until forced by competition from rival broadcasting networks in the later part of the century to adopt a more 'populist' style derived from the 'tabloid' press, the BBC clung to a mode of presentation which cherished dignity, neutrality, and even a degree of insouciance in the reporting of sport. In 1949 commentators at a soccer match between England and Italy were enjoined by their producer to stimulate a sense of partisanship whilst not 'groaning' every time a English move broke down.[18] S. J. de Lotbiniere ('Lobby'), head of television Outside Broadcasts in the early 1950s, developed a notably patrician style which he communicated to his commentators: identifying the two sides, and explaining the rules, techniques and context all formed part of an *informative* approach to describing play which eschewed any attempt to transform the process into a cheap entertainment. 'There's very little time', noted 'Lobby' in an internal memo, 'for any but the most memorable wisecracks.'[19]

Such an ethos ensured that the BBC maintained the traditions of the 'quality' press in covering a range of sports from an educational perspective. Attention to essentially participatory sports such as athletics, through coverage of the AAA championships, increased interest in, and the esteeem of, such sports.[20] Radio also helped other sports, notably cricket and boxing, to acquire a wider appeal, often among a new audience of women and young people.[21] Alongside the amateur principle was another feature of the BBC's approach to broadcasting: its emphasis on the nation. The Crawford Committee of 1926 had stressed that the BBC should be a 'trustee for the nation', and in taking up this idea the Corporation became one of the principal agencies through which an identity of the British nation was fashioned.[22] This was achieved in sport by the direct broadcasting, where possible, of national sporting occasions such as the FA Cup Final, the big horse-racing events, test matches, Wimbledon and the Boat Race. As Briggs has noted, these came to be regarded by the BBC as 'musts'.[23] Moreover, the Corporation succeeded in this without, at the same time, neglecting a sense of localism. Indeed, as Briggs has also pointed out, Reith always distinguished between centralization of control and centralisation of content, allowing regional directors much latitude to exploit opportunities for local material in their own way.[24] Until at least the 1950s there was a strong element of regionalism in the BBC's radio output. The North Region, for example, became noted for its 'exceptionally large number of outside broadcasts'. They included many sporting occasions such as the

'Roses' cricket matches between Lancashire and Yorkshire, which allowed local rivalries within the region to be given play. As part of this attachment to the sport of the region, BBC North Region executives took out membership at both Old Trafford and Headingley.[25]

Many of the themes and cross-currents in the development of broadcasting are illustrated in the relationship between the BBC and a sport which has often been overlooked by historians: rugby league. The 13-a-side code of rugby had begun as a breakaway of northern clubs in the 1890s over the issue of 'broken-time' payments; in other words, professionalism. For most of the next hundred years its development in Britain was confined to the counties of Lancashire, Yorkshire and Cumberland. The bitter enmity that characterized relationships between the northern rebels (re-formed into the Rugby Football League – RFL – in 1922) and the official Rugby Football Union (RFU) had much to do with regional hostility overlain by social-class tensions. It is not surprising that the BBC should have a special relationship with 'rugger' (union), a sport which shared similar ideas about its 'national' role, and which also possessed numerous 'establishment', especially Oxbridge, connections. Rugby league lacked all these, a fact which sometimes provoked tensions within the sport itself. In seeking, for example, to present the game on a national stage, its authorities insisted on playing the Final of the rugby league Cup at Wembley from 1929 onwards, a move opposed by many of the game's followers who understandably felt that its crowning glory should take place in its own heartland.[26] For the BBC, rugby league was not considered to be a sport whose main event should be regarded as a 'must'. Rather, like wrestling and cycling, it was seen as being unsuitable for radio, and, as Briggs notes, was 'treated very cautiously as a socially inferior local sport'.[27]

Much of this changed during the 1950s as the BBC began to develop its coverage of sport on television, and, in the face of the challenge from ITV, to cultivate a stronger emphasis on 'entertainment'. Rugby league then quickly came into prominence. It served as an excellent substitute for what had long been the most glaring omission in the BBC's sporting schedule: association football. The opposition of football's authorities, notably the Football League, to live transmissions of games on radio and television is well known. Following a brief spell of coverage in the late 1920s, it was not until after the Second World War that League fixtures were consistently broadcast on radio, and then only the second half of matches. The League, pressured especially by clubs in the lower divisions, opined that live broadcasts would drive away spectators, and it took the marked decline in spectating that occurred in the 1950s and early 1960s for the League slowly to shift its stance. There was, for example, a very brief arrangement with ITV in 1960 for the live coverage of First Division matches, but apart from the telerecordings of League football matches, chiefly by the BBC, no sustained live-coverage arrangements were made until the deal with BSkyB in 1992, by which time 'first division' soccer was no longer administered by the League. The FA's attitude had, in general, been more tolerant, with the result that games under its jurisdiction – the FA Cup and England international fixtures – were frequently broadcast, especially if they did not clash with League fixtures.[28] As television developed in the 1950s, and the BBC sought to maintain its reputation for sporting journalism with the introduction of popular programmes like *Sportsview* and *Grandstand*, so the absence of football came increasingly to be filled by rugby league. National television coverage on the Saturday afternoon *Grandstand* programme took rugby league out of its previous regional confines and made of it a sport that viewers in all parts of the country became familiar with. No longer was it necessary, as it had been until a few years previously, for the Wembley Stadium authorities to publish an explanation of the rules of the game in the programme notes for the Final Tie for the benefit of southern spectators.

National familiarity, however, was accompanied by some significant developments in the presentation of the sport by a Corporation conscious of the need to explore some of the more relaxed and intimate styles of reporting now embedded at ITV.[29] What this resulted in was the search for a rugby league 'persona'. It was found, essentially, in the game's association with the North and working-class masculinity. These themes were brought out in David Storey's novel of 1960 *This Sporting Life*, which gained some popular recognition when issued in paperback two years later, and yet more when made into a feature film with Richard Harris in 1963. In the film, in fact, close-up techniques were deployed to convey the sheer physical strength and pain of the game that came directly out of television's presentation of the sport since the late 1950s. New camera technology, which allowed sequences of play such as the scrum and the play-the-ball to be televised in medium shot, greatly added to the intimacy of the spectacle and, it was presumed, the viewer's enjoyment of the action. This further enabled producers and commentators to build the personalities of the game, from beefy forwards like Alan Prescott and Brian McTigue to sinuous half-backs such as Alex Murphy. A great deal of this, however, depended on the mediation of the personalities to the viewing audience through the commentator. This role was taken up from an early stage by the former rugby league manager and journalist Eddie Waring, a man whose success in promoting the game made him into a leading television 'star' by the early 1970s, frequently portrayed by the impressionist Mike Yarwood. By contrast with the serious-minded approach to sports reporting still adopted, for example, by the football commentator Kenneth Wolstenholme, a disciple of the De Lotbiniere method, Waring quickly settled into a more relaxed, wisecracking style. His jovial appearance and gutteral northern speaking voice seemed to cast him in the role of music-hall comedian rather than traditional BBC commentator, a part that Waring himself was all-too-ready to exploit with a store of jokes and quips: 'give 'im back his ganzy' (when a player was holding on to his opponent's shirt); ''e's a big lad – he'll be alright' (when a seemingly serious injury had occurred); 'don't kick that thing on the floor, it's 'is 'ead'. By such a combination of words and pictures rugby league became a television entertainment. Its supporters in the North had mixed feelings about this transformation. On the one hand they were pleased to see their game and its heroes receive recognition to rival that of rugby union. On the other they were often very sceptical of a process which, especially in the 'stage northerner' role assumed by Waring, seemed to be trivializing the game.[30]

The trivialization of sport as a consequence of increasingly sophisticated techniques of television presentation, has been an idea asserted by many writers. The American historian Benjamin Rader, for example, has argued strongly that the dramatization of sport on television has resulted not only in rule changes, but also in a transformation of the style and ethics of sports.[31] This idea links in some ways with the process described by Alan and John Clarke in a British context as the supplanting of the 'sporting event' by the 'media event'.[32] The traditional experience has been replaced with something manufactured in a television studio, not for a 'spectator' but for a 'viewer' and, ultimately in many cases, for a 'consumer' of advertising. Rader instances boxing as a sport where this trend is very clearly exemplified. Rugby league might, in less dramatic form, be seen as a victim of this process, especially after its take-over by global television in the mid-1990s. By this time, with the introduction of yet slicker methods of presentation to attract the viewers' attention and interest in a whole range of sports, it might be claimed that Rader's point has acquired even greater force. A number of innovations have certainly taken the experience of sport well away from what it once was for the 'ordinary spectator'. The mediating role played by the commentator has been strengthened by the development of the team of 'pundits', orchestrated by the 'anchorman', whose presence in the studio at important events is designed to tell viewers what to watch out for in the forthcoming spectacle, and how to think about it afterwards. As celebrities they also add a touch of glamour to the programme. Such production values have been clearly illustrated in recent coverage of the Olympic Games and the football World Cup. In the latter case the presentation of the 1998 competition in France even sought to bring the city of Paris into the studio alongside the experts, with the use of a huge back-projection depicting some of the city's best-known landmarks.

Visually, the pleasure of the sporting spectacle has been enhanced far beyond the early close-up to include such features as the high aerial shot from an airship, underwater cameras at swimming events, the 'camera in the stump' shot in cricket, the tracking shot from the touchline in rugby and football, and the ubiquitous action replay, either in slow motion or 'real time'. Cricket, considered to be a repository of tradition, has broken many long-established conventions in the aftermath of Kerry Packer's innovative presentational techniques in World Series Cricket (WSC) in the 1970s. The most radical was the abandonment of the traditional standby of realist drama – the '180 degree rule'. According to this convention the camera should not cross an imaginary line drawn 180 degrees between the camera itself (and therefore the viewer) and the action, for fear of unsettling the viewer's relationship to the events being presented. Cricket broke this rule simply by installing two cameras at each end of the wicket, thus providing to the television viewer a privileged perspective on events unavailable to the spectator at the ground. Though it broke with the 'authentic' experience (in which the spectator stays put and does not switch ends after each over), it nevertheless produced a greatly improved view of what was happening to the ball.

There are, however, problems with the notion that television trivializes sport. All cultural experiences and texts derive their meaning from a complex interplay of influences which serve also to change them. It is not helpful to think of the sporting experience, or any other, as being subject to a fixed, authentic 'essence' which has a prior validity. Rather, we should approach sport as a set of meanings which change according to the varied and unequal interests that are brought to bear on them. Cricket is a sport on which a good deal of such attention has been focused. Opponents of the changes in form and duration of cricket play that were introduced for commercial reasons from the 1960s onwards have pointed to what they regard as a 'debasement' of the game's essence. This they see as the slowly-evolving, artful mode of play encapsulated in the three- or five-day match. By comparison the limited-overs form, which first made its appearance in English county cricket with the Gillette Cup of 1963 (though it had long existed in the northern leagues), was regarded as lacking grace and purpose: a haven for mediocrity in the shape of the big-hitter or the tidy medium-pace seamer. An aesthetic of cricket was being constructed in this discourse which elevated to the position of the purest type of the game a version of it which had, in fact, been itself created for particular commercial, social and political reasons in the third quarter of the nineteenth century. Its 'authenticity' was historically specific. The introduction and extension of the limited-overs game has been held by some to be responsible for the decline of standards in English cricket. Contrariwise, however, others have pointed to its having injected new life, interest and money into cricket, thus resuscitating a game that was in danger of becoming moribund. However, no matter what one's personal preference might be, there can be little doubt either that this form of cricket was financially necessary, or that, over the 30 years since its introduction, it has become an accepted version of the game. It represents neither more, nor less of the 'genuine' version of cricket than does the alternative form. It is simply a changed version of the game.

Limited-overs cricket, whether in its Gillette form, or as sponsored by John Player and BBC2 in the Sunday League, or by Packer's WSC on Channel 9 in Australia, has always been closely associated with television. It represents one of the ways in which television has shaped the development of modern sport, not least through the increasing importance its contracts have for impoverished governing bodies. But whether its presentational forms, so cleverly on show in BSkyB's staging of soccer in the 1990s, have fundamentally altered the meaning of sport is open to argument. There is a sense in which many of the technical innovations of televised sport are merely cosmetic changes masking a number of basic continuities with earlier mediations of sporting journalism. There is, for instance, a strong, and possibly increasing, emphasis on the exploits of the individual player, which serves to perpetuate a form of hero-worshipping that began in the popular press earlier in the century. Moreover, the ever-present pundits signify essentially conservative values. They are usually respectably besuited and necktied, giving viewers the assurance of moral worth that used to be associated with bank managers. Their expertise is never too technical, and they are certainly not encouraged to situate their discussions of sport within any context of finance and politics. They preserve, therefore, the 'back page' place of sport as something apart from other aspects of society. Theirs is a glamourized version of male pub conversation and sociability. Women participants are rarely present in these studio analyses, except when it can safely be assumed that the sport under consideration has a female following and female stars, when the coverage might therefore exploit the erotic element for the benefit of the male gaze.[33] BBC radio made a small but significant departure from this tradition, following a step originally taken by the *Observer* when it employed Julie Welch to write on football, by enlisting a female commentator (Donna Symmonds) during the West Indies-England series of 1997–98.[34] But this is still the exception that points the rule. Sports coverage generally shows some signs of a willingness to break out of the narrow, mass-spectator limits formerly drawn by the popular press: American football, baseball (transmitted live from the USA in the middle of the night), snooker and even angling have been featured on television with varying degrees of success. In the main, however, the sports that dominated the back pages of the newspaper press in the 1920s still consume most of the time scheduled for sport on television, which, underneath its technical wizardry, continues to display a number of old-fashioned features.

SPORT AND POPULAR LITERATURE

In America the links between sport and the creative arts have been strong. In Britain the opposite has usually been true. Though cynics might assert that there has been more than enough fiction in the average newspaper account of sport, by comparison with American activity in film-making and non-fiction writing the British have not been especially energetic. There is an assumption, as Brian Glanville has noted, that sport and the arts do not mix.[35]

None the less, there have been some initiatives in the imaginative representation of sport and they have communicated important values. For example, the games ethic and the cult of athleticism to be found in the public schools of Victorian and Edwardian Britain contributed strongly to notions of manliness, social class and patriotism. Much of this was expressed through the extensive body of prose, verse and song that was centred on the leading schools. Sir Henry Newbolt's poem *Vitaï Lampada*, with its earnest refrain to 'play up, and play the game', is probably the best-known product of this public school culture. But as J. A. Mangan has shown, there were many variations on the theme that sport built character. On the association football, rugby and cricket fields of the private schools, boys were exhorted to sink their adolescent sensuality into the scrum and the tackle, to learn to take hard knocks without ceasing to behave like gentlemen, to learn a habit of leadership that was decisive yet selfless, and, in many cases, to be suspicious of overindulging in intellectualism.[36] It was all set to verse by poets such as the prodigiously athletic and literary Harrow schoolmaster Edward Bowen, whose 'Tom' captures this hearty cult of athleticism very well:

> Base is the player who stops,
> Fight, till the fighting is o'er;
> Who follows up till he drops,
> Panting and limping and sore?
> Tom![37]

Understanding upper middle-class morality without taking the influence of this literature into account is impossible. If, moroever, it was a meaning system inspired by an elite, its effects reached down to other points in the social hierarchy. Through comics, annuals and cheap fiction, often aimed at children, the ethos of the public school became a subject for popular culture. The presence over many years in the children's comic the *Dandy* of 'Lord Snooty and His Pals' testifies to this. Lord Snooty, in Eton collar and silk hat, led a group of very obviously working-class boys through a weekly series of adventures, just as Snooty's real-life counterparts led the nation through its adventures. School stories, and the place of sport within them, were an ideological staple in the mediation of gentlemanly virtues to the population at large. P. G. Wodehouse's *Mike*, published in 1909 but reprinted several times after the First World War, is generally regarded as a classic of the genre. It tells of the exploits of an outstanding boy cricketer Michael Jackson (modelled on one of the famous Foster brothers of Worcestershire) and his monocled friend Psmith, a languorous youth who articulates the games ethic in a characteristically casual manner. For all that, as Jeffrey Richards has pointed out, sport dominates Wodehouse's stories: 'Academic work plays very little part . . . Sport is the measure of a boy.'[38] Nor was it just boys who were subjected to this fixation. Popular fiction for girls also used the expensive school and its sporting activities – often exclusive ones such as horse riding and yachting – as the setting for stories of female togetherness and adventure. Angela Brazil was the leading exponent of this genre, whose heyday was the inter-war period, when weeklies like *School Friend* reached a genuinely popular readership and purveyed, as Mary Cadogan and Patricia Craig observe, 'an impeccable moral code'.[39] At the end of the century the tradition was still strong in the work of writers like Elinor M. Brent Dyer, whose stories of Chalet School centred on winter sports, or Bonnie Bryant who featured horse riding in her successful 'Saddle Club' series.[40]

Cricket has been the sport on which much of this cultural production has focused. It was, as Jack Williams has shown, a sport that articulated in many ways and through many forms ideas of England and Englishness.[41] It was made to signify tradition, the social order, the superiority of rural life and the unity of the Empire. Some of these themes were apparent in one of the best-loved fictions of the inter-war years, A. G. McDonnell's amusingly caustic *England, Their England*, which featured a celebrated village cricket match.[42] Cricket was, as many commentators have noted, more than a game. It represented a moral code, and terms such as 'straight bat', 'sticky wicket', 'bowling a googly' and 'a safe pair of hands' had strong moral overtones in a world where the phrase 'it isn't cricket' immediately denoted something beyond the pale. In his 1938 film *The Lady Vanishes* Alfred Hitchcock chose an obsession with cricket to delineate the characters of two crusty Englishmen – Charters and Caldicott – eager to return to England by train from a troubled European continent for 'the test match'. The cricket represented for them a return to normality; it stood for decency and honesty, in contrast to the sinister deceptions and cruelties to be found among some of their fellow train passengers who were Nazi spies. Cricket was the sport most associated with 'literature', though it was a literature, for the most part, of descriptive essays based on actual events and persons, rather than fiction writing as such.

John Arlott, a Southampton policeman with interests in poetry, who seized an opportunity to join the BBC at the end of the Second World War, became the writer and broadcaster most readily associated with cricket in the post-war years. With his distinctive Hampshire accent and poetic instincts he set a new style in radio commentary, and wrote furiously and well on a host of topics. Cricket was the foremost but the list also included soccer, cheese (he extolled the virtues of Dorset Blue Vinny), wine, politics and the countryside.[43] In some ways Arlott continued the tradition of the self-taught Renaissance man of journalism, Neville Cardus. In his essays, which appeared mostly in the *Manchester Guardian*, Cardus attempted to personify through cricketers certain qualities of body and mind which expressed grace and solidity. He eschewed anything that suggested quantities or measurements: 'the style is the man' was his guiding principle, and his pleasure was found in the beauty of MacLaren's or Spooner's batting, or in the subtle looping skills of the bowling of Rhodes or Blythe. His favourites, as befitted a Manchester man, were northern cricketers, men who possessed no pretensions and who evinced a down-to-earth attitude to life. Dick Tyldesley – a burly leg-break bowler for Lancashire whose formative sporting influences were allegedly 'West-houghton Sunday School, tha knows' – and the Yorkshire seamer Emmott Robinson were men who typified this rather dour outlook which refused to be impressed by social conventions. Emmott, for example, always finished his dinner with a proletarian cup of tea, because coffee 'were no good for you' after a meal.[44] It all amounted to a form of mythologising which bore slight relationship to actuality, but which formed an important ideological part of Englishness, especially its northern variations. Many no doubt felt that Cardus's work came closer to fiction than to fact. In the world of fiction proper Jack Williams has noted that only eight novels for adults were published in the inter-war period on a cricket theme.[45] No 'serious' novel has been written about cricket, and in spite of a screenplay by Terence Rattigan, the film *The Final Test* (1954), which featured a number of leading cricketers in bit parts alongside the star Jack Warner, was scarcely a landmark in British cinema history. Some 170 works of sporting fiction were, however, aimed at children in the inter-war period.

It is often assumed that sporting fictions are, like much of the popular press and the electronic media, ideologically conservative. Little research has been carried out in this field, though what has been done tends to support the common assumption. Dave Russell has commented on soccer fiction aimed at children in the 1920s, when themes included 'the crooked director, virtue rewarded by the discovery of true (usually aristocratic or upper-middle class) social origins, the importance of "fair play" and sporting behaviour and, relatedly, the centrality of the amateur tradition'.[46] There was often a romantic element in which adolescent sexual sensitivities were explored, however modestly. Some fifty years later the extensive work of Michael Hardcastle perpetuated some of these same themes in the setting of boys' local soccer leagues. Teamwork, dedication to sport, and honesty emerge as key virtues. In Hardcastle's *In The Net* (1971) Gary's devotion to football is fulfilled when he wins the respect of his teammates and, equally importantly, that of his father in a crucial match played (a concession to the women's movement here) against a team of girls, who prove to be tough opponents. In *Soccer Special* (1978) a lucky break provides Miles, whose fussy mother has persuaded him that he is too sickly for the game, with a chance clandestinely to play for his local team. He proves his ability with some impressive displays in goal, and shows unexpected reserves of strength when rescuing the injured team captain after a serious fall. Being accepted by their fellows and achieving success at sport ensure for both Gary and Miles the transition into the realm of masculinity, following periods of uncertainty brought on by doubting mothers or strained personal relationships at new schools.[47] What are prized in these stories are qualities not very different from those lauded in the public school verse of the beginning of the century.

Interspersed with these narratives, however, are fictions which hint at a more radical perspective on sport and society. In the 1950s Alf Tupper, 'The Tough of the Track', ran a good race while fighting social snobbery in the *Hotspur*, a D. C. Thomson boy's comic which had originally been launched in 1933. It was in the *Hotspur* that Wilson, 'the wonder athlete', had made his appearance. A curious emblem of asceticism, Wilson reached the age of 128 without even beginning to look middle-aged. He lived in a cave and existed on a diet of nuts and berries, which enabled him to produce some astonishing feats of athleticism, such as a three-minute mile (during the course of which he broke the world long-jump record).[48] If Wilson's mysticism, not to mention his extraordinary prowess, took a little swallowing even for the average *Hotspur* reader, Alf Tupper was closer to reality, a working-class hero whose exploits possessed a sharp edge of social criticism. Tupper himself lacked social graces, courting trouble at every turn with his blunt manner. But his saving virtue was an ability to run like Roger Bannister. His was a rare talent which his country could ill afford to squander, but Tupper faced the twin obstacles of social condescension and petty officialdom in his quest for success. In the 1950s, a peak period of British middle-distance running, the Tupper stories could almost be read as a discourse on 'modernization'. Tupper's traditional virtues of hard work, dedication and the will to victory were, in his case, thwarted by the class tensions apparent in British society. Tupper sounded an alarm, not so much at the principle of amateurism, for Tupper himself was an unpaid athlete running for the love of it, but at the climate of snobbery and social pretension which so often accompanied amateurism and which was shown as holding back Tupper and, by implication, restraining the nation's progress. Through sheer willpower and bloody-mindedness Tupper (the name is significant) usually prevailed. But, the reader might well have been led to ask, should it be necessary to fight such battles? It was no coincidence that Tupper featured in the *Hotspur* alongside another fictional hero of the common man, Matt Braddock, VC and bar, a wartime Mosquito pilot who, in spite of his skill and bravery, still remained a sergeant.

In a similar vein, but from a different era, are the fascinating stories of women and sport from the 1920s unearthed in the recent work of Alethea Melling. They, too, work 'against the grain', being aimed at young female readers and, at the same time, challenging contemporary industrial and social practices. In 'Ray of the Rovers', 'Nell O'Newcastle', 'Football Island' and a number of other stories soccer heroines of the working class make their appearance 'fighting for workers' rights, profit sharing and co-operatives'.[49] The stories, coming at a sensitive time for political and gender relations just after the First World War, appear to offer their female readers the prospect of subverting conventional gender codes and morality, and resisting the attempts by men to reassert their hegemony after the disruptions of the war.

CONCLUSION

Historians of sport have been slow to turn their attention to these issues. It is, of course, difficult to be certain about the effects of literary representations on readers. In contemporary situations we are often unsure about reader/viewer reactions to texts, and this problem becomes doubly difficult when the context is a historical one and the readers are themselves part of that history. None the less it is through such material that much of what we understand about sport – what it *means* to us – is constructed and communicated. And without wishing to suggest that the process is a linguistically determined one, in other words that the reader or viewer's thoughts about sport are created by the texts, there is nevertheless a great deal of ideological influence at work in the text–reader relationship, which is something to which as historians we should be attuned.

Key Reading

Glanville, B. *Football Memories*. London: Virgin Publishing, 1999.

Holt, R., and Mason, T. *Sport in Britain, 1945–2000*. Oxford: Blackwell, 2000.

Mangan, J. A. *Athleticism in the Victorian and Edwardian Public School: The Emergence and Consolidation of an Educational Ideology*. London: Frank Cass, 2000 edn.

Whannel, G. *Fields in Vision: Television, Sport and Cultural Transformation*. London: Routledge, 1992.

Chronology of Events

1822 *Bell's Life in London*, first national paper to include significant coverage of sport.

1859 *Sporting Life* founded, with a circulation of over a quarter of a million by 1860. A byword for horse racing, it lasted until the 1990s. It was soon rivalled by the *Sportsman* (1865) and the Manchester-based *Sporting Chronicle* (1871), the latter surviving until 1983 as an essentially racing paper.

1875 Establishment of the *Athletic News* by Bleackley and Hulton, aimed at a gentleman readership and excluding betting tips; renowned for its coverage of professional football under J. A. H. Catton. its editor from 1900 to 1921. Merged with the *Sporting Chronicle* in 1931.

1880–90s Proliferation of local football specials providing early-evening results and match reports.

1920s Greater use of photography and 'human interest' stories, pioneered by the *Daily Mail* before the First World War, brought new style to sports coverage.

1922 Opposition from newspaper proprietors to the establishment of the BBC, whose sports coverage they feared would deprive them of readers.

1927 First radio commentary by BBC on a professional football match, Arsenal v. Sheffield United; followed by outside broadcasts on major sporting events throughout late 1920s and 1930s.

1931 Football League banned radio coverage of its matches; Football Association permitted broadcasting of Cup Final, cup ties and international matches.

1938 First full televising of English Cup Final. The BBC paid a 'facility fee' for covering the game, a practice continued well into the 1950s.

1946 On resumption of League football after the war, the Football League agreed to BBC radio commentaries on the second half of live matches.

1949 BBC introduced *Sports Report*, transmitted at 5pm on Saturdays to include the latest sports results and news.

1951 Launch of *Charles Buchan's Football Monthly*.

1953 Televising of Cup Final (estimated 10 million viewers) revealed potential of television sport.

1954 Launching of the BBC's television sports magazine *Sportsview*, which featured the 'BBC Sports Personality of the Year'; show jumping had become established as a popular television sport, with Pat Smythe its greatest star.

1960 Wolfenden Report (*Sport in the Community*) critical of the approach of some sections of the newspaper press to the coverage of sport. Agreement between ITV and the Football League for television coverage of 26 live matches; because of opposition from clubs only one shown.

1964 Launch of *Match of the Day* on the new BBC2 channel, followed in 1965 by ITV's Sunday afternoon highlights.

1972 Launch of *Foul*, by students at Cambridge; the first of the 'fanzines' which were to proliferate in the 1980s, with *When Saturday Comes* leading the way in 1986.

1976 Publication of Eamon Dunphy's *Only a Game?*, the first of the 'realist' football autobiographies.

1977 Kerry Packer's World Series Cricket established as response to Australian cricket's refusal to sell him exclusive television rights for coverage of Australian test matches on his Channel 9.

1983 First televising of complete live League football matches, in deal arranged between League and BBC/ITV.

1992 BSkyB's £304 million deal with Premiership for exclusive live coverage of football matches, renewed in 1996 for £670 million. Publication of Nick Hornby's *Fever Pitch*.

1994 Introduction by BBC of Radio 5 Live, a national station covering news and sport, incorporating *Sports Report* (launched 1949).

1999 BBC outbid by Channel 4 for rights to exclusive coverage of domestic test cricket, and therefore lost the place it had held for 60 years as the televiser of cricket.

Going to the Pictures: America and the Cinema

chapter

4

The cinema, or 'the pictures' as most people called it, was one of the most important of the *public* commercial entertainments that developed in the twentieth century. H. Llewellyn Smith, updating in 1935 Charles Booth's earlier survey of London life and labour, described cinema as 'easily the most important agency of popular entertainment'.[1] When its popularity was eclipsed later in the century by domestically-based television, cinema had enjoyed a period of some fifty years when its appeal far outstripped that of sport or any other commercial leisure activity. 'The cinema slaughtered all competitors' says A. J. P. Taylor.[2] This was quite an achievement for an industry whose British foundations were always shaky, whose moral status was often questioned, and which purveyed more than any other medium of entertainment a strain of Americanism which, as Ross McKibbin notes, 'alarmed many in the country's elites'.[3]

THE SOCIAL HABIT OF THE AGE

The popularity of the cinema is not difficult to explain. It was cheap, accessible and glamorous. In its heyday between 1920 and 1950 a shilling (5p) would secure a good seat in the pictures, and a good half of the audience usually paid less than this. Until the early 1930s the venue would be a small, neighbourhood cinema hall attracting a markedly working-class audience. By the later part of the 1930s it was more likely to be in one of the larger 'dream palaces' – typified by the Odeon cinemas built by the Birmingham businessman Oscar Deutsch – that were springing up in the city centres and the suburbs to accommodate audiences in excess of 2000. As a form of popular culture the cinema is both 'text' (the film) and 'lived practice' (going to the pictures), and in the latter there was much to attract audiences, irrespective of the nature of the film itself. In fact, the perceived quality of the film was not usually the chief factor determining attendance. Sociability was probably far more important. This is an aspect of cinema culture that historians have often overlooked in their concentration on the film text and its economic context. In the smaller halls, which had grown up with the early cinema industry before the First World War, there was a convivial 'flea pit' atmosphere, sometimes best captured in films themselves, like *The Smallest Show on Earth* (1957) or, in an Italian setting, *Cinema Paradiso* (1990), which nostalgically recreate the role of the picture house as a cultural institution in the community.[4] Audience participation, sometimes of a rowdy kind, was common: cat-calls, whistles and guffaws all demonstrated interaction between audience and film, and frequently between audience and management when there was a hitch in the show, for example if the projector broke down. David Mayall has noted in his work on the early cinema in Birmingham that 'restraint, orderliness and discipline were absent features'.[5] Eating, dozing and, for young couples, courting, were all part of the experience. One cinema-goer in 1929, no doubt echoing the frustration of many millions of others over the years, complained of the distractions from 'lolling lovers, before, behind, to the left, and to the right . . . some people go to the cinema with the serious intent of enjoying the picture, and to be surrounded by a lot of dreamy youngsters bent on emulating the silly close-ups on the screen is, to say the least, repulsive'.[6] The anarchic behaviour of audiences was most evident at children's matinees, hated by the cinema managers who were forced to provide these uneconomic performances as 'loss leaders' in order to induct the next generation of film-goers into regular attendance. In spite of the attempts by the management to instil order by framing the whole experience in a community form – with a 'club' ethos which had its president, master of ceremonies, newsletter and songs – the matinees were often a byword for chaos and disorder. Irene Thomas recalled of her childhood in west London:

> Every Saturday morning there were children's shows at our dear flea-infested Roxy cinema, and the chief attraction seemed to be the competition among small boys to see who could crawl under the seats towards the front, and get *behind* the screen to read the sub-titles *backwards*.[7]

The development of the big picture palaces by the cinema exhibiting chains – ABC, Gaumont and Odeon – occurred in the 1920s and 1930s. The smaller halls seating under 500 people, which in 1914 had accounted for almost a third of all cinemas, had declined significantly by the mid-1920s. By this time over 70 per cent of all British cinemas could accommodate between 500 and 1000 customers, and ten years later the proportion of those capable of housing over

1000 had risen to 30 per cent. Such places sought to introduce a different tone to cinema culture. They were, for example, often custom-designed to instil 'atmosphere'. As McKibbin has pointed out,[8] the era of the large picture palace began in the period after the First World War with exotically designed structures intended to replicate in the audience's very surroundings some of the glamour depicted on the screen. Thus, at a time when the silent epic starring romantic idols such as Rudolf Valentino, Douglas Fairbanks, Clara Bow and Mary Pickford was a staple of the cinema repertoire, the picture palaces were conceived in a variety of sensuous styles. Westernized versions of Assyrian temples and Moorish palaces abounded, epitomized in the Granada at Tooting – 'built in the form of the Alcazar in Spain' – or the Astoria, Brixton, where the murals and freizes in the auditorium were so realistic 'you thought you were sitting in the open air at night time'.[9] They took cinema-interior design to a peak of kitsch. By the 1930s such exoticism was going out of fashion, and the new cinemas of this era displayed a more austere mixture of classical architecture with art deco embellishments, as found in the distinctive Odeon style.[10] For such establishments a disciplined audience was sought, though not always found. The performances were planned as military operations: commissionaires to control the ubiquitous queues that formed at popular times; ticket offices to take the money, with confectionary kiosks and, in the larger cinemas, restaurants to supply subsidiary sustenance; ticket collectors to monitor admission; usherettes to direct seating arrangements. The auditorium was segregated by price – cheapest seats downstairs at the front, dearest upstairs in the front balcony. Managers of these cinemas were, according to Nicholas Hiley, engaged in a 'constant attempt to move the audience up-market'.[11] They sought to maximize their revenue from ticket sales by targeting the most viable customers, who were not necessarily those who had formed the first mass cinema audiences just before and after the First World War, namely, the working class.

When A. J. P. Taylor memorably described cinema in the inter-war years as 'the essential social habit of the age',[12] he established not only a phrase which has been repeated in virtually all discussions of British cinema, including this one, but a set of assumptions about the nature of the cinema audience. The implicit belief that has been inscribed in a number of histories of cinema-going is that the audience was largely composed of working-class people habituated to attending at least once a week, often more, until the advent of television in the 1950s kept them at home. This notion is underscored by the statistics often deployed to illustrate the popularity of cinema: the survey carried out by Professor Caradog Jones in Liverpool in 1934, for example, and more emphatically, Simon Rowson's statistical survey executed at much the same time. Llewellyn Smith's survey of London found 258 cinemas in the county of London with a total seating capacity of 344 000, supporting his claim that 'the cinema is *par excellence* the people's amusement'.[13] Further, an enquiry conducted for the Ministry of Information in 1943 on cinema audiences concluded that they were made up predominantly of 'the lower economic and educational groups'.[14] Statistical information of this kind tends to be corroborated by reference to the attitudes of middle-class and upper-class observers of popular culture and leisure, who often expressed concern about the passive and uncritical habits being inculcated by cinema-going, an attitude that chimed with other concerns about the effects of commercial leisure and which focused principally on the spiritual state of the lower classes.

In fact, it does not help in understanding the popularity of cinema to start with such assumptions. Cinema-going was a complex social and cultural habit, and those who indulged in it were a highly fragmented group whose behaviour was made up of a multiplicity of individual decisions. For example, as has frequently been observed, different behaviour patterns and tastes were exhibited by different sections of the population. Older people were much less likely to be cinema-goers than adolescents, and women generally were more attuned to the various aspects of film culture than men.[15] As might be expected, rural areas were less immersed in the pictures than were the towns, simply because of the greater provision of cinemas in urban areas. McKibbin's essay on the cinema highlights age, social class, gender and geography as the main determinants influencing attendance.[16] Historians of the cinema have taken this further. Harper and Porter, for example, in their study of cinema audiences in the 1950s have distinguished between the different types, and therefore tastes, of cinema-goers in terms of categories that cut across those used by McKibbin: the 'indiscriminate', the 'regular' and the 'occasional' cinema-goer all feature in Harper and Porter's analysis, with the 'occasional' tending to predominate at this time, thus causing problems for an industry which ideally wanted a predictable market.[17] Moreover, in an important discussion of the changing nature of the cinema audience in the 1920s and 1930s, Nicholas Hiley has also challenged some well-established assumptions about the cinema 'habit'.[18] It is worth pausing over Hiley's work, since it raises some interesting propositions.

For one thing, Hiley confirms the 1920s to have been a time of concern about declining attendance. After the First World War had produced a boost of ticket sales among largely working-class audiences, reaching a peak of some 20.6 million weekly sales in 1917, there was a sharp decline by the end of the war. In 1918 it was estimated that weekly sales had dropped to 15 million seats. The explanation was to be found in the imposition by the government of the Entertainment Duty, falling most heavily on the cheapest seats, which was maintained into the 1920s in the face of constant protests from the industry.[19] In 1924 the duty was removed from seats under 6d (2.5p) but only after a period which saw huge losses of customers, many of them working-class people who baulked at paying the higher prices the duty necessitated. The duty was reimposed between 1931 and 1935, at which time average weekly sales of tickets were in the region of 17 million, significantly fewer than during the war. The fluctuating fiscal regime, combined with structural and technological developments in the form of larger cinemas with longer programmes, together with the arrival of synchronized sound in 1929, seems to have produced an overall effect of driving many of the smaller cinema halls out of business and their customers away from the pictures altogether. Although the introduction of sound caused the building of many new and larger cinemas, it did not necessarily bring back the audiences. A common feature of the 1930s was the large picture house operating half to two-thirds empty. In Bristol, for example, the local newspaper cautioned against the building of any more cinemas since '[i]t is only on a few occasions that all the cinemas have good houses'.[20] What seems to have been happening, according to Hiley, was a profound social and cultural shift in the pattern and composition of cinema-going. The small working-class picture house, with its communal audience, was disappearing (except, perhaps, in the north of England) and being replaced by a more commercialized and organized form of cinema-going, in which the core audience was less characterized by its class than its female and youth composition, and which depended far more upon a dedicated group of frequent attenders. Between 1910 and 1950, therefore, it is conceivable that British cinema experienced patronage from two quite different generations of audiences, each one's ascendancy enduring roughly the twenty or so years of the cinema-goers 'natural' life, beginning in the immediate pre-teens and lasting until the late thirties.[21]

CENSORSHIP: FRAMING THE IMAGE

The nature of the cinema audience, with its perceived class, gender and age composition, partly accounts for another feature of the development of British cinema that historians have frequently commented upon. This is the censorship that was applied to it though the operations of the British Board of Film Censors (BBFC). The BBFC was a body set up by the industry itself in 1912 as a form of self-regulation, and it maintained very close links with government and the local authorities, which themselves possessed statutory licensing powers exercised by their Watch Committees. As the timing of these developments suggests, the cinema fell under the scrutiny of the guardians of public morals at a very early stage. For example, the National Council of Public Morals, a large coalition of religious, educational and political interests presided over by the Bishop of Birmingham, conducted an inquiry into the cinema in 1913. A major concern stemmed from the belief that life might imitate art, with impressionable young children, in particular, learning criminality and other forms of depravity from the scenes they watched on the screen. These fears translated into attempts to control the image presented, though as Mayall's work on Birmingham has shown this did not happen in any crudely conspiratorial way. Censorship had to contend with both the commercial interests of the film exhibitors and the tastes of the cinema-going public in a complex set of relationships.[22]

None the less cinema entered its age of major expansion with a body of rules that ensured a careful construction of the 'reality' presented to audiences on the screen. In the inter-war years the spirit, if not the actual substance, of the rules drawn up by the BBFC in the First World War set the tone for what was acceptable. Politics, sex, religion and race relations all required careful treatment, as is shown by Jeffrey Richards' analysis of the BBFC's reports on the screenplays submitted to the censors.[23] To say, as Tony Aldgate has, that 'the censors were . . . concerned with anything and everything that might be construed . . . as posing a possible threat to the settled order of society'[24] might be putting it a little on the strong side, but they were certainly sensitive to material which dealt with potentially controversial topics in anything less than an anodyne manner. Thus, attempts to film Walter Greenwood's cele-brated novel of working-class life in Salford, *Love on the Dole*, ran foul of the censor because of the story's political and sexual themes. By contrast, an early George Formby film, *Off the Dole* (1935), made by Mancunian Films as a 'quota quickie' under the terms of protective legislation introduced in the late 1920s, was entirely acceptable. Though, as its title suggests, it dealt with unemploy-ment, it did so in comic form, and there was no suggestion in the film that economic problems might have human causes or solutions. Formby's charac-ter escapes unemployment by 'magical' intervention (a rich relative needs assistance), and even a scene at a labour exchange where men on the dole discuss the state of the world – a potentially seditious topic – is played for laughs. In this context the revolutionary bile contained in dialogue between men queuing at the labour exchange, exemplified in the line 'What is a member of parliament? . . . A member of Parliament is a man who gives *your* life for *his* country', is transformed from political indictment into a joke.[25] As a result of this form of displacement, serious subjects were left to the documentary film movement, an art form to which most film-goers did not warm.

A further motivation in the application of censorship was fear of Ameri-canization. This was strong enough by the mid-1920s, when the British film industry did seem to have become simply a vehicle for the exhibiting of imported American films, to persuade the government to introduce the Cin-ematograph Films Act (1927). It established for the first time controls over the development of the cinema in the form of a protective regime which required that a fixed proportion of all films exhibited should be British-made. This eco-nomic approach to the problem masked a further, cultural anxiety about the impact of Americanism in British society. As McKibbin has argued, 'cen-sorship existed not only to eliminate sex, violence, and politics from the cinema, but to eliminate American sex, violence, and politics.'[26] Concern about America, which was shared by a number of other European countries,[27] was not confined to the cinema. It spread to many other areas of leisure (though not sport, which mostly proved resistant to it). What worried the country's leaders was the apparent democratic populism of America and its products, which posed a threat to the traditions of social hierarchy that had built up in Britain. The problem with this attitude (apart from the likelihood that it was grossly exaggerated) was that many cinema-goers preferred American films to British ones. American films were technically superior and the acting far more natural when compared with British products, which were often made hastily and poorly to take advantage of the quota system introduced in the 1927 Act. Moreover, the culture of censorship brought a stilted style to British portrayals of social mannerisms and accents, while class relationships were treated in a stiff, conventional way which made use of social 'types'. This was true even by the late 1930s, when films dealing with overtly 'problem' issues such as health provision (*The Citadel*, 1938, an early plea for a national health service) and the state of industry (*The Proud Valley*, 1940, which examined mining and had a black star in Paul Robeson) still retained an idea of social leadership being vested in the proper hands and accents. John Clements fitted this bill perfectly in *South Riding* (1938), a film based on Winifred Holtby's consensual novel about local government. Whilst the technical proficiency of British films improved during the course of the 1930s, and some, like Korda's 1933 film *The Private Life of Henry VIII* starring Charles Laughton, became out-standing successes at the box-office, the love affair of the British cinema-goer with American films was a constant feature both of this period and through-out the century. It produced a number of effects, particularly upon women film-goers and readers of film magazines, articulating particular forms of language, ideas of family life and visions of what constituted femininity and 'glamour'.

In this climate of censorship and American influence, some British films did strike a chord with audiences. They were most often those which have been labelled by commentators as 'escapist' or 'fantasies', but to describe them in this way is to belittle their ideological significance. As we have seen in con-sidering sport, some powerful ideas can be communicated through appar-ently innocent material. Because of the political constraints of censorship, comedy often worked best as the subject for British films. Some of the leading stars of the period before the Second World War were performers trained in the music halls and variety theatres.[28] Gracie Fields, George Formby, Will Hay and others brought to the cinema techniques of singing and comedy they had perfected in the live theatre. Like many of their American counterparts of the period – the Marx Brothers are the outstanding example – they transported directly into the cinema acts that had been developed on stage. Formby's *Off the Dole* (1935), not a good film by any stretch of the imagination, was little more than a series of individual stage acts performed in front of a static camera and loosely tied together by a plot. The film nevertheless made a hand-some profit and ensured that Formby was snapped up by the big studios, for which he made a string of successful films in the later 1930s. Though he played an obviously northern character, based on his father's music-hall act of John Willie, the gormless Lancashire Lad, Formby's popularity reached through-out the country, fusing the regional with the national into a symbol of British-ness.[29] Quite different was the experience of another northern comic, Frank Randle, who also made films for Mancunian in the 1940s but whose appeal was confined almost exclusively to the North. His 1942 film, *Somewhere in Camp*, achieved 85 per cent capacity at the Majestic Cinema in Macclesfield, second only to *Mrs Miniver*, but outside the area around Manchester Randle was virtually unknown. It was perhaps just as well, for his brand of irrever-ent, bawdy, masculine humour ('by hell, we've supped some ale toneet') was not the stuff from which national icons were fashioned. Whereas Randle rep-resented the rough and unpredictable side of popular society, Formby was, as Patrick Joyce has observed, an emblem of 'the kind of working people their superiors would wish to see'.[30] In this sense, therefore, Formby's film charac-ter was a symbol of the people, part of a long tradition of 'us', rather than a specifically class construct.

Gracie Fields carried these consensual symbols to their pinnacle in the 1930s. She became probably the most-loved British film star of the period, though like Formby she lost her appeal quickly after the war. Also like Formby she exploited a northern persona, never discarding her Lancashire accent or comic style, but went further to cultivate her particular *Rochdale* origins, typified in her song 'Following the Rochdale Hunt – Tally Ho!'. With these credentials she became 'Our Gracie' to the nation. In 1934 she made *Sing As We Go* for Basil Dean at Ealing Studios, scripted by J. B. Priestley. It is a story of economic failure and class relations, handled as comedy rather than tragedy. The mill in which 'Grace' works closes down because of foreign competition but eventually triumphantly reopens with much flag-waving after a new, but unexplained British invention magically restores competitiveness. The workers face their temporary unemployment stoically, Grace, the star of the works choir, bravely announcing: 'if we can't spin we can still sing!'. Though she loves 'Mr Hugh', the boss's son, Grace knows that love across the class barrier can never work, and so reconciles herself to working for the good of all. After a series of comic escapades in the popular holiday town of Blackpool, where she has cycled to find work and location shots of which provide the film with much of its attraction, she tracks down the inventor whose new process will bring salvation. Ultimately, it is a film about reconciliation, restoration and renewal, and much of its appeal stems from the active role taken by Fields herself. Her screen persona is certainly not the passive object of the male gaze, as conventionally found in the roles played by so many other female stars of this time. She plays a resourceful woman who, whilst supportive of the *status quo*, drives the narrative forward through her dynamism and ingenuity. She is rarely bettered by the men in the film, and her independent spirit is sharply brought out in a recurring scene with a bumbling policeman, played by Stanley Holloway, whose authority she constantly bucks. In this respect she cultivated on screen the image of an admirably assertive woman, seen perhaps as more 'realistic' than that of American stars like Bette Davis and Joan Crawford, whose personalities always seemed to have too much of a neurotic edge to be 'homely'.[31]

Unlike Fields and Formby, who are frequently remembered by historians of film, Will Hay, the star of several films of the 1930s and 1940s, has been rather overlooked. With Moore Marriott and Graham Moffatt he made up a comedy trio which performed to great public acclaim in films like *Where's That Fire?* (1940), *Good Morning Boys* (1937) and *Oh Mr Porter!* (1937). As their titles suggest, Hay's comedies were given familiar institutional settings – the fire brigade, a school, a railway station – and Hay's character was set up as an incompetent authority figure who, in spite of his bombast, prevails in the end because of luck, the support of his subordinates, and the assured wisdom of his own superiors. *Oh Mr Porter!* (directed by Marcel Varnel, who also directed Formby) perfectly exemplifies a clustering of themes which could have posed problems for the censor had not the context been comedy. Hay is the bungling Mr Porter, a station master who has only been kept on by the railway company because he is related to the Managing Director. His assistants, Harbottle and Albert, are devious and workshy, scarcely idealizations of the British working man. They are sent to organize a derelict station at Buggleskelly in Northern Ireland which, the trio eventually realize, is the centre of a gun-running operation. Though not referred to by name, it is clearly the work of the IRA that provides the core of the film's plot. In view of the Irish Republican campaign against the British government, which culminated in the bombing of a department store in Coventry in 1939, this is sensitive territory for the film-maker, but once again the comic devices serve to deflect the audience's attention away from politics. The gun-runners are portrayed as 'smugglers' and are finally captured in a denouement which involves a high-speed train journey. Mr Porter's credibility is restored, and the threat to the unity of the kingdom repelled.

WAR AND DECLINE

Themes of unity were to be found in abundance in the films of the Second World War. There are a number of reasons why the 1940s, both the war years and after, can be considered a 'golden age' of British cinema. First, attendances soared to a level beyond that of the previous war, with over 25 million tickets being sold each week in 1941. This trend continued beyond the war itself. In 1946 attendances reached a peak of over 31 million a week, and did not begin to decline significantly until the early 1950s. As before, the most regular film-goers were those in the age range 14 to 45, with a marked drop in interest thereafter.[32] Second, the quality of British films, in both their technical and acting departments, had improved greatly since the early 1930s, and in many surveys the British film showed itself to be as popular as its American competitor. In professional critical terms British films were well received at this time, especially for the convergence that had developed between feature films and the documentary movement, which produced realist films such as *Fires Were Started* (1943), *San Demetrio-London* (1943) and *The Way Ahead* (1944). The film critic Roger Manvell felt that such films 'showed people in whom we could believe and whose experience was as genuine as our own.'[33] Third, many films succeeded in contributing to the efforts of the 'People's War' by achieving a propaganda effect which was uplifting without being too blatant. Fourth, and in spite of the propaganda circumstances of the time, British cinema was able to shed much of the restrictive morality that had previously characterized its censorship rules. The idea of a 'People's War', vigorously projected through both official channels and the popular media, and firmly embedded in the discourse of 'reconstruction' that gathered momentum from 1941 onwards, guaranteed that civilian morale should be maintained. Presenting the people with artificial, partial, censored images of themselves did not sit easily with this mission. Significantly, therefore, the film that had experienced most difficulty with the censors in the 1930s, *Love on the Dole*, was finally given clearance and reached the screen in 1941. The film which probably most clearly introduced a new 'realism' in the cinema of the People's War was *Fires Were Started*, which portrayed ordinary London firemen in a deliberately unheroic way, doing the kind of job which was vital for the war effort.[34]

Many of these issues converged in the film *Millions Like Us*, made by Frank Launder and Sidney Gilliat for Gainsborough Pictures in 1943. It is, as James Chapman has pointed out, widely regarded as a wartime 'classic' which illustrates the wedding of the documentary with the feature film. It, in fact, started out as a documentary at the suggestion of the Ministry of Information (MoI), and takes its cue from the anxieties felt among women who had been drafted into war work. Centred upon the experiences of a young woman, Celia, played by Patricia Roc, who is called up to work on aircraft production, *Millions Like Us* emphasizes the role of the Home Front in the war effort and the contribution to be made by women. Through its female characters, who come from varied backgrounds and are thus made to symbolize the nation together, the film helps to allay the fears women might have about war work. Initial tensions are overcome and the women not only adapt to the work routines, but form a happy alliance under the direction of their foreman, a plain-speaking Yorkshireman (Eric Portman). Tragedy occurs when Celia's new husband is killed in a raid over Germany, but in a wartime version of the old favourite of the musical – 'the show must go on' – Celia is symbolically brought back into her factory family in a canteen singsong and redirected to her factory work. Even a personal tragedy of the deepest kind imaginable can be made bearable through the support of the family/ people/nation.[35]

Millions Like Us was received sympathetically by its audience because it touched on aspects of wartime life that everyone had some experience of. But the genre of which it was part did not constitute the most popular viewing of British film-goers. American films, even quite whimsical ones like William Wyler's *Mrs Miniver* (1942), were more popular, while *Gone With The Wind* (1939) enjoyed the biggest financial success of any film during the war. Gainsborough Pictures, who produced *Millions Like Us*, were responsible for some of the most popular of the British-made films. They were not sober realist narratives, but costume dramas which in a later age became known as 'bodice rippers'. *The Man in Grey* was the most successful British film of 1943 and launched Gainsborough on an enormously profitable series of such films which portrayed a world of 'rollicking, rumbustious romps in Restoration or Regency England, of whip-wielding lords and bosom-heaving ladies, of highwaymen, gypsies, moonlit rides, of thwarted love and of steaming passion, a vivid, vibrant world inhabited by such smouldering sex-objects as Margaret Lockwood and Jean Kent, James Mason and Stewart Grainger'. The Gainsborough melodramas provided a complete antithesis to wartime realism.[36]

With this development went a disappearance of the consensual film that had developed in the 1930s and which reached its apogee in *Millions Like Us*. The Gainsborough films made no pretence to be dealing with social unity and gender equalities. When the war film made its reappearance in the 1950s as one of the most popular genres of the time, the separation of the classes and the sexes was very noticeable. Women were defined in relation to men – as wives, mothers or sweethearts. The officer class was often depicted on its own, as in the many prisoner-of-war films set in camps for officers, where other ranks, if not excluded altogether, were either servants or comic figures.[37] In *The Colditz Story* (1955), for example, the officer-prisoners exist in a culture of public school good fellowship. *The Cruel Sea* (1953), a sensitive rendering of Nicholas Monsarrat's novel, was a film about men and male bonding, with women removed to the margins. There were scarcely any women at all in the immensely popular *The Bridge on the River Kwai* (1957). It was little wonder that such films made no appeal to women cinema-goers. The mainly female readership of *Picturegoer* preferred American films, either what Harper and Porter describe as 'menopausal weepies' such as *Johnny Belinda* (1948) or *Magnificent Obsession* (1954), or the female romance typified by Audrey Hepburn in *Roman Holiday* (1953) and *Sabrina Fair* (1954).[38] Women, especially younger ones, were intensely attracted to the American singer-actor Doris Day, whose film persona recalled some of the qualities associated with Gracie Fields 20 years earlier. Though she continued to make films throughout the 1950s and 1960s, the peak of Day's career came with *Calamity Jane* (1953) in which she delivered an energetic performance interesting mainly for its bisexual nature. The part of 'Calam' requires a dualism between a rough-and-ready mannish behaviour which is gradually transformed into conventional femininity. In spite of this conservative theme, there was much admiration to be found in Day's ability to combine the two roles, which required an assertion of independent-mindedness. One woman claimed to have seen the film 88 times, 45 of them in the space of two weeks.[39]

In the 1960s a number of influences were responsible for pushing the portrayal of women in more radical directions. The social concerns with youth, first in the form of male 'juvenile delinquents', then with pre-marital sex and young women, were linked with the attempt to counter the decline of cinema attendance with films aimed at youthful audiences. Moreover, the 1960s saw a greater liberalization of attitudes, both in society as a whole and in the cinema in particular, the latter helped by the rise of the 'new wave' directors of the early 1960s and the relaxation of censorship permitted by the introduction in 1951 of the 'X' certificate. This climate produced a series of films that took a new and fresh look at subjects such as social class (*Room at the Top*, 1958, and *Saturday Night and Sunday Morning*, 1960) and gender (*This Sporting Life*, 1963), though in each case these critically acclaimed films all conformed to a cinematic British tradition of working from literary texts. Among these was a crop of films that foregrounded the social and sexual problems of younger women. In *A Taste of Honey* (1961), for example, questions of social class and traditional family domesticity were subjected to caustic scrutiny; in *Darling* (1965) the ability of a sexually attractive and manipulative young women to advance her career was examined in a setting that had undertones of the Profumo Affair; and in *Here We Go Round the Mulberry Bush* (1967) a freewheeling female character is viewed from a male perspective to achieve a reversal of conventional attitudes about sexual behaviour. It was this figure which, says Christine Geraghty, 'dominated 60s British cinema. [The] representation of an unpredictable, spontaneous, emotionally honest, sexually active young woman shows how cinema worked within the broader social context in its attempt to reflect contemporary attitudes to what was seen as a 60s phenomenon.'[40] Julie Christie's character in *Billy Liar* (1963) summed this up perfectly.

The attempt to direct attention to youth reminds us that the British cinema industry was, during the 1960s, losing its long battle for independent economic viability. Conditions for film-making had seemed propitious at the onset of the industry in the early years of the century. British cinema had a comparatively large and culturally homogeneous domestic market, with no serious overseas competition, except from America. This, however, proved fatal. Well before the First World War significant sections of the film industry had passed into American hands and there were times, especially in the mid-1920s, when it seemed that Britain was little more than a dumping ground for imported American films. This inability to compete with a better-financed American product explains the periodic intervention in the affairs of the British film industry by the state, with, for example, the protective system introduced in the late 1920s, or the attempted restriction of overseas films by the Labour government in 1947. This latter move, initiated by Hugh Dalton in his summer budget of that year, illustrated in microcosm the problems of film-making and distribution in Britain. At a time of economic crisis Dalton's plan was designed to stem the loss of valuable foreign exchange – estimated at £70 million in the case of the film industry. He imposed a 75 per cent levy on imported American films. It caused an immediate boycott by the Americans and serious economic and cultural repercussions in Britain. The demand of audiences at this time was at its peak, the British industry was completely incapable of filling the void, the cinema owners and distributors, deprived of their American staple, feared going out of business, and so stockpiled American films had to be repeatedly shown, at great cost, to keep the cinemas open. As Harold Wilson at the Board of Trade sardonically commented: 'we were actually paying out not 17 million but 50 million dollars for the privilege of seeing *Hellzapoppin'* for the third time and *Ben Hur* for the twenty-third'.[41] Dalton's measure had not only been totally ineffective but counterproductive. The levy was abandoned in 1948 and Wilson himself intervened to bring in a new quota system. It established a level of 45 per cent of British films to be shown, but this, too, proved unrealistic, mainly because the major British producer, the Rank Organization, was unable to fulfil the quota without resorting to making poor-quality 'B' films which audiences disliked. The quota was quickly relaxed, dropping to 30 per cent (its original level before Wilson had intervened) by 1950. But Wilson did make an important contribution to the film industry by instituting the National Film Finance Corporation, which provided public funds to subsidize independent producers, and the so-called 'Eady' plan, which eased the tax on cinema tickets and made money available, partly through a voluntary levy from exhibitors, for film-making. Both helped to sustain the industry and remained in existence until wound up by the Conservative government in the early 1980s.[42]

But the measures did not halt the decline of cinema-going, which was caused primarily by the rise of alternative leisure activities, especially television. The 1950s saw a steep decline in cinema admissions: by the later years of the decade the audience had more than halved, from 1.3 billions annually to around 0.3 in 1960, and some 1000 of the 5000 or so cinemas that had been in existence during the war had closed.[43] Thus began the long process, familiar to all those who lived through the 1960s, of the virtual disappearance of cinemas from the suburbs and the conversion of many premises to bingo halls and carpet warehouses, prior to their eventual demolition in many cases and their replacement by supermarkets. In the city-centre cinemas that remained the continued decline in attendance prompted the subdivision of the now over-large auditoriums into small 'mini' cinemas. In these new surroundings 'going to the pictures' took on a new experience. To begin with, the cost was relatively more expensive; the old double-bill of 'A' and 'B' film, with 'full supporting programme', was dispensed with, and with it the 'continuous show' of former days; the programme now focused on the main feature with advertising shorts. Greater emphasis still was placed on the sales of ice cream and soft drinks, often with an inordinately long interval between adverts and film in order to maximize sales; children's matinees also disappeared, much to the relief of cinema managers. But such reconfiguring did not always work, and it was only with the development in the mid-1980s of the American idea of the multiplex cinema, built on cheap land on out-of-town sites that afforded extensive car-parking space, that interest and attendance was once more revitalized. By the mid-1990s the mutiplexes accounted for almost half of all cinema admissions.[44] There was some irony in the fact that the salvation of cinema-going, a habit once thought to induce a passive, American-fed mentality, came in the form of an American model promoted by American leisure corporations.

Some of the films shown in these new venues suggest a continuing vitality in British film-making. After the critical and box-office success of *Chariots of Fire* (1981), there has been British involvement in a string of commercially-popular films – *Four Weddings and a Funeral* (1994), *The Full Monty* (1997) and *Brassed Off* (1996) being the best known. Similarly, a number of American productions such as George Lucas's *Star Wars* films were made in British studios, especially during the 1970s. Moreover, through the support of the television company Channel 4, independent producers have achieved critical (if not financial) success with films such as *My Beautiful Launderette* (1985), notable for offering a vision of a 'Thatcherite' Britain through the juxtaposition of class, race and sex themes, and *High Hopes* (1988) which similarly cast a jaundiced eye on contemporary Britain. Increasingly, however, the basis of production for British films since the 1960s has been a co-operative approach which combines American money with British acting and technical skill. 'British' films are now international products. This is characterized in the long series of films based on the James Bond novels of Ian Fleming, still capable of drawing audiences some 35 years after their original inception, by which time the Fleming material has dried up and several actors have passed through the Bond part. At the very end of the century, the effectiveness of this approach to film-making was well illustrated in the popular appeal of the film *Notting Hill* (1999). Its finance was American, and its principal players were an American (Julia Roberts) and an Englishman (Hugh Grant) supported by an otherwise all-British cast. In its plot the film recalled some of the whimsy of the Ealing comedies of the late 1940s, together with an image of Britain that came straight from the *Mrs Miniver* school of screen writing. In one sense, it unreservedly merits the overused description 'escapist'; in another, *Notting Hill* presents an amalgam of all the idealised, conservative ideologies of class, gender and nation that have traditionally found a home in British cinema, as our heroine (Julia Roberts) escapes the commercial and personal stresses of the life of a modern film star to find both peace and the solace of domestic life and motherhood in London, England. The final scene, significantly shot in a sunlit leafy park, has a pregnant Roberts in repose in the arms of Grant, as the rest of the world goes about its business. With films like this, who needs censorship?

CONCLUSION: THE INFLUENCE OF CINEMA

In spite of the ups and downs experienced by the cinema in the twentieth century it has survived as a popular leisure form into the twenty-first. Annual cinema admissions dipped below 0.3 billions in the mid-1960s and have remained below that figure ever since, although the 1990s did witness a slow recovery from the low point of 53 million in 1984.[45] The British cinema industry still occupies a role in film production, even though it is a less autonomous one than that hoped for at the beginning of the century. But even within a globalized system of finance and production, films still appear that can be classified as distinctively British in the way that they explore themes and issues particular to British life and society. And, of course, for all the travails that have afflicted the process of film-making in Britain, audiences have never suffered a shortage of foreign films. The overwhelming majority of these have been American, but by the end of the century there had developed in some urban areas a significant extension of the Bengali film industry, in the form of cinemas spefically given over to the products of 'Bollywood'. Thus, the cinema continues to be an important cultural influence in Britain, with developing multi-cultural features, though its influence is less pervasive than it was in the heyday of films from the 1920s to the 1940s.

What kind of influence, on the whole, did films exercise over their audiences? Though a fundamental question, this is a difficult one for social historians to answer. There are, to be sure, all manner of ways in which British cinema might be seen as a conservative force. For a major agency of popular culture, it was one which offered remarkably few opportunities for the people themselves to exercize any control over it. Cinema carried a distinctively 'establishment' stamp. George Perry, for example, has emphasized its preoccupation with both social class and its preference for literary adaptations; he has reminded us of the industry's unwillingness to innovate, as well as its desire for avoiding controversy.[46] The films of the French 'new wave' of the late 1950s would have been unimaginable in Britain, whereas something like

Lionel Jeffries' warmly sentimental and nostalgic *The Railway Children* (1971) could probably only have been made in Britain. The concern to project a comfortable and ordered vision of society was at the heart of the industry's long-running relationship with censorship, which only slowly moderated and has never completely disappeared. Censorship was predicated on an early belief in the power of film to persuade, especially to persuade immature minds among the lower orders. Its potency should therefore be carefully directed. This belief was very clearly illustrated in the continuing struggle over the opening of cinemas on Sunday, a struggle that was not resolved in some parts of the country until well after the Second World War.[47] British cinema has never operated in a completely free intellectual climate. Its products have been forced to comply with notions of what was acceptable at any given time. But when it is recalled that most censorship has been *self*-imposed, force is added to the argument that British cinema – middle-class controlled, 'prissy, mealy-mouthed, and sycophantic' – did not need external controls to cause it to toe the line.[48]

Example upon example in this vein might suggest British cinema as a conservative force in popular culture. But there are two sides to cultural relationships, and what is 'encoded' in the medium is only one of them; the other relates to how the message is 'decoded'. This takes the historian into far more difficult territory where the landmarks are less easily distinguishable. Put bluntly: can we know how films were received and interpreted by their audiences? Did the dominant message get through? There are various ways of attempting an answer to these questions. One is to refer to the numerous sources – contemporary surveys, readers letters to film magazines, oral history testimonies – which convey something (though often through a glass darkly) of audience reaction to films. Another is to consider the social and political context in which films were shown. If this reveals stability and consensus, it might therefore be assumed that films depicting such harmony were accepted as plausible portrayals of 'real life'. Such is the approach of Tony Aldgate, who has argued that cinema in the 1930s 'reflected a stable society, reinforced it, and sought to generate adherence to the idea that society should continue to remain stable and cohesive as it changed over time'.[49] In general, such evidence suggests that film audiences were content enough with what was being offered to them, and were disinclined to contest the messages of films (if such things could even be observed) with 'alternative' readings. Thus, it might be concluded, film did work as a means of social control.

The evidence is shaky, to be sure, but historians do not like to admit that they have no way of knowing what the effect of a particular historical process was. Determining with any kind of precision the ideological effects of cinema is a hazardous business. In the absence of anything more compelling, however, we stick with what we have, and conclude that, as a leisure form, cinema in Britain worked succesfully as a force for conservatism. But in doing so we should remind ourselves that cinema is only one ideological influence among many, and that there might be others, even within the realm of sport and leisure, with the capacity to invoke more progressive thoughts.

Key Reading ●

Barr, C. ed. *All Our Yesterdays: 90 Years of British Cinema*. London: British Film Institute, 1986.

Murphy, R. ed. *The British Cinema Book*. London: British Film Institute, 1997.

Richards, J. *The Age of the Dream Palace: Cinema and Society in Britain, 1930–1939*. London: Routledge, 1989 edn.

Stead, P. *Film and the Working Class: The Feature Film in British and American Society*. London: Routledge, 1991 edn.

Chronology of Events

1889 William Friese-Green's patent for cinema projector (Edison's in USA 1893).

1895 Lumière Brothers' first commercial film shown in Paris; 1896 in London.

1903 First 'feature' film *The Great Train Robbery* (8 minutes), USA.

1905 Cecil Hepworth's first British feature film *Rescued by Rover.*

1907 Balham Empire, London, first theatre exclusively to show films; 300 film theatres in London by 1910.

1909 Cinematograph Act introduced safety measures in cinemas; could also be invoked for censorship (against, e.g., Sunday opening).

1912 British Board of Film Censors established by the film industry, G. A. Redford its first President.

1916 Entertainments Tax introduced as wartime measure covering various commercial entertainments; affected prices of cinema seats, and lasted until the late 1950s.

1927 Cinematograph Films Act introduced protective measures to safeguard British film industry against American competition, with a quota of 10 per cent of all films exhibited to be British-made; created the 'quota quickie' film.

1933 Oscar Deutsch launched Odeon Theatres, linked with the US production company United Artists; *c.*180 Odeons by the late 1930s; Alexander Korda's *Private Life of Henry VIII* (starring Charles Laughton) the major British box-office success of this period.

1935 Of all films shown at this time 60 per cent were American.

1938 Parliament, acting on recommendations of Moyne Committee (set up 1936), introduced Cinematograph Films Act, maintaining a revised quota system to protect industry against foreign competition.

1945 Rank Organization had become the dominant force in British film production and exhibition.

1948 Labour government established National Film Finance Corporation with power to grant loans to independent producers.

1950 Eady Plan introduced reduction in entertainment duties to help cinema owners, and effected a voluntary levy on exhibitors to aid producers.

1951 'X' certificate introduced by BBFC to restrict entry to 'adult films' to those over the age of 16.

1950s Increasing challenge of television caused some 1500 cinemas (one-third of the total number) to close during this decade; technical innovations in film-making to maintain interest included 3-D, wide-screen films (e.g. Cinemascope) and stereophonic sound (ToddAO); in 1951 there had been 1.35 billion cinema admissions, in 1961 there were 0.35 billion.

early 1960s A wave of social realist dramas brought a new vigour to British film with an emphasis on the North: it included *Room at the Top* (1958), *Saturday Night and Sunday Morning* (1960), *A Taste of Honey* (1961), *A Kind of Loving* (1962) and *This Sporting Life* (1962)

1977 George Lucas's *Star Wars*, which won 7 Oscars, was made at Pinewood Studios in England and exemplified the American co-production process, established earlier with the James Bond series of films.

1982 Abandonment of the long-established quota principle.

1985 Films Act abolished the Eady Levy, and ended the National Film Finance Corporation.

1980s Growth of the multiplex cinema, and resurgence in the popularity of cinema-going; attendances reached 123 million by 1998 (after all-time low of 53 million in 1984).

1992 Of the British exhibition market 92 per cent was captured by USA.

1998 *Titanic* was UK's top box office film of all time.

'Getting Away From It All': The Holiday Spirit

CONTENTS

There can be few aspects of leisure that hold such a special place in people's minds as holidays. 'For many', according to Britain's first social historian of holidays, 'they are one of the principal objects of life.'[1] Of course, holidays come in many shapes and sizes. The English Tourist Board defines a holiday as a period of time of four nights or more spent away from home. This sounds a modest undertaking compared with the aeroplane journeys to far-away tropical locations enjoyed by many nowadays. But, equally, there are many for whom the Tourist Board definition is still a dream, and for whom a holiday might simply be an inexpensive, relaxing time spent at home.[2] No matter how it is conceived of and participated in, however, the holiday has one common characteristic: it is something enjoyed, or at least looked forward to, as a significant break from routine. Other leisure pursuits – going to football matches, for example, or simply sitting in a café chatting among friends – have this quality, but not in the sustained way that the holiday does. It is the ultimate 'change' that 'does you good'. It is the one leisure form that really is the antithesis of work. As such it offers the exceptional experiences and cultural meanings associated with those rare times in life when normal behaviour is temporarily suspended.

ORIGINS: ELITE TRAVEL

Before probing this cultural dimension of the holiday, however, we should consider its development, taking into account the historical influences that have given rise to the variety of holiday forms. First, though, let us note that at the beginning of the twenty-first century holiday-making is an extensive economic and social activity. There were 56 million holidays taken in 1998 by British people to a wide variety of destinations, a figure which represented an increase of a third in the total number of holidays taken since the early 1970s.[3] Estimates made in the early 1950s had put the figure at 26.5 million, most of which were taken in Britain.[4] Moreover, the tourist trade constituted a significant sector of the British economy at the end of the century, in terms of both employment and expenditure on accommodation and other retail services.[5] In addition to this, and rather more difficult to quantify, we should also note the immense interest in holidays stimulated by, and reflected in, the media: through television programmes, travel writing in books and magazines, advertising and tourist information, and the package-tour holiday brochure.

The extent of all this activity provides a marked contrast with the situation at the beginning of the twentieth century. To be sure there were indications in 1900 of a mass tourism to come, but for the most part holiday-making was a socially exclusive pursuit enjoyed by the wealthy. Ordinary people were only beginning to take part, in resorts like Blackpool designed to cater specifically for them. As a marker of social class the holiday worked more plainly and effectively than most leisure forms.

In many ways, therefore, the history of holiday-making in Britain is the history of class relations. The early history, which need not detain us long here, was one of pursuits enjoyed by the 'leisure class'. The mid-eighteenth century marks a starting point. The conclusion of a disruptive period of Continental warfare at the Peace of Paris in 1763 established settled conditions which enabled the first modern holiday form to develop: the Grand Tour. This was a life-enhancing experience for wealthy and largely aristocratic men and women, which rounded off their classical education by allowing them to see at first hand the architectural and artistic treasures of Italy, especially Florence and Rome. It was a time-consuming and costly business, and not always confined to spiritual matters. As the journals of the young Scottish man of letters, James Boswell, reveal, sensual, as well as sensuous, pleasures were on the itinerary. Physical restoration was a feature of the other aspect of upper-class holidays which developed at this time, and which could be pursued at home or abroad. 'Taking the waters', the contemporary therapy for over-indulgent living, became a business which produced a string a spa resorts of which Bath was probably the most famous and popular in Britain, and Carlsbad its equivalent in Europe. Sea bathing, a pastime similarly held to have curative value, was initially associated with cranky individuals like the writer Tobias Smollett. But by the end of the eighteenth century it had become a craze, with the south-coast town of Brighton the leading resort, its status dignified by the presence of the Prince Regent, the inspiration for some bizarre architecture which became a local landmark. All resorts, of whatever function, also became centres of social and political interest during the appropriate season. Deals were brokered, marriages made, civilized behaviour was perfected, and the subtle hierarchical calibrations of polite society were adjusted and rearranged according to the ups-and-downs of life, as Jane Austin's novels shrewdly observe.[6]

Intellectual changes in the nineteenth century, notably the rise of the Romantic movement with its emphasis on Nature, wrought important developments in the style of holidays. While still confined to the upper-crust, holiday-making acquired a more ethereal quality. To the Grand Tour's nourishment of the intellect and the spa town's care of the body was added Nature's invigoration of the soul. This was provided, over the course of the nineteenth century, in three forms: mountains, lakes and snow. There was, it has been aptly observed, 'morality in the oxygen'.[7] Contemplating the wonders and the force of Nature drew travellers principally to Switzerland and the Alps. England's Lake District, however, became popular after Wordsworth's effective publicizing of it, while the Scottish Highlands were fixed in the popular imagination as a result of Walter Scott's novels. And once Arnold Lunn, a century later, had educated the better-off sections of society in the athletic attractions of snow, the British briefly became the leading exponents of winter sports.[8]

For all this, however, there were many for whom 'holiday' was synonymous with 'seaside'. By the end of the nineteenth century the middle and upper classes of France and Britain had colonized a string of seaside resorts on the English south coast, Normandy, the Côte d'Azur of Provence, and the coast of the Landes around Biarritz. The British influence was strong everywhere. Some French resorts, notably Nice, were as populated in the season by visitors from Britain as by French people. But Nice, as its opulent seafront hotels on the Promenade des Anglais testify, was for big money; and Biarritz, a favourite haunt of Prince Edward (later Edward VII), was distinctly aristocratic. Even Sir Henry Campbell-Bannerman, the patrician Scot who went out to Biarritz to kiss hands on becoming Prime Minister in 1905, would have felt slightly out of place. It was in English resorts that a quintessentially middle-class taste, style and decorum was exhibited: piers, promenades, formal flower gardens, golf courses, bandstands, pavilions. Bournemouth and Eastbourne were typical. They defied the later incursion of working-class holiday-makers which lowered the tone of places like Brighton, whose twentieth-century populism is so well captured by Graham Greene in *Brighton Rock* (1938). So did Southport and Lytham St Annes on the Lancashire coast. In that part of the world, the workers headed for Blackpool. Scarborough, Yorkshire's premier resort, had been an early venue for both spa and sea holidays, and always retained a strong upper-class clientele, much in evidence at its cricket festival in September. Working-class visitors to Scarborough, and by the early-twentieth century there were many, occupied a different part of the town by the old harbour. Thus class distinctions and segregations were affirmed in leisure. There were many reasons for these variations in social tone and emphasis, the main one being the composition and stance of local corporations. In the debates over how towns should develop and respond to mass tourism the view of the majority of councillors was often crucial, as we shall see in Chapter 10.[9]

Mass tourism was decidely in the offing by the turn of the century. All the ingredients for it had been prepared in the various leisure pursuits of the wealthy over the previous century or more. Little that was new came about until the advent of air travel in the 1950s took many more people farther afield than ever before, though even that resulted in many old features of holiday-making being perpetuated overseas. It cast some doubt on the old maxim (itself redolent of the Grand Tour) that 'travel broadens the mind'. Much the same forces that we saw in Chapter 2 making popular commercial sports possible also produced mass holiday-making by the turn of the century. Rising real wages, shorter working hours, and the securing of a vacation period in the summer, either by legislation or, more commonly, by industrial bargaining, allowed people more time and more money to spend.[10] In the mid-1930s *The New Survey of London Life and Labour* estimated that 'rather more than half' of the occupied population of London were employed in trades and industries in which an annual holiday with pay was customary.[11] This was before the introduction in 1938 of the Holidays With Pay legislation, for which the trade union movement had lobbied vigorously. Moreover, the transport system had expanded by the inter-war period so that in addition to an extensive railway network, there was a growing provision of motor transport (buses, coaches, and private cars and motor-cycles), together with the ubiquitous bicycle, which enabled the urban dweller to get out into the nearby countryside. For many people, holidays ceased to be a purely local experience. The carnivals, fairs and 'wakes', which had formed the focal points of the people's holidays in the past (and which continued to be important for many), were now displaced for some by the opportunity to move away from home for a week, or even just a Bank Holiday Monday: 'charabancs arrive in Southend [on the August Bank Holiday] crammed to overflowing with East Londoners' noted the *New Survey of London Life and Labour*[12] of the annual day out to the coast, perhaps a phenomenon witnessed more in the south of England than in the north, where the week's holiday was already firmly established. It was the businessman Thomas Cook, whose breakthrough into the holiday business came through organizing trips to the Great Exhibition of 1851, who paved the way in the science of moving people around, and it was the railway that enabled him to do it.[13]

MASS HOLIDAY-MAKING, SOCIAL CLASS AND THE LURE OF THE MEDITERRANEAN

The class relationships of leisure were changed immeasurably in the twentieth century by the advent of mass holiday-making. This, of course, brought the working classes into holidays in a major way. With them came a number of the familiar moral concerns that had already been visited upon other branches of leisure. These related not only to the recurring question of whether leisure time was being spent wisely, but to newer considerations about the degree to which communal holiday-making produced 'regimented' attitudes (a concern voiced especially in the aftermath of the appearance of commercial holiday camps in the 1930s which gave rise to the phenomenon of 'Butlinism'), or about the effect of mass tourism on the natural environment. None the less, mass holiday-making was fuelled by a powerful economic imperative, and its growth produced a major new sector in the economic life of the country. Holiday-making was not just pleasure and enjoyment, it was jobs and livelihood for millions of people who worked in the services that holiday resorts provided. 'At bottom', John Walton reminds us, 'the seaside resort is an industrial town.'[14] And industrial towns are often built upon shaky foundations.

In the first half of the century many holiday towns enjoyed impressive growth, or enviable prosperity, the two things not necessarily linked.[15] Pimlott's pioneering work, written at the height of the domestic holiday trade (well before mass tourism switched its focus to foreign destinations), pointed up the economic importance of the seaside holiday. He noted, for example, the holiday capacity of some of the leading English resorts in the late 1930s: with Blackpool leading the way with a (very roughly) estimated 7 million visitors a year, and Southend not far behind with 5.5 million, around 20 million people each year might have been visiting these two resorts, together with Hastings, Bournemouth, Southport, Eastbourne and Ramsgate. The 'holiday industry' was one of the most rapid areas of economic growth in Britain after the 1914–18 war. In the decade before the 1939–45 war the entertainments industry, to which seaside towns contributed significantly, grew by almost 50 per cent – a greater rate than in any other industry.[16] The activity associated with this growth was stretched around a number of towns of varying sizes, most of them located at the seaside. Britain possessed probably a greater number of seaside resorts than any country in Europe in the middle of the century. But the labour force employed in the holiday industry was concentrated into some six towns, with populations which at this time numbered roughly (taking into account neighbouring communities) between 60 000 and 220 000: in ascending order they were – Eastbourne and Hastings (c.60 000 each), Southport (c.80 000), Blackpool and surrounding districts (c.160 000), Bournemouth and Poole (c.180 000), and Brighton and Hove (c.220 000). The ability of these places to maintain their attractiveness to visitors, and thus to retain their economic viability, depended upon a host of factors. These included: climate and natural environment, attractive buildings, a safe ambience, appropriate accommodation, the right kinds of entertainments, and, not least, perspicacious local leadership.

The precise nature of some of these attributes depended upon the kind of clientele the resort sought to attract, for class relations in leisure determined that resorts were frequently characterized by their social 'tone'. Frinton, on the Essex coast, strove hard to exclude the masses and acquired a notably 'snooty' atmosphere, as did Hove and Sidmouth. Brighton and Blackpool, on the other hand, being dependent upon volume to maintain their economic base, opened their doors to all-comers and thus acquired a rather vulgar tone. The contrast between Blackpool and its neighbour on the Lancashire coast,

Southport, is striking in this respect. Blackpool, which experienced massive investment in the inter-war years in parks, gardens, bathing pools and the Winter Gardens, had a commercially minded local council eager to place the town in the forefront of 'modern' entertainment. Its Tower, Illuminations and numerous variety shows with nationally known 'turns', and the sensational sideshows of its 'Golden Mile' made Blackpool synonymous with the hedonistic, mechanical pleasures which so many British holiday-makers equated with 'having a good time'.[17] Southport, 20 or so miles away across the Ribble estuary, was in many ways a different world. Unlike Blackpool, Southport was a dormitory town for merchants and professional people who worked in Manchester and Liverpool. In Birkdale it had a well-heeled middle-class suburb whose assured way of life has been keenly evoked in the autobiographical writings of the historian A. J. P. Taylor, born there in 1906.[18] In this way Southport prefigured a development that became common towards the end of the century, when other resort towns sought to reinvigorate a declining economy by encouraging the building of commuter and retirement homes. Southport's ground landlords, the Blundell and Fleetwood-Hesketh families, had ensured that the town was developed according to a strict grid lay-out, and this gave it a measured, orderly appearance. Significantly, although it possessed a fine sweep of promenade with some handsome mid-nineteenth-century buildings, the town rather turned its back on the sea. Its centrepiece was Lord Street, one of the most elegant main streets of any town in Britain, and perhaps even Europe. Apart from a small contingent of Scottish labour aristocrats, who holidayed there each July in boarding houses hidden away behind the main thoroughfare, its visitors were solid folks of the middle-class and above who came for the shopping and the golf: the café at Marshall and Snelgrove's and Thom's Japanese Tea Rooms on Lord Street were the places to be seen, and there were three impressive links, of which Royal Birkdale possessed the most prestige. Southport attempted to preserve an Edwardian *hauteur* well into the final quarter of the twentieth century, and succeeded at least until the 1960s when its symbol of middle-class elegance, the Palace Hotel in Birkdale, disappeared to make way for new housing. Southport never quite recovered from the local government reorganization of 1974 which placed it in Merseyside. The new address, with its suggestion of proletarian Liverpudlians, did not at all have the right social cachet.[19]

There is, perhaps, a popular notion that places like this were living on borrowed time: that as soon as mass-ownership of cars[20] and cheaper air travel opened up foreign markets, British holiday-makers voted with their feet, deserting the windswept dunes and rain-lashed promenades of their native land. To be sure, once cheap air travel made international tourism possible in the 1960s, British seaside resorts did begin finding it difficult to compete with new resorts on the Costa Brava and the Costa del Sol. The latter, though they reproduced many of the traditonal features of the British seaside, none the less offered a new exoticism which had much to do with the climate. In spite of all the charms of its bay, Morecambe, for example, simply could not offer the near-certainty of sunny days that could be found in Tossa de Mar or Torremolinos. In this new world of tourism the spectre of New Brighton, the

Wirral resort whose trade collapsed in the 1960s in a decline that was truly 'catastrophic,'[21] haunted the promenades of Britain.

This is not to say, however, that British resorts gave up without a fight. The post-war boom in holidays, when the traditional resorts recaptured the appeal they had established earlier in the century and the holiday camp enjoyed its period of greatest popularity,[22] lasted rather longer than is sometimes imagined.[23] Many British seaside resorts were able to profit from the affluence of the 1950s and 1960s, retaining much of their working-class following. The British Tourist Authority's figures for holidays taken by British residents show a clear, though not steep, decline during the 1970s, and a levelling out at around 32 million holidays each year during the last 20 years of the century.[24] Some of this was explained by the British resorts having been buoyed by the tendency of many of those taking second holidays to take them in Britain. But there was a 'sharp decline' in main holidays taken in Britain between the mid-1970s and the mid-1980s, the fall off in visitor demand partly caused by the high unemployment of the 1980s and the inability of many working-class families to afford to get away.[25] The magnetism of abroad was often confined to middle-class holiday-makers until at least the 1970s, and it was not until then, or perhaps even later, that British resorts started to face problems of re-adjustment. John Walton has shown how many of them, with Blackpool as always well to the fore, sought to 'reinvent' themselves in the last 30 or so years of the twentieth century. This process usually took one of two forms; either the redevelopment of the resort as a different kind of town, or a decision to reinvest in an updated tourist trade. The former strategy often involved housing development for the benefit of commuters or retired people, something seen clearly in seaside towns of the south east, notably Worthing which had a large proportion of retired people in its late-twentieth century population.

Resorts which attempted to revive their tourist functions often turned to new attractions such as marinas and indoor leisure centres, or to 'cultural' tourism based on heritage sites or other historical associations. Whitby's links with Captain Cook and Dracula provide a case in point. Such links could also enable places which had by no stretch of the imagination been seaside resorts to redevelop a failing local economy. Liverpool is a clear example of this with its refurbished nineteenth-century dock buildings converted into wine bars and gift shops, and much emphasis placed on the city's most celebrated sons, the Beatles. Blackpool's traditions of commercial multi-culturalism, which saw many immigrant businessmen establish themselves locally, might have been responsible for its attempts to welcome gay tourists, exploiting the so-called 'pink pound', a tactic also tried in Brighton. For all this, however, it is worth keeping in mind the fact that Blackpool Pleasure Beach has retained its long-held position as Britain's most popular tourist attraction.[26] But generally, the bigger resorts seem to have been less successful in transforming their tourist trade than do some of the smaller seaside towns. The principal post-war boom in domestic seaside tourism happened in the 1950s and 1960s with the arrival of mass car ownership, and gave rise to a different kind of holiday-making from that which had prevailed before the war. It was a more scattered form of tourism, which benefited places able to offer space for caravans or the building of chalets. Caravan sites mushroomed at this time on the coasts of Yorkshire, Lincolnshire, East Anglia, North Wales and South West England in particular. The contrast in experience between the 'traditional' resort town and the newer, more footloose form of tourism, was seen in Somerset. Whilst Weston-super-Mare struggled against muddy beaches and parking problems to maintain its traditional flow of visitors from the Birmingham area, some of the surrounding towns and villages flourished thanks to their open spaces and the ready access they gave for visits to local inland beauty spots. This change heralded the arrival of the more autonomous 'postmodern' tourist who, though still part of a mass movement of people, was beginning to reject the communal culture offered up by the urban resorts with their boarding-houses, concentrated mechanical attractions, and increasingly polluted beaches.[27]

But in spite of some success stories, the general picture of British seaside resorts at the beginning of the twenty-first century is a dismal one. High levels of unemployment, low wages and social deprivation mark many resorts out as having the same problems of regeneration as inner-city areas or former coalmining communities. At the beginning of the new century a Resort Task-force, inevitably led in the contemporary manner by a 'tourism tsar', has been set up with government support to encourage investment which it is hoped will find 'niche' markets for declining resorts. There is a sense of finality in much of this. The Taskforce was reported as saying: 'Towns which carve out a distinctive brand will receive government and European funding . . . many of these places last received serious investment in the nineteenth century. They have to have vision now or they will die.'[28]

For some, of course, holidays have not been synonymous with the seaside. There has been throughout the century a range of holiday activities which have not been dependent upon beaches and boarding-houses. Like seaside holidays, however, many of these other activities have derived their appeal from the assumed healthiness of being in the open air. Thus the Romantics' love of the countryside, and of mountains in particular, has been perpetuated in the continuing appeal of areas such as Scotland, the Lake District and North Wales as holiday destinations. In 1989 the West Country was by far the most popular of all areas for domestic British holidays, accounting for almost 20 per cent of all nights spent away from home. Some of the region's attraction for the tourist is undoubtedly to do with the seaside resorts of Devon and Cornwall, but some is also connected with the inland charms of places such as Dartmoor and 'Hardy country'. The next most popular destinations for domestic holidays were, in almost equal measure, Wales and Scotland, where rural attractions of various kinds formed a major reason for visiting. The Welsh Tourist Board's 1995 brochure highlighting the delights of Meirion-nydd, for example, included walking, climbing, fishing, pony trekking, canoeing, mountain biking and golf among the activities to be found there.[29] Hiking, rambling and cycling had all helped to open up such rural areas (especially those adjacent to large towns) in the early years of the century, when holiday-making of this kind acquired an active image which pleased all those critics of what J. B. Priestley was to describe as the 'why move from your armchair?' mentality of leisure.[30]

Frequently, such leisure had political associations. Cycling and rambling were much encouraged by the Labour left, whose campaigns to open up the countryside for popular enjoyment resulted eventually in the Labour government's Countryside Act of 1949. Leisure of this kind was felt to be good for both the individual and for the political cause. It stimulated camaraderie and intensified political commitment. Before the Second World War, as the work of Stephen Jones has shown, the Labour movement supported an impressive body of associations which existed to encourage sport and leisure.[31] The Co-op, for example, was among the first to pioneer organized travel for working people. In contrast with later years, when this kind of politically related leisure activity rather faded away, there was still in the inter-war period a commitment to Robert Blatchford's mission of the late nineteenth century to make socialism fun. In this sense, there might have been those who felt that Labour's victory of 1945 had been won, if not on the playing fields of Eton, at least on the lanes and moors of Britain, as party activists strode forth discussing social policy while trespassing on private property. It was partly this, but more usually the invasion of the countryside by the motor car in the 1930s, that prompted the owners of rural property to subscribe to the activities of the Council for the Preservation of Rural England, and to inaugurate a debate which has continued ever since on maintaining a balance between giving access to the countryside and, at the same time, safeguarding it as a national heritage.

Another element of the domestic holiday scene which has had both economic and cultural influences is the increase in overseas visitors to Britain. This is very largely a post-Second World War development. Whilst in 1946 the number of overseas visitors was less than a quarter of a million, this had risen to over 11 million by the end of the 1970s, with the steepest rise occurring between the early 1960s and mid-1970s.[32] It not only brought valuable foreign exchange into the country in the form especially of dollars, deutschmarks and yen, but it caused the British tourist industry to think hard about providing good attractions and services, and it might also have helped to introduce a more tolerant and cosmopolitan attitude into British society. In terms of holiday destinations it brought a tourist who was not especially interested in the seaside, but who certainly did want to indulge in 'Britishness' of both a rural and an urban variety. It helped to revive as resorts some of those inland towns which Pimlott had noted in the 1940s[33] as having benefited as touring and stopping-off centres from the arrival of the motor car. Since Pimlott's day some of them have been by-passed, and not just by roads: Brotherswater (Cumbria), Caterham and Chiddingfold (Surrey), and Yeovil now seem names from the past as tourist halts. But others, especially if located in or near the Cotswolds, are still buoyant – Cheltenham, Ludlow, Ross-on-Wye, Tewkesbury, and of course the nonpareil of historic centres, Stratford-on-Avon. The historic associations of such places help them to profit from the 1980s upsurge of the heritage industry, now also seen as a lifeline for many a declining industrial area, from Wigan which sought to exploit its 'Wigan Pier' myth, to Tyneside which seized on the popularity of a romantic novelist and restyled itself 'Catherine Cookson Country'.[34] The destination which has benefited most from international tourism, however, is London, which Pimlott described as 'the outstanding inland holiday resort'.[35] This was still the case 40 years later when 45 per cent of all holiday nights spent in Britain by foreign tourists were spent in London.[36]

As might be expected there has been a marked increase in the number of holidays taken abroad by British residents. The British Tourist Authority's estimates for holidays taken by British people at the end of the 1990s reveal that the number of holidays taken in Britain, which had remained the majority until the mid-1990s, had by 1998 dropped below the figure for holidays abroad; whereas in 1971 the difference between the number of holidays taken in Great Britain and those taken abroad had been wide (c.35 million and c.8 million) the gap had closed by 1997, with domestic holidays falling below 30 million, and overseas holidays for the first time exceeding that number (c.32 million). Moreover, social class differences were noticeable in the consumption of holidays. The proportion of those (mainly social classes AB and C1) who were accustomed to taking more than one holiday a year had also increased sharply; by the end of the 1980s, for example, whilst almost half of those in class AB took more than one holiday each year, barely 20 per cent in that class took no holiday. By contrast, in class DE at the opposite end of the social scale, nearly 60 per cent took no holiday, and only around 10 per cent took more than one.[37]

In keeping with the patterns of foreign travel established in the days of the Grand Tour, the principal destinations of those who took holidays abroad were in Continental Europe. But the focal point had shifted. Italy and Switzerland had now given way to Spain and France. Throughout the final third of the twentieth century these two countries accounted consistently for around half of all overseas holiday destinations. The numbers travelling to France increased from approximately 15 per cent to around 20 per cent, whilst those visiting Spain, over a third of all foreign holiday-makers in 1971, were still 27 per cent at the end of the 1990s.[38] No other country remotely matched these proportions. British visitors to the Irish Republic, which had accounted for some 7 per cent of foreign travellers in the early 1970s, had fallen to half that proportion 30 years later. The United States had, on the other hand, increased from a low level in 1971 (estimates vary from 1 per cent to 4 per cent) to around 7 per cent in 1998, to be the third most popular destination after Spain and France, though of course still a long way behind.

HOLIDAYS AS CULTURAL TEXT

Economic explanations might be advanced to account for the annual exodus to the Mediterranean. There is no doubt that the development of cheap air travel, usually supplied by charter companies rather than scheduled services, and the organization of package holidays by tour operators geared up to achieving economies of scale through the block-booking of both flights and hotels, have enormously facilitated the growth of international tourism. But the other aspects of this process are sometimes forgotten. These relate to an attitude that has only recently developed of people convincing themselves that they 'need a holiday'. Whence does this mentality originate? An important cause is to be found in the cultural negotiations that take place in the whole 'discourse' of holidays and tourism, which is created and made available to consumers through advertising and its related activities. It is this cultural process which sets up expectations in the minds of travellers.

John Walton's work reminds us that holidays are as much as anything 'imagined events'. They exist in the mind as well as in actuality. Indeed, as anyone who has taken a family holiday knows, the actual holiday can be a stressful and far from relaxing experience. But as an imagined event that same holiday is capable of generating immense pleasures of anticipation and remembrance. The holiday snapshot, which in spite of its supposed spontaneity is, in fact, a carefully framed and composed artefact with the purpose of memorializing the 'pleasure' of being away, is the characteristic contemporary personal record of holiday-making. The holiday is therefore a cultural activity in the sense that it is about meanings. John Urry has described the way in which going away involves a new way of looking – a 'tourist gaze' – which opens up new and different scenes with an infinite range of associations: 'reading the landscape for signifiers of certain pre-established notions or signs derived from various discourses of travel and tourism'.[39] These gazes are not simply individual reactions, but are also positioned by the tourist industry itself, of which a large part is devoted to various ways of representing holidays.

Thus the tourist, in embarking upon the process of holiday-making, enters a world given over to the construction of imaginings. This world of modern mass tourism has a number of characteristic features, which have been seized upon by commentators interested in creating a sociology of tourism. We may reflect briefly on some of the more salient of these features. First is the notion that tourism involves for many a process of 'de-skilling', in which the autonomy of the individual traveller of old has been replaced by the commercial relations and authority of organized travel – the 'package tour'. In this context, the tourist is shepherded, initiative taken out of her/his hands by the package tour operator.[40] Second, mass tourism is seen to have transported many of the features of the nineteenth-century seaside holiday overseas, thus locating within a foreign setting familiar and reassuring features and institutions. The most obvious examples of this are the seafront cafes on Spanish coasts which advertise cups of tea and English Sunday dinners. But in a broader context the foreign holiday is often dependent for its attraction on its ability to reproduce the communality or 'togetherness' that was the vital ingredient of Blackpool's success as working-class resort. Third, there has often been thought to be a degree of 'otherness' about holidays. Urry, for example, has claimed that the tourist gaze is framed by 'difference', constructed in relation to its opposite.[41] Thus, the holiday involves new experiences which might be welcomed, though they might also provoke anxiety. Fourth, the holiday also has been held to contain a suspension of normal rules of behaviour. This 'liminality', first observed by Turner[42] and since underlined by many other commentators, is a necessary part of tourism, bestowing much of the pleasure associated with 'getting away', dispensing with the routine of everyday life. Ferdynand Zweig summed this up perfectly many years ago in his observation that for many an older working-class mother the holiday offered an exceptional opportunity to shed the habitual responsibility of looking after others and, for a brief time, to be 'waited upon' herself.[43] Fifth, associated with liminality is the indefinable quality of 'authenticity', a feature of holidays first remarked upon by two early theorists of tourism, Boorstin and MacCannell.[44] Essentially, the discussion of 'authenticity' centres upon whether modern mass tourism offers simply 'pseudo-events' (a term originally coined by Boorstin) contrived by the tourist industry, or more genuine experiences of 'real' life. There is an implicit suggestion in much of this debate of the 'de-skilling' notion of mass tourism and its stage-managed artificiality. Finally, however, in considering these various aspects of modern holiday-making, we should bear in mind that the holiday experience is fashioned in a structure where the different and possibly conflicting aspects are brought into a compromise: between, for example, the familiar and the strange, the urban and the rural, the old and the new and the individual and the collective. The successful tour operator will strike this balance, and thus make profits.

This kind of amalgamation of experiences is most clearly illustrated in the package holiday brochure, one of the characteristic cultural texts of contemporary society. Produced by the package holiday companies, it is available free either from high-street travel agencies or through the post. It is, alongside the increasingly popular television consumer programmes featuring holidays and the travel pages of the newspapers, probably the most influential channel through which 'imaginings' are created. Though all brochures conform to a similar basic idea of conveying information about travel arrangements, destinations, accommodation and, above all, costs in a simple style, they none the less are directed at different markets, and therefore communicate a multiplicity of nuances of meaning. Social class differences are perhaps their fundamental distinguishing difference, however, clearly evident from the outset in the very texture and imaging of the brochure. Representations of 'life-style' vary between readerships assumed to want cheapness, neighbourliness and conviviality, and those to whom notions of exclusiveness, discernment and culture are offered. There is no doubt that, to this extent, holiday brochures both reproduce and construct ideas and images of social class. Sometimes, these are overlain with other meanings.

An interesting case in point is the holiday literature produced by the Saga company, whose products are aimed at those in later middle-age. Saga holidays are presented as an amalgam of comfort (if not luxury), convention and a quest for the new. They therefore typify the problem of balancing the various aspects of tourism, in the context in this case of a defined age group. In the Portuguese Algarve, for example, Saga offers a holiday to the resort of Albufeira. Its brochure text and pictures construct an image of traditional and modern, urban and rural, active and relaxing. Saga holiday-makers therefore have a choice of giving their own emphasis to their holiday, though within the organized structure created by the company. That the experience is not mere hedonism, however, is indicated by refernces to the opportunities to engage in 'cultural' activities, whether they be visiting Moorish sites, museums, playing bridge, painting or going bird-spotting. These educational pursuits therefore set the Saga tourist apart from the masses, a distinctiveness which is reinforced in the emphasis on quality in the hotel descriptions. This whole narrative is framed by a photograph depicting convivial and attractive 50-somethings in, significantly, an *uneven* gender mix: three men, two women. The meaning is clear. At this age widowhood or, equally likely, divorce is a strong possibility, but the Saga picture emphasizes that single people need have no anxieties about being isolated on one of their holidays. Social inhibitions are therefore erased by the comforting image of the group.[45] By contrast, varied images of youth are represented in the brochures of a number of companies whose product is clearly aimed at the 18–30s market. These range from the hedonistic, lotus-eating pleasures of Club Med holidays, which sum up the cliché of 'sun, sea, sand and sex', to the more recently marketed forms of physically active 'back-packing' tourism, which harks back to the idea of the individual traveller creating her/his own intrinsically 'authentic' experiences. There is an earnestness about such representations which recalls socialist rambles and holiday camps of the 1930s.

The complex amalgam of meanings in holiday literature is interestingly present even in casual texts. Figure 1 is a cheap flyer picked up by the author from a tourist information office near Malaga. At first glance it is an obviously 'home-made' piece of advertising put out to entice package tour holiday-makers into something a little different from the usual day at the beach. Its bold main text promises authenticity (the 'real Spain') and tradition ('time stands still') which will create a big impression ('a day you will never forget'). The crudely drawn picture offers ideas of rural solace, and this is underlined by the detailed text which describes a riding centre 'hidden amongst olives', away from 'tarmac roads', where 'forgotten paths' lead to views of 'lone eagles' and people tilling the fields by hand. The very name of the centre, Romanie Farm, has associations with gypsies and travellers. Thus, in a few cliched phrases, the tourist is presented with an image of a world which stands in complete contrast to the modern society in which s/he lives life for the bulk of the year and which, moreover, is still present in the international hotels of the Costa del Sol. Geographically, the distance between the two worlds is not great, as the detailed directions to Romanie Farm indicate. But in the mind there is an immense chasm. Much of the appeal of this text derives from the sense of difference it conveys, a difference which might offer an exciting experience in itself, or simply an opportunity to tell friends back home about the 'real Spain' rather than the 'pseudo-events' on offer on the coast. For even half a day, Romanie Farm provides 'authenticity'.

The text raises many intriguing points. First, there is the obvious contradiction between the pleasure of 'difference' and the many reassurances given that the experience will be a 'safe' one: 'British-owned farm', 'British standards', 'bombproof horses', 'no previous riding experience necessary'. This is authenticity without any attendant dangers. Second, there is the assumption

DISCOVER THE REAL SPAIN

Romanie Farm Riding Centre is hidden amongst the olives in the picturesque valley of Entrerrios.
Escorted rides leave daily for the surrounding hills - we need never touch a tarmac road.
Discover forgotten paths watched only by the lone eagle soaring overhead. Escape into a world gone by as you pass at a lazy pace through idyllic farms where country folk still till the fields by hand.

- And stop at a character country inn for lunch or tapas and a welcome drink for horse and rider.

WHERE TIME STANDS STILL -

Romanie Farm is British owned. Our guides and riding instructors are young and friendly and trained to the best British standards.

Our bombproof horses are specially chosen for their quiet temperament and are ideal for beginners or nervous riders -no previous riding experience is necessary.

A DAY YOU WILL NEVER FORGET !!

ROMANIE FARM. ENTRERRIOS. FUENGIROLA.

TO BOOK LESSONS, HALF DAY RIDES, AND PUB RIDES
PHONE 211-9127 (OR MOBILE 908-954699)

We can provide transport to and from your hotel.

To find us by car - Exit from N340 motorway at Fuengirola by the Aquatic Park (km 209) and head inland. Pass Mijas Golf course. Pass St. Anthonys College then after 300 m turn left (signed to Entrerrios). Pass over big new bridge then follow road to left back under the bridge. Continue for 5 km until you pass "Albergue" Entrerrios on the right. after 500 m turn right onto track by small sign to ROMANIE FARM.

Figure 1

in the text that tourists will be attracted by notions of the rural. Though many holiday-makers in this part of Spain will come from urban areas in northern Europe, it is a reasonable assumption to make that they will associate the rural with peacefulness and rest, and perhaps even with a 'good' life, against which the urbanized and industrialized society of northern Europe might be regarded as artificial and alienating. This idea is not new. It has been encour-

aged by many currents of thought in Europe during the course of the nineteenth and twentieth centuries, not least by the stream of literature put out by
the tourist industry itself. On occasions the attempt to equate the rural with
'purity' has fuelled political movements, often with disastrous consequences.
It is, however, not an idea likely to receive uncritical acceptance by those
Spanish 'country folk' who 'still till the fields by hand'. They have too often
voted with their feet against rural life. Third, the text builds on this notion of
the authentic with the idea of the 'real Spain'. Such an image is, of course, the
stock-in-trade of brochure writers throughout the tourist industry: the 'real
Greece', the 'real Italy', even the 'real USA' constantly confront the tourist,
whose gaze usually locates the signs that confirm her or his pre-ordained
vision of the authentic.

Spain particularly attracts this form of representation. It draws heavily
upon a familiar inventory of images found in travel writing, especially of the
kind practised over the years by authors such as Gerald Brenan, Laurie Lee
and, more recently, Chris Stewart.[46] In their writings each has evoked a deeply
rural, seemingly changeless, and often poverty-stricken Spain which none the
less is held to nurture certain essential qualities of honesty, community, neighbourliness and sturdiness; qualities which modern society has to its detriment
lost. The fact that some Spaniards have themselves struggled since the nineteenth century to liberate their country from the intellectual ignorance and
economic oppression found in the country districts is often overlooked. It is
certainly overlooked in the de-politicized versions of the 'real Spain' reproduced in travel brochures, where there is a suggestion that the rural is
superior, though for most of us now unattainable except perhaps for brief
glimpses as part of a holiday experience. For many Spaniards, whose livelihood depends upon the foreign exchange brought in by tourists, the 'real
Spain' is to be found in the hotels, bars and beaches of the costas. But for
tourists perhaps there is a sense that leaving the coast behind them for a day,
and visiting an inland village where the visitor would certainly not wish to
live her/his normal life, is not just a pseudo-event contrived by the tourist
professionals, but a truly authentic experience which really does climax the
entire process of 'getting away from it all'. This is quitessentially what the
concept of the 'tourist gaze' seeks to convey.[47]

CONCLUSION: HOLIDAYS AND HISTORIANS

There are many dimensions to holiday-making which are of interest to the historian. In addition to the quantitative aspects – the sheer number of holidays
and the importance they hold for economic life generally – there are several
qualitative dimensions to be explored. They have to do with the influence of
holidays on the individual's sense of well-being, on social relationships, and
on the development of society. Is Britain, for example, a better and more tolerant place as a result of the increased awareness of others that mass holiday-
making has brought? Has the civilized behaviour that was once thought
to characterize the upper classes, and which was in part cultivated through

travel, been extended to the masses, whose holiday experiences are, after all, made up of many of those features which originated in elite tourism? There might be a case for looking at holiday-making as part of the 'civilizing process' which the Weberian sociologist Norbert Elias claimed characterized modern society.[48] There might equally be a case (though I would not especially wish to press it) for seeing tourism as a form of social control which keeps society stable by keeping people happy; if not very happy all the time, then at least reasonably happy for part of the time. Grand interpretations of this kind have been left largely to the sociologists who have made most of the running so far in the study of tourism. The point for historians to bear in mind is that the historiography of holiday-making, in spite of the herculean exploratory efforts of John Walton, is still under-developed territory, and that, like many other aspects of leisure, there are several avenues that beckon. There is, for example, no doubt that holidays are intimately bound up with class relations; but what is less clearly established is their effect on gender relationships. For those fortunate enough to be able to take a family holiday, their destination would, in the vast majority of cases, have been determined by the male 'head' of the family. In this sense, holiday-making simply reinforced an existing age and gender power relationship within the family. And while being on holiday might, in some circumstances, have been a liberating experience for many women, allowing them to escape temporarily from the tyranny of domestic chores, in others it no doubt bound them yet more firmly to their 'traditional' role. John Benson has pointed to the toils of the self-catering holiday for many married women and mothers, who 'merely exchanged one kitchen sink for another'.[49] Claire Langhamer's work shows how this was a constant refrain throughout the middle years of the century, and no doubt it carried on into the 'gite' holidays in France which became so fashionable in the 1980s.[50] Similarly, there are questions about the effect of holidays on age relations. Until the exploration of these themes gets fully underway and starts to yield its results, the conclusion of this chapter remains a basic one. The holiday is writ large in both the individual and the national psyche. It is important economically, as well as for the meanings inscribed in its cultural dimensions. Historians certainly cannot afford to ignore it, for like many other parts of popular culture it is simultaneously a window through which British society can be viewed, and an important medium in the construction of the view.

Key Reading

Inglis, F. *The Delicious History of the Holiday*. London: Routledge, 2000.

Pimlott, J. A. R. *The Englishman's Holiday: A Social History*. Hassocks: Harvester Press, 1976 edn.

Urry, J. *The Tourist Gaze: Leisure and Travel in Contemporary Societies*. London: Sage, 1990.

Walton, J. K. *The British Seaside: Holidays and Resorts in the Twentieth Century*. Manchester: Manchester University Press, 2000.

Chronology of Events

1841 Thomas Cook's excursion for temperance reformers from Leicester to Loughborough.

1851 Great Exhibition in Hyde Park attracted many millions of visitors, a large proportion on day excursions – the London and North Western Railway carried over three-quarters of a million.

1892 Henry Lunn organized tour to Rome for ministers of religion and their families.

1889 Savoy Hotel, London, opened.

1894 National Trust founded.

1911 Automobile Association published its first hotel guide.

1913 Some three-quarters of a million British tourists, mostly middle class, visited Europe.

1919 Daily air service London–Paris introduced.

1924 Establishment of the Workers' Travel Association; Civil Service Clerical Association established holiday camp near Lowestoft.

1930 Founding of the Youth Hostel Association (YHA), which had 80000 members by the late 1930s; 1 million cars on British roads.

1937 Following lengthy pressure from the TUC, the Amulree Committee was appointed to look into the issue of holidays with pay; Butlin's holday camp opened at Skegness.

1938 Holidays With Pay Act introduced to extend paid holidays to workers not already covered by collective bargaining agreements.

1939 Access to the Mountains Act; 2 million cars on British roads.

1939–45 Because of wartime restrictions governments encouraged people to take 'Holidays at Home'; by 1945 some 80 per cent of the workforce was entitled to paid holidays.

1948–49 Berlin Airlift encouraged formation of small independent airline companies which later moved into the charter flight holiday business.

1949 Labour government's Countryside Act designated National Parks.

1950 First package holiday organized by Horizon to Corsica.

1954 Travel allowance for people travelling abroad raised to £100.

1958 Introduction of economy-class air fares.

1968 Countryside Commission established.

1969 Development of Tourism Act set up the British Tourist Authority (BTA) and the English, Scottish and Welsh Tourist Boards.

1970 Merger of Trust Houses (founded 1903) and the Forte hotel and restaurant company.

1974 Collapse of Horizon and Clarkson travel companies.

1979 Exchange controls removed in Britain.

1999 25.5 million overseas visitors to Britain, by comparison with 5 million in 1969.

part two

Leisure, the home and voluntary activity

chapter 6

Leisure, the Home, Radio and Television

CONTENTS

The overlap between the main 'sectors' of sport and leisure provision – the commercial, the voluntary and the state – becomes evident when we move away from commercial leisure and begin to look at voluntary activity. This has received less attention from historians than have those giant leaps in the commercialization of leisure that occurred from the middle of the nineteenth century, especially in that 'climacteric' of change which produced a 'mass culture' in the 30 or so years before the First World War. But there is good reason for thinking that a great deal of leisure, if not sport, is best understood by considering the changing nature of the home and family. It might be tempting to imagine that commercial leisure displaced a prior family-based focus, and that this was one of the reasons why its presence incurred so much concern on the part of reformers. In fact, however, changes in both commercial and domestic leisure were taking place at much the same time, resulting in new leisure forms in each sector. Home-based leisure was as historically specific as market-based leisure.

The changes are expertly charted in three studies of nineteenth-century leisure that have become classics of the historian's craft. To begin with, Hugh Cunningham's analysis of a broad sweep of changes has observed a fundamental shift in leisure relations in the mid-century.[1] Leisure became implicated in the process of class consciousness at the point when middle-class people began to seek control of formerly public spaces in order to 'privatize' them for approved activity. In a process that had to do with wider middle-class fears of the mass, much of the old cheek-by-jowl public culture of the eighteenth century was reshaped and became demarcated by social distinction and exclusion. It was a process that frequently invoked state power to achieve its objectives; by-laws removed allotments, for example, to make way for housing or railway development; drinking hours were curtailed; popular sports were driven off the streets in the interests of public order and the protection of property. In one direction, the process produced a new, domesticated middle-class culture, its distinctive symbols of respectability enshrined in the piano, essential for the cultivation of refined tastes (especially among the family's female members), in the improving press such as the *Saturday Review*, in dinner parties, gardening and, if the household's resources ran to it, private tennis courts and billiards tables. Working-class households could sustain few of these accoutrements of cultivated domesticity, except perhaps the new popular sporting press with its racing tips.

Working-class leisure developed its quintessential features in a more public and collective form. The neighbourhood public house and the music hall were important focal points, though hardly 'respectable'. Alongside Cunningham, Peter Bailey, in his influential *Leisure and Class in Victorian England*, has located the emergence of middle-class ideas of 'rational recreation' in this process. Bailey sees them partly as a response to the guilt felt among the bourgeoisie that the culture of the masses had been driven away and neglected. Through rational recreation, it was believed, the minds and habits of the working class would be elevated by inculcating a belief in 'time-budgeting and money management' and introducing them to 'the satisfaction of mental recreation, thus immunising them against the contagion of pub and the publican, and the animal regression of "sensuality"'.[2] It was a movement which, on the whole, failed. Gareth Stedman Jones, focusing these initiatives and changes on London in the later nineteenth century, has seen significant developments in the separation of leisure and the creation of a distinctive and self-absorbed working-class culture, related to changing patterns of work and residence in the capital. He notes, especially, the decline, by the 1870s, of the old artisan tradition, which had produced a male sociability with a unique radical politics and a work- and pub-based culture of heavy drinking. In its place developed a more suburbanized, privatized working-class culture, with leanings towards the music hall, racecourse, football match and seaside excursion, conservative in its philosophy, but none the less resistant to attempts by outsiders either to understand or to change it.[3] It was a culture, says Jones, summed up in the characters played by two of its best-known products, the music-hall performer Dan Leno, and Charlie Chaplin, also a music-hall artiste but whose name was forever to be synonymous with the cinema:

> little men, perpetually 'put upon'; they have no great ideals or ambitions; the characters they play are undoubtedly very poor, but not obviously or unmistakably proletarian; they are certainly products of city life, but their place within it is indeterminate; their exploits are funny, but also pathetic; they are forever chased by men or women, physically larger than themselves, angry foremen, outraged husbands, domineering landladies or burly wives; but it is usually chance circumstances,

unfortunate misunderstandings, not of their own making, which have landed them in these situations, and it is luck more than their own efforts which finally comes to the rescue.[4]

Class tensions over leisure continued to be a feature of British society, and until housing changes provided better material foundations for a home-based leisure for all, the ideal of respectable domestic leisure was always going to be out of the reach of many. In some senses such material changes did not occur until after the Second World War. However, one technological development of the First World War did provide the basis for a significant change in the the relationship between home and leisure. It was the wireless.

LISTENING TO THE RADIO

The development of wireless telegraphy during the war had made it possible to broadcast programmes to large numbers of people, though the opportunities to do so were not grasped until, in 1922, the press baron Lord Northcliffe arranged a promotional broadcast which aroused widespread public interest.[5] The establishing in that year of the BBC (initially the British Broadcasting Company, which became the British Broadcasting Corporation in 1926), was, as we saw in Chapter 3, a move of some importance in national life. It took off in quite spectacular fashion. Some dozen years after the creation of the BBC's monopoly, over 70 per cent of British households had licences.[6] Wireless, or 'radio' as the Americans called it, was potentially a family form of leisure though, in both practice and theory, before the Second World War it was addressed to individuals. This meant far more than the fact that, in the early days when wireless came in the form of crude crystal sets, it was 'father' who called for quiet while he fiddled with the set to 'tune-in'. Scannell and Cardiff have pointed to clear gender differences in early wireless usage: for men it was something akin to fixing motor cars, a piece of weird gadgetry promoted to catch the supposed male fascination with machines; women, on the other hand, were expected actually to enjoy what was broadcast.[7] But until wireless sets were improved in the early 1930s their technological eccentricities, including the 'interference' that tuning-in produced, made them a source of both household and neighbourhood discord. In the conception of public broadcasting that was enshrined in the Corporation's monopoly, wireless was an individual cultural experience, almost a personal tutorial between the broadcaster and s/he who 'listened in'.

It was into this relationship that the state entered. What was available for listeners to hear through the BBC's programmes was a curiously mixed fare of material, served up in a tone of social superiority devised by the BBC's Director General John Reith. Considering some of the features of Reithian broadcasting culture, it is surprising that radio survived as a popular leisure pastime at all. To begin with there was the Corporation's 'establishment' image ('tone' might be more exact) exemplified in the cultured accents of its announcers. As Ross McKibbin has pointed out, the BBC consistently failed before the Second World War to find a popular 'voice', completely unable to represent the working class in its programmes except through monstrous caricatures.[8] This upper-class bearing extended to a close moral supervision of the content of programmes, with anything that smacked of populism or vulgarity immediately suspect. Radio comedians, for example, were given a list of 'dont's', which included jokes about the Scots, Welsh, clergymen, drink and medical matters, a ban which, as McKibbin notes, included the subject matter of virtually all English humour.[9] Further, there was the enforcement at Reith's insistence of a particularly dull, evangelical regime of Sunday programmes. Listeners were expected to be 'attentive', and the habit of easy listening, with the radio simply a backgound noise, was strongly discouraged. In the 1930s both radio channels, National and Regional, promoted mixed programming consisting of a variety of different features, which meant that neither became stereotyped according to a particular output. It meant that listeners had to select carefully what they wanted to hear. This somewhat austere service, designed as the very opposite to the way broadcasting was developing in America, was moderated by certain activities within the Corporation that ran counter to its main mission; the *Radio Times*, for example, which had become a popular weekly magazine capable of selling over 2 million copies by the late 1930s; the coverage of sport through high-quality outside broadcasts which ensured that the BBC represented all the major sporting events; and the output of the BBC's regional services, less suffocated by the Reithian doctrine (because seen as less important) and therefore able to strike a more authentic popular tone, as well as helping to preserve regional identities. But by the eve of the Second World War, this new means of communication, which administered to listeners in their own homes a dose of medicine that was considered to be good for them, was experiencing some of the same reactions that had been found to earlier forays in 'rational recreation'.[10]

Reith's stern regime is easy to criticize, and even easier to caricature. What is often overlooked in doing so, however, is the democratic and national thrust in the BBC's mission. By regarding listeners as being capable of assimilating, at choice, a wide range of quality programmes, Reith – for all his undoubted social snobbery – avoided the construction of the listening audience according to social classes who were presumed to have different cultural tastes and capacities. 'Mixed programming' to an 'attentive listener' ensured that the cultural richness and variety that wireless was capable of mediating was communicated to many people, and that the medium was therefore employed to stimulate and educate. It was a notion of cultural improvement that had been developed in the nineteenth century by intellectuals such as Matthew Arnold, and which had since then been at the root of the many concerns expressed about the nature of popular leisure. To be sure, what was provided for listeners owed nothing to popular demand – the law of the market place had no role in broadcasting relations – and Reith certainly thought he knew better than his audience what should be broadcast. In these senses, the BBC's operation could be described as elitist. But to do so would mask the genuinely radical purpose implicit in the Corporation's mission, which was to address its listeners equally and to form them into a national cultural entity, unified

through its diversity. Fortunately, or unfortunately, the response of some listeners to this mission was lukewarm before the Second World War, although
many positive responses were elicited in the survey of listening habits carried
out by Hilda Jennings and Winifred Gill in a working-class district of Bristol
just before the outbreak of the war.[11]

A sign of the BBC's relationship with the general public is provided by the
popularity achieved by the commercial radio stations based in Continental
Europe in the 1930s. They were able to broadcast in English to large areas of
the southern part of the country. Both Radio Normandie and Radio Luxem-
bourg, established in the early 1930s, and later Radio Internationale, which
broadcast to the troops of the British Expeditionary Force in France in 1939–40,
offered a diet of programmes featuring popular British and American entertainers. They achieved a far more relaxed style which struck a chord with their
audience. Programmes were, on the whole, short, based mainly on popular
music and financed by advertisements. They captured a younger audience,
recognizing that the BBC's style was often not attractive to young people, who
were repelled by both the dullness of its programmes and the fact that they
had to be listened to at home, a location that many young people failed to
find exciting. At least the foreign stations were able to overcome the dullness.[12]
Whether the BBC, bearing in mind its greater technological resources and
secure financial base through the licence fee, would have been able to with-
stand this challenge without modifying its content is difficult to say. As it was,
the question was only posed for a short while before it was suspended for
some 30 years. What changed the BBC's relationship with its audience, and
also claimed for it a more legitimate place as a popular *national* institution,
was the war.

Two characteristics served the BBC well during the years of conflict. One
was its impartiality. As a public corporation it had never assumed a political
position, though critics were aware that its relationship with government
was a close one. During both the General Strike of 1926, and then when the
National (Conservative) Government's policy of Appeasment in foreign
affairs was being conducted in the late 1930s, the BBC had refrained from challenging the official government position. Appeasement was never posed by
the BBC as a *party* issue; because it was to do with foreign policy it was presented as a matter of national interest, even though there were those who dis-
agreed with it.[13] Such neutrality, craven though at times it was, nevertheless
gave the BBC an aura of trust which the state broadcasting services in totali-
tarian regimes did not possess. In wartime it helped the BBC to present itself
as a beacon of truth and democracy. Shorn of the taint of being an instrument
of government propaganda, the BBC was thus able to cultivate its second
major wartime characteristic – as a promoter of civilian morale. David Cardiff
and Paddy Scannell have illuminated this role very clearly in their excellent
research on wartime radio for the Open University.[14] What is pointed up in
their work is the recognition by the BBC, in co-operation with government,
that a broadcasting authority with so marked an 'establishment' provenance
needed to make concessions to its audiences if it was effectively to play its
part in the necessary construction of a positive civilian morale to fight the war.

To its credit, the BBC achieved this by resisting attempts by the Ministry of Information to turn it into a channel of propaganda. But not before programmes such as *Good Luck War Workers* and *Award For Industry* (later re-titled *Worker of the Week*), intended to portray a harmonious industrial community pulling together to fight the war, had been foisted upon producers by the Corporation's leadership. When referred to Listener Research, they were revealed as being obvious stunts, greeted with derision by workers who knew the actual state of affairs in industry. To continue with them jeopardized, as Head of Features Lawrence Gilliam pointed out, 'the BBC's credit with the working class public'.[15] Commenting upon requests to inject 'pep talks' into the popular radio programme *Workers' Playtime*, its producer John Watts noted:

> It would be a grave error to insert propaganda or exhortation into the middle of this entertainment programme. Workers are always throroughly suspicious of 'welfare' in any shape or form, invariably thinking the employer or the Government is only giving them entertainment, or the canteen or whatever the amenity may be, in order to get something out of them . . . We've had several examples recently where the superintendent or boss or proprietor has come on after the show – which had been enthusiastically received – and talked to the men about absenteeism or a fall in production. The atmosphere created by the programme has in every instance been completely lost.[16]

It was as a consequence of the efforts of producers like Watts, closer to the audience and its tastes than were those at the top of the BBC hierarchy, that the Corporation gradually began to accelerate the trends that had begun in the late 1930s towards a form of radio which contrived a more authentic popular voice. From seeking to *direct* the public's taste, the BBC moved towards a position where it sought to *reflect* more of the popular mood.

This change involved not only a transformation of the BBC's attitude towards its audience, but a recognition that radio was used by its listeners in ways quite different from those envisaged in the Reithian philosophy. The major consequence of these changes was the dilution of the twin pillars of the traditional broadcasting edifice – the idea of the 'attentive listener' and the practice of 'mixed programming'. In their place was created a style of broadcasting which was aimed at particular audiences, with particular tastes, who listened to radio in a sociable, communal form. For example, groups of soldiers in canteens or billets; factory workers on the shopfloor or in their lunchtime canteens; families sitting around the radio set at home in the evening; groups of people in air-raid shelters or pubs listening to radio publicly, their own set having been broken, perhaps, and not repairable because of the shortage of valves. It was the decision to construct a more entertaining form of radio for the troops of the British Expeditionary Force in France in 1939–40, following an influential report by the BBC's A. P. Ryan, that resulted in the new initiative of the Forces Programme. Ryan's report had, in so many words, posed a clear choice for the BBC: adopt a more popular approach or risk losing the audience, with all the repercussions for wartime morale that such a loss might entail.[17] Initially directed at soldiers, the Forces Programme was soon extended to include other types of listeners such as factory workers, for whom the popular *Music While You Work* and *Workers' Playtime* were devised. Favourable reactions reported through Listener Research encouraged further experiments with 'light' broadcasting, using the model of the Continental stations of former days (now closed). Out of many initiatives sprang some of the most popular programmes in the history of British sound broadcasting. *The Brains Trust* (or *Any Questions?*) was an unexpected hit which produced in its resident panellists, Professor C. E. M. Joad, Julian Huxley and Commander Campbell, three of the unlikeliest national celebrities of the war; and an outstanding intellectual joke uttered by the venerable Gilbert Murray – 'Veni, Vidi, Vichy – I came, I saw, I concurred' – which was recirculated among the public countless times thereafter. Its immense popularity posed an intriguing question for those concerned with the appeal of radio: spontaneity, debate, the mixture of the serious and the trivial, the personality factor coupled with the catchphrase (Joad's 'it depends what you mean by . . .'), and the producer's willingness to include one female panellist once the original threesome had been expanded – all were ingredients in its success. *The Brains Trust* became a national institution that really did seem to pull people together during the war, and perhaps its capacity to act as a focus of communal life was the programme's greatest attribute.[18]

The other seminal contribution by the BBC's Variety department to wartime morale and broadcasting history was *ITMA* (*It's That Man Again*), a vehicle for the fast-talking comedian Tommy Handley and a superabundance of catchphrases, of which Mrs Mopps's 'Can I do yer now, sir?' was probably the best loved and most repeated. *ITMA* was slick and topical (its scripts often rewritten just before the show went out to include up-to-the-minute references) with a keen satirical eye. The bureaucracy of the legion of wartime regulations and officials was its main target, and the show achieved, in the manner of Will Hay, subtle caricatures of pompous officialdom.[19]

The war was responsible for other experiments. With the arrival in 1942 of American troops in Britain, opportunities were taken to introduce more American programmes such as the Jack Benny and Bob Hope shows, and to streamline presentation and continuity, innovations which Cardiff and Scannell feel brought 'a new kind of professionalism in the management of entertainment'.[20] A quite different initiative was seen in the introduction of what later would have been called 'open access' programmes. They allowed listeners not only to participate in the programme by writing in with questions (as with the *Brains Trust*) or making requests for music, but to present and contribute to the programme themselves. The factory programme *Works Wonders*, which featured amateur 'turns', was one example of this, as was the show aimed at anti-aircraft units, *Ack Ack Beer Beer*.

Such experiments, a concession to the idea of the 'People's War', did not outlast the conflict. Any implication there might have been in programmes such as *Ack Ack Beer Beer* that the BBC was about to be handed over to the democratic control of its listeners was stifled when the war came to an end. The Corporation's leadership sought to reassert as much as possible its former position. Its organizational structure remained hierarchical in every sense.

Wartime changes in the understanding of radio audiences were retained, notably in the establishment of the famous tripartite division of the Home Service, the Light and the Third Programmes, a strategy of which Reith himself disapproved. But, as Sian Nicholas has pointed out, much of the old cultural mission was still there and Reithian aims 'were not so much removed as redefined'.[21]

The war and the immediate post-war years represented the pinnacle of radio as a leisure form. Thereafter it declined as television grew. By the late 1960s listening habits had so changed under the impact of television that it was no longer possible to apply even the modified wartime interpretation of Reith's 'attentive listener' to the radio audience. No longer was listening a communal activity. In some senses the use of radio reverted to the individual, though in a very different form from that envisaged by Reith. With developments in the transistor, radio became a portable personal possession, not fixed to home use, and could be employed for a range of immediate, short-span listening forms – news, music, sport, gossip and many more. The audience for this kind of broadcasting became predominantly a young one.[22] Programming by both the BBC, in its local and national forms, and its commercial competitors launched in the wake of the Sound Broadcasting Act of 1972, adapted to these new circumstances.[23] 'Format' radio came into being. Not only were stations characterised by a particular type of output, but programmes themselves were 'deconstructed'; the traditional carefully built programme gave way to one in which there was a sequence of 'segments' or 'bites' focused around a personality presenter, and into which listeners were able to dip in and out as the fancy took them. Thus, instead of having a beginning, middle and end, each programme became simply a collage of bits and pieces. The format approach accommodated advertising, was adaptable to a variety of broadcasting genres, but worked best with music, which by the end of the century occupied the commanding height in sound broadcasting. At the BBC Radios 1, 2 and 3 were given over largely to music of different kinds. Radio 3 (reformed in 1970 from the old Third Programme) notably lost its high cultural richness and innovation, not to mention the rather precious persona which was the butt of every comedian, and only Radio 4 retained something of the old 'mixed programming' philosophy; current affairs, plays, comedies, sport and magazine features (but no music) made up its daily provision. A popular part of it was the enduring soap opera *The Archers*, which had first gone on the air in 1950. It threatened, as A. J. P. Taylor once said of the West End production of Agatha Christie's *The Mousetrap*, to 'run for ever'.[24]

WATCHING THE 'TELLY'

Writing of the quarter century after the Second World War, Harold Perkin described a Britain in which:

> There came into being a kind of average lifestyle, home-centred, family-oriented, servantless, with leisure time devoted to home-based activities, television watch-

ing, gardening, do-it-yourself decorating and home improvement, with weekend car trips to the country or the seaside, and annual holidays in Britain or abroad, a lifestyle which encompassed a growing majority of the population.[25]

It was a life-style that continued into the final quarter of the century, faithfully recorded in the statistical returns of the *General Household Survey* and *Social Trends*. One habit recorded there soars above all the rest: television watching. 'The biggest single leisure activity of the majority of all British people', says Arthur Marwick.[26] Surely, here was a leisure form to unite the nation.

The rise of television was a post-war process. Though a public television service had been introduced by the BBC in 1936 (suspended during the war), it reached only a handful of rich households in the London area. The masses had to wait until the 1950s for television to reach them, which, until a national network of transmitters was completed, it did sooner for those who lived in the South than for those in other regions. As with radio the growth of television sets was rapid. In the early 1950s less than 5 per cent of households possessed them. Two decades later this was the proportion of those which did *not*. But more so than with radio, the emergence of television was accompanied by familar laments about the state of popular leisure. These went much further than frustrated parents complaining about how much time their children spent watching the set. They reflected a concern that the state's role in setting the tone of broadcasting might be waning. In contrast to radio, which had been launched as a monopoly to the general approval of most of the vested interests concerned, television broadcasting came into being amidst a flurry of debate about the commercialization of the airwaves. The Television Act of 1954 ensured that this would come about, and commercial broadcasting (euphemistically named 'independent television') began with Associated Rediffusion's programmes on 22 September 1955.

The ending of monopoly broadcasting had been debated fiercely since a report by the Beveridge Committee on the BBC, published in 1951, had produced a minority report from the Conservative politician Selwyn Lloyd which strongly favoured commercial broadcasting. The lobby which formed to promote his views was composed of various interests, including Conservative MPs, electrical and entertainment companies, advertising groups and theatre managers, all of them clearly interested in opening broadcasting to the advertising opportunities which would stimulate demand for their products at a time of blossoming consumer markets. This alliance of forces caused Herbert Morrison, former Labour Home Secretary, to describe the commercial lobby as 'a Tory plot on behalf of big business against the little man'.[27] But whilst some members of the Conservative government supported the lobby, the debate for and against commercialization was not exactly aligned with political parties, as became evident in the 'anti' lobby. Though orchestrated by a Labour MP, Christopher Mayhew, it contained a broad section of opinion united in the belief that the ending of the BBC's monopoly would result in a deteriorating quality of programmes: it would 'vulgarise, bowdlerise, and coarsen' according to one critic.[28] In the debates on the Television Bill in the

House of Commons there was much concern expressed, especially by Labour members, over possible Americanization of programme content. The wish to maintain a British tone to broadcasting was strong and David Maxwell Fyfe, introducing the bill as Home Secretary, promised that the great sporting events such as the Cup Final, the Derby and the Boat Race which were 'part of the British way of life', would not be monopolized by any one programme contractor, since such a thing would lead to 'great public dissatisfaction'.[29] In the end, as Jean Seaton has commented, the bill was passed because 'most Tories believed that in some way it would promote industry, commerce, and the free market'.[30] Many doubts were assuaged when controls, inspired by the Reithian philosophy, were instituted to prevent unbridled free enter-prise. The Independent Television Authority (ITA), a body not unlike the BBC's Board of Governors, was to oversee the operations of the contractors (programme-makers); advertising time would be limited in duration and placement; programmes could not be 'sponsored'; and franchises were granted on a short lease, initially nine years.

Seaton's analysis of these developments, however, brings out a deeper concern about the way not only broadcasting, but British society itself was developing at this time. One of the features of the early 1950s, which had been responsible for triggering the interest in commercial broadcasting, was the notion of 'affluence' – the idea that the British economy and society was poised for 'take-off' into sustained consumer growth after the privations and controls of the Attlee years.[31] Indeed, what made the deregulation of broad-casting attractive to some Conservatives was the fact that, with their leader-ship subscribing largely to the main lines of Labour strategy in a consensus that the financial journalist Sam Britten was to describe as 'Butskellism', com-mercial television offered at least one tangible example of a return to authen-tic Tory values. Seaton shows that television was both cause and effect of some of the most important economic, social and cultural changes of the 1950s.[32] It was a cause in the sense that, as a cultural medium of rare influence, its output was helping to create a new homogeneous, classless and increasingly com-mercialized culture, thus eroding some of the former life-styles of British citi-zens. Notable in this was the supposed decline of 'traditional' working-class culture, with its robust and community-based institutions and practices, a problem to which Richard Hoggart turned his attention in *The Uses of Literacy* (1957). But television was also an effect of these changes because it was the symbol of the new material affluence based on consumer durables and motor cars, all affordable through hire purchase schemes because of the high levels of employment that lasted until the late 1960s. Rather than being simply another form of leisure, therefore, television occupied a central place in the discussions of the 'condition of England' which became increasingly common towards the end of the 1950s. One small though illuminating example of this came in the inquest conducted by the sporting press after England's spectacu-lar defeats at football by Hungary in 1953 and 1954. Among the many 'expla-nations' adduced for this was the power of television over the country's young people. It was observed by some experts interviewed in the *Daily Express* that young men no longer wanted to work hard at football practice, preferring instead to 'watch television'. This led the paper's columnist Desmond Hackett to conclude that 'affluence' had removed the spur to succeed that had characterized sportsmen in the past; his conclusion was that life was now too easy, and the ready-made entertainment provided by television epitomised this new-found complacency. From decline at football, it could be inferred, Britain might expect to slide into decline as a nation.[33]

It was in a mood if not of decline, then at least of uncertainty about the nation's future that one of the most detailed scrutinies of broadcasting took place. The Pilkington Report, published in 1962, connected with this mood through the growing fear of a national cultural malaise, which was felt by some to have descended on the nation as a result of the growth of commercial television.[34] The 'populist' nature of ITV's programmes – which included a large proportion of old American films and situation comedies, together with game shows which handed out large cash prizes ('give-away shows') – and the handsome profits made by the commercial contractors (which caused one, Roy Thompson of Scottish Television, to claim in 1957 that an ITV franchise was 'a licence to print money') appeared to some critics to be a baneful influence on national life which needed to be checked. There was a feeling, common at the time and which scarcely abated in later years, that the persuasive power of television over the individual was immense; that it exercised a drug-like effect on a passive (working-class) audience. It was about this time that the term 'goggle box' began to be used to describe television. Its assumed effects were held to be responsible for a range of ethical and criminal problems of the day, including sexual behaviour, violence and theft, and susceptibility to advertising, an issue forcibly raised in the influential American writer Vance Packhard's *The Hidden Persuaders*.[35] The appointment in 1960 of the Pilkington Committee focused attention on many of these issues, bringing once again to the surface of public debate a wave of anxiety over the leisure and tastes of the common people, and giving an 'elite'/'mass' dimension to the Committee's proceedings. The inclusion in the Committee's membership of Richard Hoggart, well known by this time as a critic of contemporary developments in popular culture, led some observers to believe that the Committee was predisposed to favour a vision of broadcasting that matched the traditions of the BBC, rather than the newer position adopted by the commercial system.[36]

As many expected, Pilkington found in favour of the BBC. The quality and balance of its programmes was endorsed, no radical recommendations for a change in its overall structure were proposed, and the Corporation was wholeheartedly backed to be the provider of the third television channel expected to be introduced in the near future. Independent television, on the other hand, was a different matter. Though its rise over the previous few years was praised for technical and administrative achievement, in terms of the quality of its product ITV was considered to fall 'well short of what a good public service of broadcasting should be'.[37] It was, therefore, singled out for root-and-branch transformation, with a call for its supervisory authority – the ITA – to exercise a far stronger influence in the overall shaping of its programmes and advertising. A number of features were held to exemplify the poor standard at which commercial television was operating. These included the portrayal of violence in programmes, which prompted Pilkington to recommend the development of a 'family viewing time', the giving of cash prizes in game shows ('where programmes or games call for no skill, prizes should be of nominal value only') and, especially, advertising, where the ITA was enjoined to monitor advertisments 'which appeal to human weakness'.[38]

The Report drew widespread condemnation from the press, especially its Conservative elements, and as Asa Briggs notes: '[T]here was little surprise when the Government which had commissioned the Pilkington Report did not accept many of its most important recommendations.'[39] Whilst the BBC was granted the authority to introduce the new 'third' channel, which became BBC2 in 1964, there was no overhaul of the ITV system except for a nod in the direction of the control of advertisements. Crisell is undoubtedly correct in ascribing electoral considerations to the Government's decision to ignore Pilkington.[40] ITV was popular, and any attempt to dilute or change the nature of its schedules might have backfired politically. For a government experiencing adversity at the polls, as the swing against it at the Orpington by-election in March 1962 had shown, such a move could have been fatal.

'ACTIVE' OR 'PASSIVE' VIEWERS?

This gets to the heart of the problem of television. For all the censure directed at ITV from Pilkington and other intellectual and academic sources, commercial television was popular. As an article in the *Observer* newspaper highlighted, at the point when Pilkington's committee was about to hold its first meeting, there was not one BBC programme in the 'top ten' of TAM's (Television Audience Measurement) ratings for the week ending 18 September 1960. (The BBC's last challenger for top of the ratings had been the long-forgotten *Ask Pickles* in 1956.[41]) This was by no means an uncommon situation; indeed, it was a regular feature of television viewing from the mid-fifties to the end of the century. Many households, especially working-class ones, had the television set permanently tuned to the local ITV channel. This should not have surprised observers who knew anything about the content of British commercial popular culture as it had evolved since the late nineteenth century. ITV programmes were liked because they mined a vein of popular culture which encompassed both the homely and the escapist, and drew upon themes and genres which had been developed in the popular press, the music hall and cinema, the sports field and the seaside holiday since the beginning of the century. It was rather blousy and vulgar but, like Graham Greene's Ada in *Brighton Rock*, it embodied an honest vulgarity which constituted a down-to-earth British populism. The BBC had not been insensitive to this notion of entertainment, but in its attempt to create a culturally rounded listener/viewer the Corporation had rather subordinated popular pleasures beneath a stratum of more earnest material. Though the BBC could produce programmes which achieved both popular and critical acclaim – *Z Cars*, *Maigret*, the *Black and White Minstrel Show* and *Dixon of Dock Green* were all examples of such, and all were showing at the time the Pilkington Committee was sitting – it possessed a degree of 'moral authoritarianism'[42] (a phrase used in the Commons debates on Pilkington) which linked it to 'them' rather than 'us' (to use Hoggart's famous opposition). When commercial television gave many viewers what they liked, without hedging that notion in Reithian obfuscations about viewers not really knowing what they liked, it was warmly and perhaps rightly embraced.

Coronation Street, the Granada TV soap opera which made its first appearance in December 1960, summed up much of ITV's affinity with its audience. In many ways the regular soap opera was the hook that caught the loyal audience, and *Coronation Street*, with its consistent capturing of some 20 million viewers, has fulfilled this function for ITV with spectacular success for 40 years. It might be worth pausing briefly to consider its winning formula, for this will take us close to what constitutes 'popular television'. Though the programme has changed in significant ways over the years, principally in the quality of its *mise-en-scène*, it retains enduring features which might explain its appeal. At its core is the family, represented at different levels – household, neighbourhood ('the street') and, by implication, nation. The mainstay of the family is found in its female members. The men are often marginal, whimsical, untrustworthy, or indecisive, and a series of redoubtable women have driven the *Coronation Street* narrative forward – Ena Sharples, Annie Walker, Elsie Tanner, Bett Lynch. At the end of the twentieth century the programme still employs visual signifiers of a 'traditional' northern English working class: the terraced houses, corner shop, pub and cobbled streets. All were dated when the programme first went on the air, and large parts of working-class Manchester were falling under the hammer of urban redevelopers. The 'street' is therefore an anachronism, just as its community is a sociological fiction. Though vaguely 'working class' in mores and speech, the inhabitants are no modern proletariat. Independent occupations predominate – window cleaner, garage owner, shop owner, bus driver – rather than factory hands. Until recent years this was also a *white* community, multi-racial influences notable only by their absence. Just as unlikely is the retention in the street of its potentially most upwardly-mobile member – Kenneth Barlow, a schoolteacher-cum-intellectual. In the first programme this character was deployed to illustrate generational and cultural tensions between working-class parents and grammar-school/university-educated children, soon to be fleeing the nest in search of a new and better future. Forty years later Kenneth Barlow is still there. He provides a counterpoise of rationality to the activities of the less-formally educated though still 'knowing' street members who face life's ups and downs with a steady British resilience and a ready quip. *Coronation Street* has a romantic nostalgia for the idea of the North which was invented through various popular cultural forms, especially dialect literature, in the nineteenth century and carried on in music hall and film by entertainers such as Gracie Fields and George Formby. It is a conservative 'realist' vision from which pleasure is derived through its familiarity and predictability, and which represents the nation to itself in a comforting form. It is in every sense the archetypal *family* programme and uses television as a family medium. Its essential formula has been taken and successfully adapted with a more realist edge in numerous copies, principally *East Enders* (BBC) and *Brookside* (Channel 4).

The Pilkington Committee did not despise programmes like *Coronation Street* (indeed Hoggart might well have felt some affinity with its portrayal of a 'traditional' working class); it simply felt that there was more to be aspired to. Pilkington subscribed to a view of television which attributed to it a strong influence; the medium was powerful, the viewer passive. And yet this is an issue about which, after a half-century of television viewing and the growth of an entire academic industry devoted to studying media effects, there is still much uncertainty. Academics are sceptical of the 'hypodermic needle' view of television which sees it as a 'drug' injected into the passive organism of the viewer, to work its effects for good or ill. Such had been the slant of early American studies, influenced by Frankfurt School notions of popular culture, and they have continued to exercise a powerful hold over the public imagination, notably at times when crimes of violence or riotous behaviour are under scrutiny. It seems all too obvious that violence on the television screen produces violence in the streets, as the idea of 'copycat' killings indicates. However, detailed empirical work into the processes of 'encoding' and 'decoding' the messages that are present in television production and viewing has different inferences. David Morley's important studies of audiences, for example, have revealed a complex 'reading' of programmes by different kinds of viewers.[43] The studies suggest a relationship between programme and viewer in which there is no simple 'meaning' being communicated, and certainly not in a one-way direction.[44]

Interesting though this research is in problematizing the impact of television, it points up a gap which should be evident to historians. Most studies of television have been concerned with the production process, the 'text', and its impact. This is illustrated very clearly in Conrad Lodziak's study of television, written in the mid-1980s, and intended to show that the influences attributed to the medium have often been overestimated by theorists. Lodziak, emphasizing the expanded social and leisure context of television, was none the less unable to call upon any empirical examples of television viewing. His tendency therefore to see television watching as a passive activity which 'colonizes' people's leisure time and creates obstacles to progressive social change thus reproduces a conventional wisdom which tends to give viewing a bad name.[45] A more positive outlook on the effects of television was provided by the mass-observer Tom Harrisson. Noting the intellectual's general dislike of television, Harrisson raised an interesting question, seldom asked: '[W]hat *did* people do on a winter's day or a Sunday afternoon of rain before TV – especially if they hadn't much money? The short answer for millions of people then: "NOTHING MUCH".'[46]

Television occupied these dreary spaces as a novel and glamourous entertainment which created new cultural habits in the home. Though social historians have been slow to probe this issue, sufficient exploratory work has now been done for us to be able to ask whether television in any sense created an 'active' viewer, of a kind similar to the active listener of radio found in Jennings' and Gill's survey of listening habits in the late 1930s.[47] Initially, because television sets were in scarce supply and also expensive, viewing was something done in common. Television therefore perpetuated the habit developed in the theatre, music hall, cinema and workers' canteen of enjoying the programme in the company of others. One woman interviewed on this recalled of her first sight of television that it was

> like going to a cinema in Aunty Betty's house, it was in a room about as big as this – just packed full of people. The picture had a snowy effect – it wasn't very good.[48]

Much of the audience for the first big media spectacles – the 1953 Cup Final, closely followed by the coronation of Queen Elizabeth II – viewed on sets in neighbours' houses or in pubs and clubs. The collective experience of these events gave substance to the idea that they were 'national' occasions when the crowds shown on the screen, at Wembley or outside Westminster Abbey, became a microcosm of the nation as a whole. Nor did this viewing form completely die out with the proliferation of television sets. It is continued at the end of the century by BSkyB's football viewers, many of whom do not receive the broadcasts in their own homes and for whom therefore the pub is the natural meeting place for watching the match. As sets became common possessions, however, most television came to be viewed in the home and, unlike radio for the most part, by family groups sitting in their living rooms. It was a scenario captured well in the BBC's own *Royle Family* sitcom at the end of the 1990s, with the family half-watching and half-conversing, the television set almost a supernumerary family member, its comforting presence in the room providing a reassuring, though not necessarily dominant focus of attention.

Ownership of television sets in the early days was an important status symbol, the aerial on the roof becoming almost a sign of having 'arrived' in the affluent society. Acquisition, which often involved costly hire-purchase arrangements, was sometimes justified (like the later purchase of home computers) on the grounds that it would help children with their homework. Many of of the respondents in research carried out by Tim O'Sullivan claimed to have been careful over the amount of time they allocated to television watching, though others acknowledged that it was a release from the boredom of 'staying in' – 'it was not like staying in because there was television to watch. It could be relaxing and it could send you to sleep. It was another option . . . and we worked out what was worth watching pretty quickly.'[49] The new medium thus served importantly to heighten the attractiveness of the home as a focus of leisure.[50] Television clearly became a key influence in the lives of all these people, transforming their habits and relationships profoundly. But in all kinds of ways – as a financial commitment, a focus of domestic space, a source of negotiation between parents and children and men and women, and as a subject for decisions about choice and taste – it became an agent of new domestic relations which, it might be suggested, both rein-vigorated the home and secured television as a domestic leisure form free from the legacy of Reith.

The *Royle Family* image of the family unit seated around the set has, however, following constant developments in media technology, become an anachronistic one for the early twenty-first century. Television sets by this time had proliferated within the home, alongside other electronic devices such as videos, computer-based entertainments, television information services and music centres, to create a centrifugal process in which each family member might be pursuing his or her own particular interest in different rooms. With such a choice of habits available, it takes a strong effort of will in many house-holds to bring the family members together to view television as the Royles do. In some senses, though, it does mean that the role of the individual in relation to the medium is more active.[51]

The diverse end-of-century culture of electronic media consumption contrasts sharply with the premises from which the Pilkington Report proceeded. Pilkington was, in fact, a final gesture towards the idea that broadcasting should have a mission to produce a rounded individual listener or viewer; that there were cultural standards which the broadcaster should define and uphold. Much had changed by the time the next major report on broadcasting appeared in 1977. The hallmark of the Annan Committee's delib-erations, commissioned by the Labour government in 1974, was 'regulated diversity'. Annan recognized that standards were important, but that they sprang from quality programmes aimed at a diverse audience range, and should be supervised by a devolved structure aimed at opening access to broadcasting for many different groups of viewers. No overall moral arbiter was proposed. 'Our society's culture is now multi-racial and pluralist . . . the structure of broadcasting should reflect this variety . . . We prefer editorial independence tempered by the recognition that mistakes in taste or policy should be frankly and openly acknowledged by those responsible. Pennies and pounds should be put into programmes, not into policing them.'[52] The Annan Report proposed the end of what had come to be called the 'duopoly' of BBC and ITV, and although its recommendations would have created a thicket of new bureaucracies its intention in spirit was to empower the indi-vidual consumer. It too, in its way, therefore subscribed to an idea of the 'active' viewer. Many of its recommendations were roundly ignored by the new Conservative government which took office in 1979, but during the course of the next two decades a number of developments, some technical, others the result of political exigencies, did ensure that at least some of Annan's ideas were adopted. Channel 4, for example, though given to inde-pendent television and not, as Annan had proposed, created as an 'open' broadcasting service, did develop a new style of programme, often catering for minority tastes and interests. Programme making, because of the oppor-tunites that new technology gave to 'cottage industry' production, extended to a far wider range of companies. And, for reasons of financial restraint imposed by government, the BBC was obliged to farm out much of its production to such companies, whose lower overheads enabled them to make cheaper programmes. Moreover, the introduction of satellite, cable and digital channels, together with a host of radio stations, in the deregulated broadcasting market created by the 1990 Broadcasting Act, has resulted in a variety of options available to the individual, who now inhabits a global media environment far different from that of the constrained national schoolroom envisaged by John Reith.

CONCLUSION

Radio and television have together been the twentieth century's most popular and enduring leisure form. Though both originated amidst fears that they would engender a *passive* form of entertainment, their history reveals interesting changes in the way the leisure form has been used by its audience, and the century has ended with the notion of the *active* listener/viewer having as much validity as at any time over the previous 75 years. This point reinforces a theme that we have observed in other areas of sport and leisure; namely, that although a leisure form might be beyond the reach of what would normally be considered 'popular control' (in the sense that it is owned by big business, or subjected to strict governmental regulation) this should not be taken to mean that its audience are simply passive consumers. In various ways the consumer can affect the way in which the leisure form is marketed or made available, and the history of the BBC shows a constantly changing relationship in this sense between the Corporation and its audiences. Like many other leisure forms, moreover, broadcasting illustrates the tensions that exist between commercial, state and individual interests; and although each of these interests is invested with different amounts of power with which to pursue their goals – it is not an equal contest – the individual or group to which the product is directed is not without some influence in the contest.

Histories of broadcasting have been relatively silent on these issues. Asa Briggs's monumental history, for example, presents a 'top down' view in which the organizations themselves, rather than their audiences, have pride of place. This has been the model adopted subsequently by most historians in studying radio and television. In some respects this reflects a British view of broadcasting as a public service passed down to the population, and it is not surprising that Briggs gives much emphasis to the BBC. Briggs's work was conceived in the 1960s. Changes in the last 30 years of the century suggest a different, more listener/viewer centred, approach with the BBC only one player among many, and perhaps not the most important. The gradual loss of the BBC's monopoly, indicating a loss of faith in that idea of broadcasting as a public service, has served to point up the difficulty of seeing leisure as a form of social control. The general picture is too fragmented for this notion to operate in any clear way. But we need more 'bottom up' social history of broadcasting, written from the perspective of the ordinary listener/viewer, before we can pronounce on these matters with a surer voice.

Key Reading ●

Bailey, P. *Leisure and Class in Victorian England*. London: Routledge, 1997 edn.

Briggs, A. *The History of Broadcasting in the United Kingdom*.
   vol. I *The Birth of Broadcasting*. London: Oxford University Press, 1961.
   vol II *The Golden Age of the Wireless*. London: Oxford University Press, 1965.
   vol IV *Sound and Vision*. Oxford: Oxford University Press, 1979.
   vol V *Competition 1955–1974*. Oxford: Oxford University Press, 1995.

Crissell, A. *An Introductory History of British Broadcasting*. London: Routledge, 1997.

Cunningham, H. *Leisure in the Industrial Revolution c.1780–c.1880*. London: Croom Helm, 1980.

Scannell, P., and Cardiff, D. A. *Social History of British Broadcasting, vol. I, 1922–39*. Oxford: Blackwell, 1991.

Chronology of Events

1896 Marconi's patent for wireless filed at Patent Office.

1904 Wireless Telegraphy Act brought wireless under public control through Post Office and required wireless operators to purchase a licence.

1922 Post Office authorized Marconi company to transmit wireless broadcasts; in **October**, Marconi, GEC and other manufacturers of wireless sets formed together in the British Broadcasting Company, with daily broadcasts from London; in **December** John Reith appointed General Manager.

1923 *Radio Times* launched; Sykes Committee recommended broadcasting be financed through licence fee under control of the state.

1925 Crawford Committee recommended establishment of a public corporation for broadcasting in the national interest.

1927 British Broadcasting Corporation (BBC) founded; Reith as Director-General.

1936 November: BBC television service started from Alexandra Palace, transmitting to the London area.

1939 At outbreak of war National and Regional Programmes merged into a new Home Service; setting up in January 1940 of Forces Programme (which became the Light Programme in 1946).

1946 Resumption of BBC television service, discontinued for duration of war (14500 licences issued in 1947); Third Programme established.

1951 Beveridge Committee recommended continuation of BBC monopoly in broadcasting.

1954 Television Act established commercial broadcasting in the form of Independent Television (ITV) under the supervision of the Independent Television Authority (ITA), chaired by Sir Kenneth Clark.

1955 22 September: first ITV transmission in the London area, with first commercial television advertisement (for Gibbs toothpaste).

1962 Pilkington Report critical of the record of ITV; recommended a third television channel; July: first transatlantic television broadcast through Telstar satellite.

1963 All existing ITV franchises renewed.

1964 Inauguration of BBC2.

1967 July: colour television introduced on BBC 2 (extended in 1969); September: introduction of Radio 1 as popular music station, and renaming of other stations as Radio 2, 3 and 4; experiments in Leicester with local radio.

1972 Sound Broadcasting Act enabled creation of local commercial radio stations, first of which opened in the autumn of that year.

1977 Committee on the Future of Broadcasting (Annan Committee) recommended public accountability in broadcasting, the creation of a fourth public channel, and greater accessibility to broadcasting for listeners and viewers.

1979 Conservative government's Independent Broadcasting Act created Independent Broadcasting Authority (IBA), to which new fourth channel granted (Channel 4 – opened November 1982).

1984 Developments in new forms of satellite and cable broadcasting reflected in the inauguration in January of Sky Television.

1986 Peacock Committee recommended deregulation of television to broaden viewers' choice and extend opportunities for programme makers.

1990 Merging of British Satellite Broadcasting and Sky Television to form British Sky Broadcasting (BSkyB); Broadcasting Act included a new Independent Television Commission to regulate all commercial television services, the right to bid for exclusive rights to cover sporting events, a radio Authority to supervise the expansion of independent radio, and the requirement that all television broadcasters allocate not less than 25 per cent of their broadcasting to 'independent producers'.

1996 Broadcasting Act established the Broadcasting Standards Commission, and made provision for digital terrestrial television.

1997 Setting up of Channel 5 as new television channel.

chapter

7

Youth, Age and the Problem of Leisure

CONTENTS

As we saw in the opening chapter, there is a long history in Britain of 'problematizing' leisure. As a result the topic cannot, either in academic or social discussion, be detached from a clutch of attendant preconceptions. More than most issues it comes trailing clouds of prejudice. A great deal of this has to do with social class relationships, and when to these is added the subject of youth, a concept which has come to be so thoroughly imbued with fears of physical and moral threat, the mixture becomes a most combustible one.[1] But the matter of age and leisure, which a consideration of youth brings to the fore, is not limited to young people. In the later twentieth century, with a greater proportion than ever of old people in the population, it extends also to the leisure activities of the senior members of the community.

YOUNG PEOPLE AND LEISURE

Nevertheless, the most dramatic aspects of age and leisure relate to young people. Although concerns about youth, class and leisure seem to have been ever-present in British society, their elevation to the status of sociological theory occurred in the United States in the inter-war period. It was here that the Victorian notion of 'juvenile delinquency' first took firm theoretical hold. Explanations for what seemed aberrant and dysfunctional behaviour by youths were varied, ranging from the Chicago School's quasi-biological 'social ecology' theories to functional interpretations based on the Durkheimian concept of 'anomie'.[2] In the popular imagination, fuelled by cinema representations of youth, the teenage years were felt to possess a particular kind of psychology/pathology which was held to account for their tendency towards delinquency. However, attributing such characteristics to young people might not actually be a helpful way of understanding their predicaments. If indeed there is something distinctive about this period in the life cycle it may be that, rather than psychology, anthropology can provide some clues. One such is in the idea, contained in the concept of 'rite of passage', of being in a socially transitional state. The adolescent and youth years might in this sense be seen as a 'rite of passage' when young people are, to use Victor Turner's phrase, 'betwixt and between'. Beyond childhood and its dependent status, but not yet into the stage of 'settled' behaviour and career aspiration demanded of adults in modern Western societies. Thus, for example, students might be regarded as experiencing this transition. Turner, following van Gennep, the originator of the 'rite de passage' concept, sees this as a stage of 'liminality'. In traditional societies it represents a phase when individuals are temporarily removed from social norms prior to be their being reintegrated as full members of society. Liminality is thus dislocation, and can therefore be a period of risk when the individual might reject social behaviour and lose bearings, suffering a state of 'normlessness' when the customary codes of conduct are dispensed with. In any event liminality is a time for reflection, of standing outside conventional life, and in this respect could be adapted to serve as a description of the social adjustments undergone by teenagers in Western societies. When we also recognise that leisure can be a social activity in which excitement is derived through testing rules to their limits, it is perhaps the young who are more likely to find themselves in such liminal contexts, undergoing a modern 'rite of passage'.[3]

Certainly there have been several cases of youthful leisure activity in twentieth-century Britain, from rock music to drug culture, sexual behaviour and football hooliganism, which seem to reinforce this idea. Whatever the value of such conceptual approaches, much of the activity they highlight has been perceived, in leisure studies as in anthropology, in an implicitly gendered way. It has been represented essentially as activity concerning *males*. This results not from the empirical evidence, which extends as much to women as to men, but from the ingrained assumption that youth culture is masculine culture. To change the assumption requires a change of perspective. The feminist writer Angela McRobbie, in the course of a critique of this tendency in studies of sub-cultures, has pointed out that by the early 1980s the entire study of 'youth culture' and the 'sociology of youth' had been conducted from a male perspective. It was a perspective that she, and others, began to alter only quite recently.[4]

So, like the poor, young males seem always to be with us, and constantly to be presenting society with their problems. Indeed, attention was focused on youth in the post-war years partly because the poor no longer seemed to pose the problem they once had. What has primarily identified youth has been its leisure activity. Examples of youth culture can be found at almost any point in our period, and before it. But the 1950s have been conventionally regarded as the time when the presence of a youth culture that was not only distinctive, but enduring was first witnessed. It arrived in the form of the 'teenager'. It was at this time that a combination of full employment and imported American popular culture created the conditions for the emergence of what the market researcher Mark Abrams memorably described as the 'teenage consumer'.[5] But whether the phenomenon arose at this juncture, or earlier, is now debated. The historian David Fowler has made a strong case for locating the emergence of the process in the inter-war years, when opportunities for young people in the labour market allowed them to start earning decent wages, often in 'blind-alley' jobs which would later be converted into apprenticeships with longer-term prospects. Fowler is able to cite instances from the 1930s of most of the features normally assumed to have developed after the war: the easing of parental control, teenage spending on music, dancing and cinema, and the emergence of 'a hard-sell youth market'.[6] Though much of his evidence is drawn from the Manchester area there is no reason to suppose that Fowler's geographical focus represents an exceptional case, and his work deserves closer attention than it has so far been given by historians interested in the mainsprings of this important social process.

As it is, though, the attention of the majority of social historians remains fixed on the post-war period. Arthur Marwick's influence is strong here. He attributes to the war and the economic conditions that followed it a fostering of independence among young people.[7] Abrams, writing at the end of the 1950s, also explained teenager-ism as rooted in economic circumstances, especially the greater disposable income available to those in the age group 15 to 25. They made up some 6.5 million of the population, the vast majority of them unmarried and possessing, Abrams estimated, around 8–9 per cent of all personal income in Britain. They were for the most part *employed* people, rather than those in education, where numbers had increased significantly since the raising of the school-leaving age in the 1944 Education Act. But for Abrams, the 'teens' really started at 15, when most people had left school. Because these young people lived with their parents they had minimal domestic overheads – mortgages and the acquisition of consumer durables scarcely concerned them – and had a significant amount of money to spend after paying for their keep. It was spent on the conspicuous consumption of relatively cheap fashion items such as clothes and records, produced for the teenage market by entrepreneurs guided, in the absence of any domestic traditions in this particular market, by American models. Abrams also noted a feature of this culture which served further to problematize it: it was largely working class in its composition. 'The aesthetic of the teenage market is essentially a working-class aesthetic.'[8] Thus the old concerns over working-class leisure use, typified after the war in Ferdinand Zweig's studies with their recurring theme of the relationship between leisure-spending and poverty to create 'secondary poverty', were renewed in the context of the teenager.[9] It was not so much the rise of a new consumer group that presented problems; after all, teenagers were in this respect dutifully taking their place in the newly found consumer society of post-war Britain, whose affluence depended upon the purchase of goods. It was what teenagers did with these goods, or rather the kinds of behaviour that accompanied their consumption, that provoked unease.

Teenage behaviour was regarded in a multitude of lights, from shallow and materialist to, at its worst, violent and disruptive. Much of this thinking was derived from the more exaggerated forms of youth culture: the easily identifiable 'Teddy Boys' of the mid-1950s, for example, with their reputation for violence, sometimes directed against black immigrants; the Mods and Rockers of the early 1960s, and the street battles they fought with each other at otherwise peaceful seaside resorts on bank holidays; and, subsequently, the apparently relentless succession of bizarre youth movements which followed them – from Skinheads, Suedeheads, Rudies and Punks of the late 1960s and 1970s, to the football hooligans who seemed ever-present in the later years of the century. One interesting similarity between these otherwise divergent youth cultural forms is that they were, for the most part, the product of working-class youths. Whether employed or, as was increasingly the case from the mid-1970s onwards, unemployed, the exponents of the culture appeared not to be in Turner's 'betwixt and between' state. They had already taken a first step on the career ladder which, for many, might prove to be their last step. Their behaviour, unlike that of the student-based youth culture evident in the mid- to late-1960s, seemed much more an attempt to stake a place for themselves in society through their leisure, since their economic standing was so lacking in status.

How far was there, in any case, a distinctive youth culture? The economic historian John Benson's scrutiny of these developments raises some interesting and original thoughts which set the teenage phenomenon in a slightly different perspective from that usually taken.[10] Approaching youth culture from the direction of consumption – in particular shopping, tourism and sport – Benson finds that there was, as most people imagined, an increasing relationship between consumption and youth: 'by the 1960s young people seemed to be among the most active, enthusiastic and independent of all consumers'.[11] But whether this contributed to the growth of a distinctive culture of youth seems to be another question, to which Benson gives a largely negative response. The culture of consumption was just as likely, it seems, to fragment as to cohere youth. Apart from shopping, which probably did mark out teenagers in terms both of the kinds of goods purchased and the manner in which shopping activity was conducted, other forms of consumption were embedded with various class and age influences. Tourism, for example, seems to have manifested few independent teenage forms, and this general pattern has probably altered little in the 20 years or so since the point in 1980 at which Benson's study concluded. Sport is also particularly interesting in this respect. Although the 1980s and 1990s might have seen some changes in styles of consumption which show a more distinct youth presence – in the purchase of T-shirts, track-suits and especially trainers – little else has happened that might cause Benson's main conclusions to need modification. Sport is an activity in which young people are highly visible as participants, yet it functions in an overall context where age-mix is a controlling principle. Young people cannot use sport to proclaim their difference because the whole activity is so thoroughly bound by cross-generational ties. Even gambling, which has been such an important feature of the fascination with sport, attracts little attention from young people. With the exception of disorderly behaviour ('hooliganism') at football matches, which does seems to have been a uniquely youthful pastime, sport and youth culture do not go together.

Benson's rather sceptical analysis provides a healthy correction to some of the assumptions that are often made about teenagers. But, of course, much of the problem about youth culture stems from what is assumed rather than what actually happens. As with the bigger subject of working-class leisure, there developed with the question of teenagers a middle-class (and middle-aged) fascination with the phenomenon. It claimed much attention in one form or another, producing what Stanley Cohen was to describe in his work of the early 1970s as 'moral panic'.[12] The fears instilled in 'respectable' society by manifestations of youth identity and independence such as Teddy Boys and Skinheads first emerged, as we have seen, in the United States with the concept of 'delinquency'. This suggested not only a form of behaviour which departed from normal standards, but equally significantly one which therefore needed to be policed, 'corrected' and reformed.[13] It was an idea present in a number of American films shown in Britain in the 1950s, notably *Blackboard Jungle* (1955) and the more popular *Rebel Without A Cause (1955)*, the film which elevated the actor James Dean to cult status as the era's favourite tormented youth. The visceral thrill for audiences of *Rebel* stemmed from the fact that Dean's torment was rooted in an otherwise respectable middle-class environment, where all the material problems of life appeared to have been solved. Later, similar fears played their part in the orchestration of the 'law and order' discourse of the 1970s which made an important contribution to the emergence of a distinctive brand of Conservative politics, embodied in Margaret Thatcher.[14] But concern over youth was not confined to right-of-centre opinion. In a brilliantly original and seminal study of working-class life published in 1957, the university lecturer Richard Hoggart famously drew attention to the 'juke-box boys'.[15] These were youths, aged between 15 and 20, many of them awaiting call-up to national service, whose leisure time was spent in a soulless imitation of perceived American life-styles. In a subsequently much-quoted passage from *The Uses of Literacy* Hoggart offered a gloomy picture of teenage mores:

> I have in mind . . . the kind of milk-bar . . . which has become the regular evening rendezvous of some of the young men. Girls go to some, but most of the customers are boys aged between fifteen and twenty, with drape-suits, picture ties, and an American slouch. Most of them cannot afford a succession of milk-shakes, and make cups of tea serve for an hour or two whilst – and this is their main reason for coming – they put copper after copper into the mechanical record player. About a dozen records are available at any time . . . almost all are American; almost all are 'vocals' and the styles of singing much advanced beyond what is normally heard on the Light Programme of the BBC. Some of the tunes are catchy; all have been doctored for presentation so that they have the kind of beat which is currently popular;

much use is made of the 'hollow-cosmos' effect which echo-chamber recording gives. They are delivered with great precision and competence, and the 'nickleodeon' is allowed to blare out so that the noise would be sufficient to fill a good-sized ballroom, rather than a converted shop in the main street. The young men waggle one shoulder or stare, as desperately as Humphrey Bogart, across the tubular chairs.[16]

Later generations who have either forgotten or who never knew Humphrey Bogart are likely to read this description of seemingly innocuous behaviour with astonishment; how could this be perceived as a threat? To Hoggart, however, the milk-bar and its 'nickleodeon' was a threat; not so much a physical one, but a threat to the spiritual life of the country. 'Compared . . . with the pub around the corner', an institution which symbolized much of the robust working-class culture of Hoggart's youth, the milk-bar represented 'a peculiarly thin and pallid form of dissipation, a sort of spiritual dry-rot amid the odour of boiled milk'.[17]

Hoggart's ethnographic observations of northern working-class life in *The Uses of Literacy* were not quite what they seemed. His descriptions of lived culture, as of the passages from American pulp fiction quoted elsewhere in the book, were largely his own confections, drawing heavily from his own experiences. But they are no less interesting for that. There is no reason to suppose that, being 'fictions', they do not capture the essential features of popular culture. Moreover, whether he faithfully reclaims this world through a middle-class intellectual's image of ordinary working-class life in the mid-century is, perhaps, a matter of less importance than the fact that he provides his readers with a clear view of what he valued and deplored in British society as it was developing at this time. Weaving together themes of class, culture and Americanization Hoggart offered a particular view of British 'declinism'. He saw the sturdy and (partly) self-generated working-class culture of his boyhood under threat from an imported commercial mass culture whose nature was summed up in his characteristic phrase 'candy-floss world' – lacking any substance, sugary and, above all, American in origin. He echoed D. H. Lawrence in seeing mass-entertainments as 'anti-life', 'full of corrupt brightness, of improper appeals and moral evasions'.[18] This was a persistent charge of the cultural critics, and had been levelled against cinema in the 1930s. Unlike the literature of Leavis's 'great tradition', popular culture often failed to pose moral problems, leaving its consumers incapable of making critical and aesthetic judgements. It was a theme to which Denys Thompson warmed in a popular Penguin of the early 1960s with the ominous title *Discrimination and Popular Culture*.[19] Hoggart, and those who followed his lead, make an interesting illustration of a moral panic over youth culture at the end of the 1950s.

Hoggart's critique came at a time when other trends were converging to produce a crisis of confidence in British society. Many of these were of an international nature. The urbane British presence of the late 1940s – when, Kenneth Morgan claims, Britain played 'a confident Greece to the American Rome'[20] – had evaporated ten years later. Much had changed. Britain's reduced international role was dramatized by the Suez affair of 1956, and further underlined by a series of related events and influences: the retreat from the African colonies, the restoration of Continental power symbolised in the formation of the European Economic Community in 1957, the pervasive American cultural imperialism, and even the failure of England's football team. All combined to create a mood of self-doubt which intensified as the 1950s came to a close. Critical eyes were being cast upon many aspects of British attitudes and institutions, and, indeed, upon the very condition of Britain itself. Nowhere was this more evident than in international relations, where it became commonplace for British shortcomings to be compared with the more dynamic and imaginative qualities perceived in overseas countries, especially Continental European ones. An entire discourse of 'modernization' had developed, characterized by a public mood which the authors of the Nuffield study of the 1964 general election described as one of 'self-doubt and angry introspection'.[21] 'Declinism' – the concern with why Britain had failed to maintain its position in the world – had become a major issue in this discourse, exemplified by Michael Shanks's astringent analysis, *The Stagnant Society* (1961).[22] It was to be a central theme of politics in the early 1960s.

Two characteristic products of this climate of opinion, both of them juggling themes of youth, leisure and modernization, appeared at the very beginning of the 1960s. They were the reports published in 1960 by the Central Council of Physical Recreation on 'Sport and the Community' (The 'Wolfenden Report')[23] and the report of the Ministry of Education on 'The Youth Service in England and Wales' (the 'Albemarle Report').[24]

Wolfenden, discussed more fully in Chapter 9, covered a wide range of issues. It was particularly concerned with the improvement of resources for sport, and broke new ground by making the first serious plea for state intervention in this area. Much of this was stimulated by concerns for the leisure of youth, and at several points the Wolfenden Report made cross-references to the recommendations of the Albemarle Committee, which had reported a few months previously. The report of the Albemarle Committee (of which Richard Hoggart was a member), commissioned in 1958, concerned itself with the youth service in England and Wales. There had been a growing unease with the efficacy of this service, orchestrated as it was through voluntary organizations and local educational authorities, and part of the Committee's task was to find ways of restoring to it a much-needed morale, especially given the congruence of a new adolescent culture which, in the Committee's words, 'adults find puzzling or shocking'.[25] As may be imagined, its perspective on the problem was a 'top down' one, exemplified in its methodology. In the fact-gathering process typical of such committees much emphasis was placed by Albemarle on talking to organizations and individuals charged with administering or studying the 'problem' of youth. Thus, though individual members of the Committee did visit youth groups in various parts of the country, the 'voice' of youth was notably absent in the report. Attention was directed to the creation of an effective national organization of both public and voluntary provision under the aegis of a Youth Service Development Council respon-

sible to the Minister of Education. Further attention was given to the resourc-
ing of youth centres and the training of youth leaders, both of which required
finance. It was to government that the Committee looked, at a time of relative
economic buoyancy, to provide the funds. By contrast with end of century
tightness of public funding, it was a common assumption in the early 1960s
that government would be in a position to 'throw money' at the problem (as
later politicians disparagingly described such a tactic).[26] This was a notion
repeated in another influential exploration of the youth problem, and another
contribution to the moral panic over youth, T. R. Fyvel's *The Insecure
Offenders* (1963), a book of genuinely international proportions informed by
the dark threat of 'delinquency'. Fyvel's left-wing perspective, which found
sympathy for the dead-end prospects of many young people at this time,
proposed a solution in the form of a marriage between the old principle of
voluntarism and the newer one of public funding. Its offspring would be a
reinvigorated youth club movement, whose future prospects Fyvel envisaged
in terms that seem, looking back some 40 years later, naively utopian:

> I believe that in 1970 . . . each medium-sized town should have its . . . youth centre;
> . . . an essentially modern building, with imaginative facilities for music, dancing
> and play; for more elaborate hobbies like a cine-photography club, real jazz,
> amateur acting, or boat-building; the complex might be geographically-linked with
> the local public library or swimming-pool.[27]

If all this smacked of adults attempting to shape youth culture in an
'approved' fashion it was, of course, because youth was all too readily capable
of fashioning its own styles and tastes.[28] A timely reminder of this came from
Ray Gosling, later a well-known broadcaster but in 1961 the organizer of a
youth club in Leicester. Gosling's riposte to the Albemarle Report was the first
'Young Fabian' pamphlet put out by the left-wing Fabian Society. It expressed
an unease with the generally patronizing and deferential relations that official bodies sought to create in dealings with youth, which, Gosling claimed,
tended to be seen as a category rather than a collection of individual people.
A successful youth service, in Gosling's eyes, would be one which young
people ran themselves, something that Gosling had tried to encourage in his
own club in Leicester.[29]

YOUNG WOMEN AND LEISURE

Because much of the discussion and perception of youth was framed within
a specific notion of youth as a masculine threat, large areas became overlooked. As was sometimes pointed out, most young people went through life
without doing any of the things that so troubled older observers of the youth
scene.[30] 'Respectable' youth, whether or not involved in 'approved' youth
organizations like the Boy Scouts and Girl Guides, probably constituted the
majority of young people, just as in later years the 'ordinary' football fans
vastly outnumbered those 'hooligans' whose activities consumed so much of

sociologists' attention. Even the middle-class student youth of the late 1960s, occupying university registries and demonstrating againsy US action in Vietnam, represented only a small proportion of a student population which was itself far smaller than it had become by the 1990s. This did not prevent shadowy figures in government regarding student protests as being led by militants who were 'frighteningly radical'.[31]

A consideration of what has thus been 'hidden from history' in youth culture brings us back to McRobbie's point about the emphasis on the male. Most of the distinctive sub-cultures of youth have foregrounded the male, whether acting in an aggressively masculine way, as with the Teds and the Rockers, or in a more restrained and sometimes epicene form, as with Mods and Glamrock.[32] Girls and women have seemed to occupy a marginal and decorative role in these groups – literally as 'pillion passengers' in biker groups – confirming their general social role as subordinates to men. In the matter of 'deviance', which was what prompted most discussions of youth leisure, males seemed to be the chief actors. In fact, much of the attention that was directed both by academics and others to the cultural experiences of young women was to do with their 'socialization' into femininity. Carol Dyhouse's important study of both middle- and working-class girls in the late-Victorian and Edwardian period emphasized the place of the home and the schoolroom – but especially the home – in preparing females for the sexual division of labour and leisure that characterized gender relations in society as a whole in this period. In leisure time the popular Girl Guide movement provides an interesting illustration of contemporary mentalities. Though apparently initially the product of autonomous action by young women themselves, the Guides were carefully incorporated into a 'feminine' counterpart of the scouting movement. This was a process which involved, among other things, the adoption of suitably feminine names for patrol groups, and the focusing of the girls' attention on beauty and appearance. Once Lady Baden-Powell had taken control of the movement during the First World War, there developed an emphasis on the cultivation of a respectable self-reliance that taught girls to resist the lures of sex and mass culture, whilst at the same time being 'efficient women citizens, good home-keepers and mothers'.[33] Similar regimes were installed through the paternalist work programmes of some employers, the Rowntree factory at York being a prime example.[34] Commercial leisure also played its part in fostering what McRobbie has termed the 'feminine career'. Her excellent close reading of the magazine for teenage girls, *Jackie*, shows how in the 1970s similar ideas of femininity, domesticity and early marriage were still being reproduced,[35] though by the 1980s they were undergoing changes of content and tone which clearly reflected the influence of feminism in encouraging a greater awareness of gender equality and 'realism' in the representation of women.[36] Such ideological constructions of 'femininity' nevertheless put up a powerful barrage against attempts to bring young women into athletic leisure, as Sheila Scraton found in her study of secondary schoolgirls in Liverpool. In a number of ways to do with dress, discipline and physicality, the girls found physical education lessons distasteful and, to their teachers' dismay, simply 'dropped out'.[37]

At some indeterminate point in the 1960s the emphasis on females in the discussion of youth and leisure shifted from the problem of socialization to that of 'deviancy', a notion that had conventionally been associated with males. In other words, young women were beginning to carve out a life of their own, and leisure habits to go with it. Among them was a general tendency for sex to move out of the privatized, disapproved-of, under-the-counter position it had occupied in British society, and become a more openly discussed and enjoyed activity with its own leisure culture. This change had a number of causes, of which the expansion of higher education after the Robbins Report of 1963 and the gradual emergence of a women's movement were important in framing middle-class attitudes. But the most significant was undoubtedly the atmosphere of greater sexual freedom that accompanied reforms in the laws on abortion, homosexuality, and divorce and matrimonial property. Together with this came a relaxation in theatrical and literary censorship (the latter following the celebrated trial in 1960 over Penguin's publication of *Lady Chatterley's Lover*) and the introduction of the female contraceptive pill. As a result of all this there was, says Arthur Marwick, 'a new hedonism abroad in the land'.[38]

Female leisure had changed immensely since Pearl Jephcott conducted her sensitive studies of post-school girls from working-class homes during the Second World War. Jephcott's concerns, like those of Hoggart some ten years later, were with issues of 'quality' in leisure habits; popular leisure, especially cinema and much of the reading matter available to working-class girls in the form of magazines and books, was considered not to stretch their minds, and to offer only shallow and false values. Jephcott's girls were a new generation, experiencing in dancing, the pictures and pub-going a regular daily leisure habit which to many of their mothers, and certainly their grandmothers, would have been unknown. It was an experience that was often carefully supervised, more so than for boys of the same age, by strict fathers who insisted upon the girl's returning home at a given time. But for Jephcott, the whole fare left much to be desired; her summary of one girl's leisure represents the central thesis of the study: 'she uses the cinema to escape from the sordidness of her own home whereas she ought to be learning to fight against those bad conditions. But neither the pictures, nor her weekly "love books" encourage her to protest, they merely provide her with dope.'[39] Some 40 years after this the nature of the moral crisis over the leisure of young females had altered. Quite apart from the appeal the growing feminist movement might have had for women, the new more liberal climate encouraged a view of them as autonomous persons, individuals in their own right and not merely people who acquired their identity in relation to men as wives, mothers or daughters.

One aspect of these changes was a different, and more relaxed, attitude towards sex and sexual behaviour. When Geoffrey Gorer studied this in the early 1950s, he found a population which was conspicuously dull and inexperienced in such matters; possibly, Gorer surmised, the most chaste and faithful in the developed world. 'Sexual compatibility' came well down Gorer's list of factors making for a happy marriage, a state of affairs whose chief attributes – 'give and take', 'making a home together', 'making a life together' – were reminiscent of Sydney and Beatrice Webb's description of 'our partnership'. It made marriage sound like a business venture. Sexual gratification did not appear to have a high priority. Significantly, Gorer did not enquire into exactly what 'having a good sex life in marriage' involved for those who answered affirmatively on this point.[40] By contrast, the survey conducted by Kaye Wellings and others in the later 1980s and early 1990s points in its coldly utilitarian tone to a newly found wealth of experience and experimentation among its respondents. The sexual 'repertoire' (so called) had become varied; homosexual relationships were experienced among 6 per cent of men and just over half that percentage of women with, in almost all cases, exclusively homosexual behaviour rare; and, above all, premarital sexual experience was common, with the age of first intercourse at before 16 being reported by almost a fifth of those in their late 'teens (i.e. born in the early 1970s). Wellings and her team show an undoubtedly more active population sexually, but one in which some conservative attitudes still prevailed: heterosexual, monogamous partnership was the predominant ideal; casual sex was frowned upon, as was infidelity; and homosexuality (at a time when AIDS was becoming widely publicized and, indeed, provided the rationale for the Wellings study) was the subject of widespread condemnation, especially by men.[41]

The way in which these changes produced female-specific reactions was less to do with the emergence of female groups analogous to the Teds or Rockers of old, though Punk women acquired some notoriety, than in the construction of new figures of disapproval which had as their common theme the image of the aberrant woman. The most trumpeted, which endured throughout the 1980s and 1990s, was that of the single female parent. Its existence owed more than a little to Cohen's idea of 'folk devils' and 'moral panics'. Studying the emergence of the 1960s sub-cultures of Mods and Rockers, Cohen noted the existence of a chain of events, beginning with the creation in the mass media of a campaign which labelled the 'folk devils' and generated a 'moral panic' around them. This led on to a situation of 'deviancy amplification', wherein the folk devils sought to live up to the image of themselves presented in the media. Thus intensified, the phenomenon called forth yet more strident demands for action to control it. McRobbie noted the emergence of just such a moral panic in the 1980s over single, teenage mothers, whose crime was the double one of having breached moral rectitude and, at the same time, having become dependent on the state for financial benefits, at a time when reducing taxation and rolling back the frontiers of the state were the twin pillars of popular Toryism. Which was regarded as the greater sin depended on one's imagination and politics. McRobbie's case study of teenage mothers in a working-class area of Birmingham creates a bleak picture of young women with few prospects of either work or settled relationships, who from an early age have been pitched by social and economic circumstances into a joyless and, what is interesting from the point of view of this chapter, a *leisure-less* life. There was no opportunity for these young women to participate in those new 'life-style' leisure forms of the 1980s which depended upon regular income and consumption – for example, shopping, home decoration and renovation, and beauty therapy. 'From being fresh-faced 16-year-olds they became impoverished-looking clients of the state.'[42] Economic deprivation excluded this section of the population from leisure.

Before leaving the area of youth it is worth commenting on one leisure form that was common to all the disparate aspects of youth culture, and which, like the issue of the single female parent, provoked much concern. Since the 1960s youth culture has been associated with the leisure use of drugs of various kinds. In the 1960s cannabis was, according to Marwick, 'the characteristic drug of youth and the older figures who identified with youth culture'.[43] It was closely linked with the more middle-class 'hippie' and student-intellectual elements of youth culture, which also experimented with the mind-expanding 'psychedelic' drug LSD. Amphetamines acquired some popularity at this time, too, especially with groups such as the Mods, whose culture was exalted in the song by The Who, 'My Generation', with its recurring stuttering diction meant to represent the effects of 'speed'. In the 1960s and 1970s drug use, illegal of course, seemed confined to youth of university or working age. By the late 1980s, however, increasing concern was being expressed that it was spreading down the age range and becoming prevalent among schoolchildren, in some cases even those in their early teens or below. The presence of drug dealers outside schools, the cult status achieved by films like *Trainspotting* (1996), which highlighted the increased use of 'hard' drugs like heroin, and the apparently everyday use of the drug ecstacy by young people at nightclubs and 'rave' venues, all fuelled an anxiety on the part of parents and the forces of law and order which grew into another moral panic. In some respects it seemed that drug taking was threatening to become as endemic in British society as drunkenness was in the Soviet Union. It all linked with the big fear of the 1980s – AIDS – the causes of which were in dispute, but the effects undoubted. AIDS was a killer disease, and had connections with drug use, among other things. The century thus came to a close with youth as much a problem as it had been at any time over the previous 50 years.

This takes us to a final dimension of the 'problem of leisure'. It has historically been conceived of as an area in which self-appointed critics have claimed to perceive the shortcomings of other people's leisure and, further, to know what has been required to 'improve' it. This position has manifested itself in many different ways and in varying degrees of formality. It has traditionally been concerned with male leisure, indeed it has often proceeded on the assumption that leisure is a male prerogative. With the growth of feminist history, especially since the early 1970s, this paradigm has been challenged, an attempt has been made to place women's leisure more prominently on the map, the attempt has had important implications for related issues of race and age, and the cumulative effect of all this has done something to ensure that the previously excluded will not be overlooked in the future discussion and provision of leisure.

BRINGING OLDER PEOPLE INTO LEISURE

The relationship between leisure and youth has none the less been so intimately constructed that the broader issues of leisure and age have been almost
completely overlooked. In Western societies, where old age has in some social
circumstances been associated with a decline of production and achievement,
the elderly have traditionally not possessed the same levels of respect
accorded to them in non-industrial societies, where their experience and accumulated wisdom place them in high esteem.[44] Earlier in the century, in manual
labour particularly, men reached their peak of productivity at around the age
of 40. The later years of life were a period of declining labour power which
had to be stretched out as far as possible because of the absence of any adequate retirement pension. Thus the conventional social concern in Britain with
the connection between old age and poverty; the workhouse in Victorian times
was usually populated not by the unemployed, but by the old. Moreover,
there were signs in the later twentieth century that in those fields where geron-
tocracy had endured – business, education, politics – leadership was passing
to a notably younger age group. This is clear in the high-profile leadership
of politics. British prime ministers, for instance, are getting younger, with
Tony Blair elected in 1997 in his early forties, and a Leader of the Opposition
younger still. At the same time, people are living longer and the proportion
of elderly people in the population is increasing. At the beginning of the
century just under 5 per cent of the population was aged 65 and over. By the
end of the century the figure had increased steadily to almost 16 per cent, a
greater proportion of whom were women. It was estimated that by 2021 the
proportion of people aged 65 and over in the population would total almost
20 per cent, with 2.3 per cent being aged 85 or over (compared with 0.2 per
cent in 1901).[45] This in itself has given rise to panics, if not yet of a moral nature
then at least of a fiscal one. In the 1980s the prospect of a large public welfare
responsibility for the care of the old in the twenty-first century was being
anticipated by governments committed to a reduction of direct taxation. An
image was communicated through political discourse of a helpless, degener-
ated and above all costly group of elderly people who would be a 'burden on
the taxpayer'; it helped to create a stereotype of old age that suited political
strategies, but which was not necessarily consistent with the reality of later
life. It nevertheless justified the shifting of provision for old age over to the
private sector, with a consequent rise in the business conducted by insurance
and financial companies and private retirement homes. Such fears of a large
and unproductive group of the elderly were confounded by the reality of old
age in the late twentieth century.

Like youth, age is a socially constructed category that changes with
historical circumstances, and the fact was that many of the old were active
citizens with much to contribute socially and culturally to their community.
The middle-aged, a group whose chronological definition has shifted over the
course of the twentieth century from the 30–50 to the 40–60 band, have been
particularly identified as an important market, for whom life-style choices are
provided in sports goods, motor cars and a wide range of leisure products

and services, from food and drink, to music and holidays. John Benson, one of only a small group of historians to look closely at age in historical terms, has significantly entitled his book on middle age *Prime Time*.[46]

For those who have reached an age where regular salaried work has ceased – late middle or old age – their lives might seem to represent endless 'free time': 'I always reckon my life's one long holiday. We can do what we like, and have a cup of tea when you feel like it, have a walk round the garden. . . .'[47] Leisure for the old, however, is curtailed by a variety of factors, the chief ones being finance, infirmity and isolation. It is a common feature of ageing that people are relatively less affluent than when in work, and also enjoy more limited physical mobility. In fact, a good deal of an elderly person's day might be taken up sleeping or dozing. Not least in importance is isolation, bearing in mind that some 20 per cent of men and almost half of all women over the age of 65 live alone.[48]

These constraints shaped the daily round of hobbies and pastimes enjoyed by a group of 55 elderly people who formed the core of a study of ageing carried out by Paul Thompson, Catherine Itzin and Michele Abendstern in the 1970s and 1980s.[49] The sample is, of course, not typical, especially in that all its members are by definition survivors into old age and have therefore displayed some degree of resourcefulness in giving meaning to their later life. But the accounts given to the research team illustrate a rich variety of leisure activity: gardening, walking, golf, motor trips and holidays, in addition to home-based hobbies and the ubiquitous television watching. For some, around a quarter of those interviewed, making leisure in retirement was a struggle, and for these people the television presumably consumed much of their 'free' time. The majority, on the other hand, showed a capacity to use their time creatively, even taking up new hobbies such as dancing and toy making in their 70s. Though sociability was important for all of them, there was a refreshing resistance to the idea of old people's clubs; the notion of being organized was treated with scorn and, indeed, the researchers concluded on the basis of this that age-related leisure is something to be avoided in public policy. 'Ghetto-izing' the elderly through assumptions about a culture of old age is perhaps not a good idea. Thus a study of leisure helps in some ways to demythologize the process of ageing.

CONCLUSION

The issue of age and leisure should have reminded us that historians have often neglected the concept of age in studying society. Where social class, and more recently gender, have attracted much interest and debate, age has been at the margins. Yet it is so clearly important. In leisure we have seen how the physical opportunites and limitations of age have affected what is and is not possible for people to engage in. More importantly, perhaps, we have seen how some sections of the population are, because of their age, likely to be viewed with alarm, and to become the object of ameliorative action. The persistence with which older groups, arrogating to themselves some kind of moral superiority, have set their sights on 'youth' has been a striking feature of the twentieth century, as of earlier ones. Young people have long been everybody else's favourite folk devils. This aspect of age relations has been one of the main themes of this chapter. It might be criticized for not focusing enough on the creative activities of young people themselves. Their energies and contribution to a wide area of leisure, and other areas of social life, are not underestimated. Indeed, they are assumed in the main argument of the foregoing discussion, which is that age relations have changed over the course of the century. The moral and intellectual leadership (in Gramscian language) once exercised by older people over the young, many of whom were their (grand)sons and (grand)daughters, was lost at some point in the later 1950s and into the 1960s. A 'crisis of hegemony' ensued. This sounds cataclysmic, but all it amounted to was the creation by many young people of their own space, their own style, and their own set of values. In many ways the Punk movement provided the most exaggerated example of this process. They were no longer just 'apprenticed adults', or at least they thought so. In the last analysis, however, all the youth sub-cultures were reabsorbed by the commercial system. All the breakaway bands which had sought to express themselves individually outside the controls of the record-producing companies were brought back, or their styles were, into what became a new mainstream. The power of money prevailed in the end, utilizing the ideas of rebellious youth.

Key Reading

Benson, J. *Prime Time: A History of the Middle Aged in Twentieth Century Britain*. London: Longman, 1997.

Brake, M. *Comparative Youth Culture: The Sociology of Youth Culture and Youth Sub-cultures in America, Britain and Canada*. London: Routledge and Kegan Paul, 1985.

Cohen, S. *Folk Devils and Moral Panics: The Creation of the Mods and Rockers*. London: MacGibbon and Kee, 1972.

McRobbie, A. *Feminism and Youth Culture: From 'Jackie' to 'Just Seventeen'*. Basingstoke: Macmillan – now Palgrave, 1991.

Osgerby, B. *Youth in Britain Since 1945*. Oxford: Blackwell, 1998.

Chronology of Events

1855 Foundation of the Young Women's Christian Association.

1876 Foundation of Girls' Friendly Society

1883 Foundation of Boys' Brigade.

1891 Foundation of Church Lads' Brigade.

1908 Foundation of the Boy Scouts (Wolf Cubs started 1916); some 140 000 scouts by 1913.

1910 Girl Guides formed (1913 YWCA formed a Guides section, which affiliated to the Girl Guides, as did the Girls' Friendly Society in 1915).

1923 Formation of the National Association of Boys' Clubs.

1939 Board of Education established the Youth Service to bring together the work on youth of voluntary organizations, local education authorities and the central state.

1944 Education Act, confirming many existing local education authority practices, established grammar and secondary modern schools following a test at age 11 (the 'eleven plus'), and raised the school-leaving age to 15 (put into effect in 1947).

***c.*1953** Appearance of the Teddy Boys, the first distinctive (working-class) youth movement of the post-war years.

1956 John Osborne's play *Look Back In Anger* established the 'angry young man'; first showing in Britain of *Rock Around the Clock*, accompanied by riotous scenes in cinemas, followed by tour of Bill Hayley and the Comets in 1957.

1960 Report of the Albemarle Committee on the Youth Service in England and Wales; end of National Service (men born after September 1939 not called up).

1961 Contraceptive pill widely used in Britain.

1962 Beatles' first hit, *Love Me Do,* followed by their second, bigger hit *Please Please Me* (1963).

1963 Robbins Report on higher education proposed an increase in the number of university places, on the principle that those qualified should be entitled to take up a place in higher education.

1968 Demonstrations and occupations by students at various British universities.

***c.*1976–79** Emergence of the Punk youth culture.

1980–81 Riots in major British cities involving young people, often from Afro-Caribbean families.

1984–87 Government sponsored campaign against drugs and AIDS.

1993 Establishment of the Child Support Agency to help single mothers and their children by enforcing maintenance payments from absent fathers.

chapter 8

The Club

Principle

CONTENTS

Marx considered British working men to be great 'joiners': their support for clubs of all kinds outstripped even that of their mutualist-inclined French counterparts. It was a habit that prompted the French literary brothers Goncourt to remark that the first thing two Englishmen would do if cast away on a desert island would be to form a club. Voluntary association was, indeed, a classic British cultural form, stretching back at least to the eighteenth century.[1] A report commissioned by the National Council for Voluntary Organizations in 1996 estimated that there were somewhere in the region of 200 000–240 000 voluntary bodies in Britain, involving some 21 million people. On this broad reckoning of voluntarism, around 14 per cent of all bodies were concerned with 'culture and recreation'.[2] Of all the sectors in which British sports and leisure pursuits are to be found it is the voluntary – the one created by people themselves as part of everyday life – that is the most extensive and deeply embedded, reaching into the very fabric of social life. In 1973 the House of Lords Select Committee on Sport and Leisure noted that voluntary clubs had been the 'life blood' of sports provision, with over 100 different governing bodies having some 110 000 affiliated clubs.[3] For a sense of the range of interests on which clubs and societies are habitually based across the whole range of leisure, the following list from an Open University publication captures something of the comprehensiveness of British voluntary association:

> model-building, brass band playing, singing, amateur dramatics, arts and crafts, dancing, wine-making, sweet-pea growing, various ethnic arts, flower arranging,

bell-ringing, archeology, astronomy, family history, folk music, gardening, natural history, rambling, stamp collecting, public speaking – and so on almost indefinitely.[4]

Indeed, as Bishop and Hoggett have observed in studying this area of leisure activity: 'people will join together to form groups around anything which provides the slightest opportunity for organization'.[5] The club as a focus of sport or leisure exists in numerous forms and for varied purposes. There are, as the authors just cited have also pointed out, differences between those clubs which are formally organized as self-help groups, where collective action and mutual aid to generate a specific outcome is the purpose, and those which rely on an 'external' form of organization such as evening classes. Furthermore, they note the existence of the more informal group, a 'fraternity' rather than a club – trainspotters are the example given – but which none the less depends strongly on self-organization.[6] Beyond this it is possible to perceive different levels of activity, in the sense that some such groups form associations which operate in a national context whilst others, perhaps the majority, are best understood as fulfilling a local purpose. A clear example of the former would be the Marylebone Cricket Club (MCC) which, until the 1960s, was effectively the governing body of cricket in England, though remaining a private and very exclusive male club.[7] It was one of only a few examples of this type, others being the Jockey Club and, for a time at least, the British Olympic Association, the All-England Tennis and Croquet Club, and the Royal and Ancient Club of St Andrews. Other governing bodies – the Football Association or the Amateur Athletics Association – were not clubs in this sense, although they might informally have developed something of a club ethos as a result of their lengthy existence and the limited circulation of personnel among their leading officials. In all cases, however, such associations shared with the multitude of local sports and leisure clubs a feature which distinguishes this leisure sector from the other two with which we have been concerned; namely, that of making their own sport or leisure associations subject themselves to a process of democratic governance. They have a constitution and a continuing existence, and they are run by committees which, at least in theory, are responsible to the membership, and which must therefore submit themselves periodically to re-election by popular vote. This process depends, of course, upon a willingness on the part of members to give active participation to the democratic spirit. Participation, however, is not always given, which explains why associations, both national and local, can become self-perpetuating oligarchies run by the committed minority.

CLUBS, COMMUNITIES AND LEISURE

Given the seemingly all-embracing nature of its activities, and a constitutional foundation which is common to all clubs and societies, the question then arises as to whether voluntary association has the capacity to bring a broad social mix under its umbrella. Marx's observation on the working man's predilection for clubs is an apposite one in this context, though perhaps less applicable for the twentieth century than it might have been in his own day. It prompts the thought that, contrary to what Marx was implying, it has been the middle classes who, in recent British history, have been most closely involved with voluntary association. In their 1950s survey of the suburb of Woodford, a largely though not exclusively middle-class area on the northern margins of London, Willmott and Young identified an interesting feature in the relationship between social class and clubs. They found a distinct difference between middle- and working-class residents in the area; a far higher proportion of the latter did not attend and did not take out membership of clubs and societies, even though there was a wealth of such organizations to be found in the community.[8] The explanation for this difference is doubtless explained by the investment of time and money needed to sustain club life, the better-off social groups therefore being privileged in terms of the resources they are able to commit to voluntary association. Moreover, the institutional sociability of clubs and societies helps to make up for the more privatized lifestyle of middle-class suburbs like Woodford, where people were much less in contact with relatives than they had been in the older communities from which many residents had migrated. When working-class communities are considered it has often not been clubs that have characterized their cultural activity. They exist, to be sure, but it is the more informal ties of neighbourhood, family and work that provide the foundations of communal life. 'Sociability, in such a setting, needs no organization', observe Willmott and Young.[9] 'Sociability' was something that happened in street, market, pub or work – rarely at home, though for everyone family ties were the essential bond of communality.[10]

That other great popular institution the public house (of which Marx also had inside knowledge[11]) has played a much bigger part in working-class leisure. In fact, the relative paucity of voluntary associations in older urban working-class neighbourhoods might be accounted for by the existence of the pub, and particularly by its subsuming of many of the functions of clubs and societies into its own extensive range of sport and leisure activities.[12] Although in one sense a commercial enterprise, the pub has exercised since Victorian times a far firmer cultural hold on its habituees than other commercial outlets such as shops and cinemas, performing a number of roles which made of it a focal point of community life. The modern leisure centre has not matched it in this respect. To begin with, it was a place of essentially male sociability. Although, as Andrew Davies's research on Salford has shown, the pub could in some neighbourhoods be an important source of women's leisure, it was generally a place where strict boundaries were drawn between male and female spaces.[13] *Coronation Street's* portrayal of the 'snug' as a sanctuary for the older women drinkers, who for reasons of respectability would not have ventured into the public bar, was a fairly accurate depiction of the lines of segregation in most older pubs, especially in the North. For the men, whose homes probably offered little in the way of leisure opportunities before the arrival of television, the pub provided not only drink but companionship and a host of links with the community at large. Social historians have surprisingly said little, except in work specifically directed to the problem of 'the drink'[14], about the pub's general functions. But in the valuable survey carried out by Mass-Observation in 'Worktown' (Bolton) just before the Second World War, some interesting features emerge which are no doubt typical of pubs in many places at this time.

In Bolton the pubs were important as locations for certain sporting pursuits. Pigeon-racing, fishing and dog-showing were all sports carried out in venues away from the pub, but which used the pub as their base. Within the pub a number of other sports were practised: cards, darts and dominoes were the most popular, whilst it was observed that the old pastime of quoits seemed to be dying out. Bowls was commonly played on greens attached to pubs. As well as physical games of these kinds, pubs were places where people placed bets, sang, played the piano, listened to others doing so, or simply drank their beer. They served as meeting places for mutual-aid societies such as the Oddfellows or the 'Buffs' (Buffaloes). Mass-Observation did *not* encounter in Bolton pubs the activities of billiards, whist, skittles, shove-ha'penny or dancing, though presumably these would have been found elsewhere. To these pastimes could be added, for pubs on the outskirts of towns with access to open spaces, games like knur and spell, or the organizing of annual carnivals and processions. Pubs did not promote sports such as football, cricket, tennis or golf in Bolton; these were either based on works premises or had their own clubs which, for tennis, golf and cricket were described as 'pubs for middle classites'. In a wider social and economic sense pubs fulfilled a variety of non-leisure functions such as job-seeking, the holding of trade union meetings, venues for criminals and the hatching of crimes, and the hosting of special neighbourhood events such as weddings and funerals.[15]

Mass-Observation, as with so many of the other objects of its attention, drew a somewhat romantic inference from the activities of pubs. They were regarded as a form of working-class life that by the time of the Second World War was changing, possibly for the worse. The pub's communal omnipresence, its spontaneous sociability, and the 'democratic' nature of the play associated with it ('it is the only kind of public building used by large numbers of ordinary people where their thoughts and actions are *not* being in some way arranged for them'[16]) was felt to be under threat from new leisure forms – motor cars, dance halls, the cinema – where a less collective experience was being offered.[17] To an extent this was a fair assessment, vindicated at least by evidence from some of the newer working-class housing estates that were beginning to appear in the inter-war period. Problems of isolation were particularly acute for married women in such an environment, but more generally, the kind of sociability that had characterized the working-class districts from which the residents of the new estates had removed seemed to be disappearing, replaced by a home-based existence. The marginalizing of the pub summed this up. On housing estates the pubs were fewer, indeed some local authorities refused to allow them at all. When they were encountered they were less gender specific, but also less friendly, often large establishments some distance away which catered for a motorized clientele and lacked the intimacy of the old neighbourhood beer shop, the 'local' as it was usually and accurately known.[18]

Alongside the pub as a focus for working-class leisure was the working-men's club. It combined some of the features of the pub, though possessed many distinctive qualities of its own; it was not 'tied' to a particular brewery, it was run by its own committee, and it therefore retained the profits accruing from its activities. In many areas, particularly in the north of England, the clubs were affiliated to the Club and Institute Union (CIU), an organization founded by the Unitarian clergyman Henry Solly in the 1860s as part of an attempt to instil 'improving' leisure in the working classes by combating ignorance and intemperance. By the 1940s the CIU had some 3000 affiliated clubs. When Brian Jackson conducted a survey of the clubs in the 1960s he found 70 affiliated to the CIU in Huddersfield alone.[19] Their official purpose was, as McKibbin has noted, 'to promote mutuality, improvement, and rational recreation' and thus meet the approval of the Registrar General of Friendly Societies.[20] In practice they were havens of male drinking. During the Second World War the Trades Union Congress, as part of a wider campaign on the 'problem of leisure', approached the CIU for its views on this issue; the enquiry elicited a reply from the CIU secretary which was revealing about the organization's activities. Clearly feeling that he should emphasize as far as possible the movement's moral purpose, the secretary assumed an apologetic stance:

> [T]he great majority of working men, perhaps because their school education finished at the early age of 14, or possibly before then, are not inclined, having reached manhood, to engage in any form of education which involves study, and the promotion of education by the Union has been an uphill struggle.[21]

He went on to say that the greatest interest was to be found in games and sports, along with concerts, flower shows, and dances. He acknowledged that women were not generally admitted in their own right, attending the clubs only as guests of the men. Writing of clubs some 20 years later, Brian Jackson found them still hanging on to their special masculine character, though now more receptive to the presence of women. He found only one club in Huddersfield that did not admit women into its main building (only into the adjoining concert room).[22]

The vitality of pubs and working-men's clubs paradoxically points up the narrowness of club life within working-class communities, and reinforces the notion that the classic *locus* of voluntary association is in a different social milieu. This is not to deny that its importance in organizing sport and leisure in Britain has been high. Indeed, a British 'ideal type' of sport and leisure development, if such a thing can be characterized, would be one in which initiative rests with private people in their self-organized groups, rather than in a market provision and certainly rather than in the hands of the state. This, as we shall see, has given rise in Britain to a particular ethos in sport which is best described as 'amateurism' – the notion that sport should be organized for the athletic pleasure it provides for individuals and groups, and that this is its chief purpose, rather than winning or money making. It is an ethos which has at times been strongly expressed in leading associations such as the MCC, the FA and the AAA, and which is closely linked to a particular class position.[23] But before taking up this theme, it is important to examine the nature and purpose of voluntary association at the level where it actually generates the activity upon which the national associations are built: the locality.

Perhaps the most startling fact about local associations of all kinds at this level is their sheer number. Some 4000 active associations were recorded in Birmingham in the 1970s, whilst in Milton Keynes, a town of 90000 population, there were around 500 at the same time.[24] At Kingswood, Bristol, with a population of 85000, there were around 300 such groups; 228 in north-west Leicester (population 68000), the majority of them formed in the 1970s; over 70 in the small market town of Banbury (population 20000) in the 1950s. One survey, conducted at the end of the 1960s, concluded that over half of all adult men and a third of all women in Britain held club membership of some kind.[25]

The history (as opposed to the contemporary sociology) of this aspect of sport and leisure development has not been given much attention, especially when compared to the interest displayed in the commercial sector. One exception is the work of Helen Meller, which examines the organization of leisure in Bristol in the half-century before the First World War. Meller uncovers a rich seam of voluntary association, much of it concerned either with the provision of leisure for middle-class groups, or with the dissemination of good leisure habits to the masses. The former tended to claim priority and Meller sees the 'sporting revolution' of the late nineteenth century as essentially a middle-class suburban one, 'not a means for promoting social integration and the civic spirit, but . . . a reflection of the socio-economic division in society'.[26]

Sociological analysis tends to underpin Meller's conclusions. One of the most fruitful subjects of sociological work has been the detailed local community study, devoted to a careful dissection of the structure, function and relationships of institutions and people. A series of such studies conducted mainly in the 1950s (the timing is interesting in itself) are now celebrated as classics of their type. They cover a range of different communities, small and large, new and old, urban and rural, and though their vision is more panoramic than the subject of sport and leisure, they are none the less revealing about the workings of clubs and associations in this particular domain. A brief detour through this canon of sociological study will be valuable for us in establishing the place of the club and society in local life.

Beginning with the smallest community, there is Frankenberg's analysis of the North Wales village of Glynceiriog in the early 1950s.[27] It portrays a community of some 200 people, strongly bound by ties of kinship, chapel and the Welsh language, which created in this small environment a group of clubs in the sphere of leisure alone which covered football, garden produce, sheep-dog training, sewing and the village carnival. The football club and the village carnival committee were particularly important because they provided the village with a symbol of identity and unity in relation to other places. In the quite different Yorkshire mining town of 'Ashton' (Featherstone), studied by Dennis, Henriques and Slaughter in their study of the mid-1950s, the dominance of mining as an occupation produced distinctive features of cultural life.[28] Most leisure activities were bound up with work and the pit, and were severely masculine. Leisure, for miners and their families, was sensuous, a pursuit of hedonism. It was based either on the miners' lodge (trade union branch) or on the Miners' Welfare, a cultural institution formed nationally in the aftermath of the First World War and run jointly by the coal owners (the Coal Board from 1947) and the miners' trade union. Drinking played a big part in leisure, and thus the various pubs together with the working men's clubs, of which there were six, were the centres of attention. Sport (cricket) and the St John Ambulance Brigade were also significant voluntary activities, but the other big leisure interests, rugby league and bingo, were offered through the commercial sector. In Ashton only the Labour Party's women's section catered for women's voluntary leisure. A community of slightly larger size – Glossop, a Derbyshire textile town a dozen or so miles from Manchester – was the subject of a study conducted by a team led by A. H. Birch.[29] Birch estimated there to be around 100 voluntary associations in the town,[30] the population of which was just under 20000. Those concerned with leisure included a variety of sports clubs – golf, tennis, bowls, for example – and, as in Ashton, associations which existed specifically for female leisure, the Townswomen's Guild and the Women's Institute being the main ones.

In contrast to these communities, each of which was settled in the sense of having established institutional forms and a mixture of social groups, there were newer communities where the studies conducted were designed in part to determine how far a sense of community had developed. In the study made in the early 1950s by Lupton and Mitchell of a Liverpool housing estate established during the Second World War, it was perhaps not surprising that few voluntary associations came to light.[31] As in Ashton, though in different form, a variety of recreational activities was organized in this community under the auspices of one body, in this case a Residents' Association. Its events tended to take place under one roof, a Community Centre whose main attraction was its bar.[32] This example followed a similar situation that had arisen in Watling, an estate set up on the fringes of north London in the 1920s and studied by Ruth Durant in 1939. Here a residents' association had also endeavoured to cohere the activities of the new residents, initially with some success, but later subjected to factionalism.[33] The lack of individual autonomous clubs on such estates, in contrast with other places, is explained by their relative newness and the absence of prior activity; for example, only three separate associations were in being at the time of the Liverpool study – the British Legion, and clubs for catering, poultry-keeping and drama. As we have seen, there was a problem on housing estates of maintaining the forms of communal sociability found in older working-class neighbourhoods, and in both Watling and Liverpool the attempts by the residents' associations to create a collective culture met with only partial success.

Perhaps the most intimate account of the daily operation of voluntary associations in a single community was Margaret Stacey's study in the 1950s of the Oxfordshire town of Banbury.[34] Excluding formal religious or political organizations Stacey found 71 voluntary associations in Banbury, a town of similar size to Glossop. They ranged from 'a sweet pea society to a rugger club, from university lectures to tropical fish keeping, from charitable organizations to trade unions'.[35] Stacey divided them into eight categories: sport, hobbies, cultural (such as music societies), social (e.g. Townswomen's Guild), social service (e.g. Toc H), charity, mutual aid (insurance societies) and occupational associations (e.g. trade unions).[36] In the main these associations were peopled and run by men, those concerned with sports and hobbies especially so. Frequently, however, there was a distinctive age characteristic, with the sports clubs being middle-aged and constantly therefore seeking to reproduce themselves by acquiring new recruits.

All of the studies underline the fact that voluntary association was, in one form or another, not only an important ingredient of sport and leisure, but a vital feature of community life in general. In fact, the purpose of the studies was to examine the significance that voluntary associations had in the totality of social life in the chosen communities. In this the timing of the studies, with a significant clustering of them in the 1950s, suggested not simply a case of academic fashion, but also a concern about the nature of the society developing in post-war Britain, particularly the social strains and tensions present in the so-called 'age of affluence'. There was implicit in these enquiries an awareness of social bonds, and the effect on them of changes brought about by social mobility. Fundamentally, the issue was one of what the later American social scientist James S. Coleman described as 'social capital' – the system of social networks, norms and trust which provide a basis of mutual organization and benefit. At its most sublime level this issue can become one about the very foundations of democracy itself, as in Robert D. Putnam's celebrated case of the decline of American 'civic engagement', epitomized in the rise of solo-bowling – 'bowling alone'.[37]

In this respect the presence of so many clubs and societies in Britain might have had a reassuring effect, suggesting that they existed to provide access to all who wished to join, and that voluntary activity in its entirety therefore bore witness to a pluralist society capable of encompasssing the views and interests of all its members. However, each of the studies so far examined revealed this to have been far from the case. The over-riding effect produced by the operations of voluntary associations led much more to social differentiation, and in some cases to social exclusion.

Perhaps the most striking instance of this process comes, not from Britain itself, but from Britain's recent colonial past, and the complex hierarchies of race and class constructed around club cricket in the Caribbean. C. L. R. James has noted his dilemma, as an educated black man in Trinidad, over which cricket club to join: Queen's Park was for wealthy whites and mulattos; Shamrock catered for white Roman Catholics; Shannon was for black lower middle-class people; Stingo for working-class blacks; and Maple was a brownskin middle-class club.[38] Brian Stoddart's analysis of club cricket in this region, particularly Barbados, shows that this subtle alignment of clubs with both race and social status was pervasive throughout the Caribbean. It created hidden separations in otherwise united combinations. Thus the greatest of all white batting partnerships for the West Indies, that of Challenor and Tarilton before and after the First World War, masked a status distinction between the two men off the field; Challenor was from a wealthy planter family and could play for the prestigious Wanderers club, whilst Tarilton, a Parochial Treasurer in Barbados, had lower social status and played for Pickwick. '[I]n Barbados such different social circles rarely mixed.'[39] Neither club contained a black cricketer. None mixed black and white. And yet, as Stoddart points out, cricket worked alongside economic and political power to reproduce the cultural values and therefore leadership of the white elite well beyond the First World War.

In Britain itself similar distinctions of class and status, gender and ethnicity attended the operations of club life. In Ashton, for example, the most working class of the communities studied in the 1950s, it might be expected that work and leisure would take on a strongly proletarian and masculine character. The main divisions therefore seemed to hinge around gender. There was little work available for women, and thus marked barriers between the male and the female spheres developed. Most of the leisure activities in the town were for men – the colliery band, sports teams, the working men's clubs and the angling club. Women's leisure was far more restricted, indeed 'for many women with young children the cinema is the sole relaxation outside the home'.[40] 'Callin' – visiting other people's houses for a chat and a gossip – was the principal leisure activity for Ashton women. Even when the sexes were apparently taking leisure together, in the selection for example of the local 'Rugby League Queen', a popular ritual which displayed that Ashton 'possesses beautiful women as well as stong and skilful men', a clear distinction between the functions of the sexes was created.[41] In Glynceiriog, on the other hand, the distinctions that operated in voluntary associations were mainly around status and class. 'Outsiders' – those who either came from outside the physical confines of the village, or who did not share the social class, linguistic and religious culture of locals – were none the less accepted into village life according to their status and money. Thus, positions as presidents or patrons of clubs were filled by higher status outsiders, whilst 'working' roles like that of club secretary, were occupied by 'intellectuals' (teachers, doctor, chemist) who lacked status, but were none the less accepted for their clerical skills.[42]

In Glossop the lines of demarcation by status were even plainer. Birch found that membership of most voluntary associations was fairly evenly divided amongst the social classes, but a small group of industrial and public service leaders and managers, with no local background and few social connections in the town, colonized a series of clubs through which they preserved their social separateness; the golf club was the prime example. Other status distinctions were noticeable, for example in the contrast between the Brass Band (industrial workers) and the music and repertory societies (professional and white collar). On the whole, though, the major difference in membership was a gender one: men rather than women joined clubs and societies.[43] Similar patterns were evident in the Lancashire industrial town of Nelson, a community in the 1920s of some 40000 people. The cricket club, which played an important part in civic life and which was a mark of Nelson's identity in the outside world, possessed a large membership. In many respects it spanned the town's social range. But its leadership was notably middle class, and politically it expressed a position that was at variance with that of the town council, which was solidly Labour.[44] In some respects Nelson was like Ashton, though it differed in that the work available to women gave them a status in both the economy and social life that would not have been possible in coal mining. Thus leisure in Nelson was less rigidly subjected to the gender divisions seen in Ashton. What it did develop, especially following migration into that area of north-east Lancashire from the Indian sub-continent in the early 1960s, was a racial demarcation. It was noticeable that in cricket, one of the most popular sports in the area, Asian people formed their own teams and played in their own leagues.[45] In nearby Bolton, which has been the subject of detailed research by Jack Williams, there was a rapid increase in the numbers of Asian cricket clubs in the 1980s and 1990s. Though there was no separate Asian league, there was a restriction of the Asian clubs to a particular stratum of local cricket, with none of them playing in the leagues which were recognized as having the highest standards of play. Moreover, among the Asian clubs themselves there were many religious, linguistic and geographical differences reflecting the various identities at work within the overall 'Asian' community. Bolton, some 7 per cent of whose population in the early 1990s was of Asian descent, is clearly not a typical town, but its leisure patterns reveal some of the influences of race that were first discerned by Ruth Glass in her pioneering work of the late 1950s.[46]

In Banbury, in addition to the gender and age profile already noted, there was also a marked social-class divergence in club membership. Stacey sums this up, and simultaneously illuminates what is possibly the central function of voluntary association, when she remarks of Banbury's sports clubs: 'Banbury people do not engage in sport as an exercise in competitive athleticism but as an occasion for social intercourse: as a competitor remarked of a tennis tournament in which he was playing, "these do's are 75 per cent social and 25 per cent tennis".'[47] Students of electoral behaviour have noted that voting preference is dictated less by what people vote *for* than by whom they vote *with*, and we might adapt this observation to the study of sports and leisure clubs: they exist to preserve social identity as much as to purvey athletic activity.

Stacey's examination of the complex interplay of voluntary association membership in Banbury brings us to a point which takes the discussion of sport and leisure into a different sphere. In a manner reminiscent of Lewis Namier's microscopic analysis of the eighteenth-century House of Commons, Stacey traces the 'connexions' and 'networks' that came into being between different elements of Banbury's voluntary associations. What is equally important, she makes the connections between voluntary association and the town's political life. To give a small illustration of her otherwise lengthy and detailed deconstruction, we might take the example of Banbury's sports clubs, of which there were several, though none, significantly, which bore the town's name. Stacey found two levels of clubs, which she named Sports I and Sports II. The first was composed of rugby, cricket, tennis and hunting clubs. It had two distinctive characteristics. One was the high proportion of committee members who lived outside the borough, which showed that these clubs served to bring farmers from the outlying districts into contact with the social life of the town. The second was the high occupational status of the group's members – who either owned above-average size farms or were professional and business people from the town itself. Freemasonry was present in this group, and while they did not have any formal links with political or religious organizations, the members of Sports I were 'overwhelmingly' Conservative and Anglican. The other category of sports clubs – Sports II – was made up of a different cricket club, the table tennis league, Post Office sports, and the Comrades' Club; all sports requiring little in the way of expensive equipment, and all therefore accessible to the less well off. Societies such as the Foresters, Oddfellows and Buffaloes were represented. Stacey included Sports II in the 'lower part of the Conservative connexion'. Conservatism thus emerged as the centre of gravity of much associational life, with Liberalism acting as the focus for a second, but much less powerful network. Except for trade union activity, Labour possessed scarcely any network of its own, and what it did have was made up of low-status, immigrant (non-Banbury) workers.[48]

CLUBS, CLASS AND STATUS: THE AMATEUR ETHOS

The Banbury case study brings out important points about the function of club life in class formation, and has been used by Ross McKibbin to illustrate profound shifts that were taking place in British society in the middle years of the century.[49] Clubs of the kind found in Banbury were central to a social process in which the middle classes were re-formed into a more homogeneous, though certainly not monolithic, grouping, over a period which stretched from the 1920s to the 1950s. Crucial to this process was the fashioning of an a-political consciousness that enabled some of the continuing fractions within the class – principally those connected with religion – to be overlain with shared values. Some of these were supplied by the sense of 'other' arising from the growth of Labour as a political force at this time. The haste with which hitherto opposed elements of the middle class, their political allegiances previously divided between Conservative and Liberal, conjoined in anti-socialist alliances during the 1920s testifies to the influence of external forces in shaping these shared values.[50] But internally, so to speak, middle-class consciousness also depended upon the existence of an ethos which voluntary association provided. The strictly hierarchical world of local clubs and societies generated this ethos. As McKibbin puts it, the clubs operated on a set of conventions about 'proper' behaviour among the 'right sort' of people, who would not be 'embarrassed', and qualities such as 'niceness' and 'humour' could be encouraged.[51] It was a code that eschewed violent or impassioned commitment, and in which politics was in effect depoliticized. The Conservative Party under Stanley Baldwin in the 1920s aligned with it perfectly, making Conservatism the 'natural' home for all 'neutral' opinion. 'I give expression', proclaimed Baldwin on a famous occasion, 'in some unaccountable way, to what the English people think.'[52]

Sports clubs fitted this ethos perfectly. It is McKibbin's contention that within a middle-class milieu, sport existed to promote sociability and minimize the disruptive consequences of competitivism. At a local so at a national level this credo applied, sustaining outmoded conceptions of amateurism and ultimately doing much harm to the international competitiveness and standing of British sport.[53] There is certainly much evidence at the national level that a gentlemanly, clubbable atmosphere prevailed in British sports. It was responsible, most obviously, for the maintenance until the 1960s of a social divide between amateurs and professionals in cricket. Much of the public display of social difference (separate changing rooms and points of entry on to the field of play for amateurs and professionals, for example) had disappeared by the late 1940s,[54] though one revealing linguistic ritual remained: the granting to the amateur in the press results of matches of full initials *before* the surname (thus P. B. H. May), as against the designation of professionals either by initials *after* the surname, or simply by surname. There is a good story about the first appearance by Fred Titmus for Middlesex at Lord's in the late 1940s, when the printers of the match scorecard had made a mistake which gave to Titmus, a professional, amateur status (F. J. Titmus). The mistake was spotted by the ground authorities, and rectified by hourly announcements on the public address system to the effect that 'F. J. Titmus' should read 'Titmus, F. J.'[55] Amateurism was discontinued in 1963 mainly because it was becoming increasingly difficult for amateur players to play the game in an unpaid capacity. Many were having to resort to covert professionalism by taking paid sinecures on the staff of the county clubs.[56] As may be imagined, however, it took some time for old social habits to die out, and even in the 1970s the selectors of the England test team were looking for a captain who displayed amateur characteristics, which chiefly meant being 'the right sort'. It was doubtful whether Ray Illingworth, a Leicestershire and former Yorkshire cricketer who enjoyed some success as England's captain between 1969 and 1972, really lived up to this image, and the selectors clearly favoured the counter claims of the Glamorgan player Tony Lewis. He had made his first appearance as an amateur (A. R. Lewis) and had been educated at Cambridge University, where, moreover, he also played rugger.

Even in the more commercialized game of soccer the amateur spirit prevailed for a long time. It manifested itself both in the Football Association, which had an upper-class, old-school-tie atmosphere reflected in its elegant headquarters at Lancaster Gate opposite Hyde Park, and in the more provincial and down-to-earth world of the Football League. Soccer had accommodated professionalism without suffering the splits that affected rugby, but the professional players were treated without much respect for the most part, and there were a number of ways in which 'professionalism' in the sport was resisted: club shareholders placed a ceiling on the dividends they paid to themselves, betting and the football pools were opposed, radio and television were regarded as threats to attendances at matches and therefore held at arm's length, and overseas developments in the game were largely ignored. It was in this last respect that the amateurism of British football was most starkly exposed, for it resulted in the decline of British teams in international competition, a fact made plain by the England team's mediocre performance in the 1950 World Cup competition, followed by its humiliation by Hungary at Wembley in 1953. This match, astounding to most soccer supporters as much for the manner in which Hungary's victory was achieved as for the margin (6 goals to 3), called forth a torrent of criticism from the popular 'modernizing' press. Roy Peskett of the *Daily Mail* captured the mood of reform which seized most sports correspondents at the time when he saw in the match an implicit contrast between a dynamic European continent able to learn, adapt and innovate, and a moribund England in danger of being left behind in the world.[57] The target of much press criticism was the gentlemanly and outmoded attitudes of the Football Association, now clearly overtaken by the rational planning evident in the Hungarians' approach to football. One incident drew down hoots of derision; Stanley Rous, the FA secretary had, in an unguarded moment, told the press that England should not fear losing to Hungary because 'losing can be fun'. Such a Corinthian attitude seemed weirdly outmoded, and the cartoonist Roy Ullyett of the *Daily Express* took up his pencil in excoriating manner at Rous's expense. Bob Ferrier in the *Daily Mirror* felt equally outraged, urging:

> We must sweep away those plumbers and builders and grocers who select national teams, and give the responsibility to men who have played and know the game. And above all, our League set-up must make sweeping and immediate sacrifices to our international game.[58]

One of the problems had been, and remained, the priority claimed by League clubs over the requirements of the national team. The modernizing Alan Hardaker, who took over as secretary of the Football League in 1957, achieved many things during his stewardship, but few in this area.[59] Changes, less radical than those suggested by the press and many soccer supporters, were set in train by both the FA and League during the course of the 1950s and early 1960s. England, of course, won the World Cup in 1966, though as host nation without the need to qualify, and ultimately with the benefit of a much-disputed goal. But some of this singular success must be attributed to changes at the FA in the later stages of Walter Winterbottom's period as national coach, and to the tactical insight of his successor Alf Ramsey. The achievement of 1966 was not repeated, nor did the mentality observed by Hardaker among directors of soccer clubs disappear: 'a football directorship ... provides business contacts, a built-in opportunity to do favours for others, a chance to exercise and to gain social prestige and reflected glory'.[60]

Rugby union was the sport most imbued with a middle-class spirit, indeed rather defiantly so. Its hostility towards those clubs which had broken away from the Rugby Football Union in 1895 over the 'broken time' issue to form the Northern Union (later Rugby League) was implacable.[61] Rugby Union's great expansion during the inter-war years was linked to that process of class formation which so benefited the Conservative Party. The local rugby club, patronized by its *nouveau riche* membership of dentists, solicitors and estate agents, became a pillar of anti-socialism in many British towns, complemented by the embracing of rugby by so many of the private schools, together with a host of both the older grammar schools and those newly established in the municipalities in the 1920s.[62] It was a reaction to the increasing association of soccer with the working class – its 'Woodbine' image as some called it. The present author distinctly recalls one municipal grammar school headmaster in the 1960s justifying the playing of rugby union at his school (when most of the pupils would have preferred soccer) by reference to 'political reasons'. East Lancashire was one enclave of immunity in this national trend; its leading grammar schools kept faith with soccer, a sport that they, alongside the big public schools, had helped to create. Wales, as we saw in Chapter 1, together with Cornwall and parts of Devon, were the only places not to manipulate rugby for social exclusiveness.

Golf, a game of 'relentless amateurism and petty snobberies',[63] might have outshone even rugby in this respect. John Lowerson's account of the game's development makes clear that its expense confined golf to an affluent middle class, though it was probably never just the 'suburban' game often imagined. Its late-Victorian expansion – a spectacular one when in the 1890s alone over 500 clubs were founded in England and close on 200 in Scotland – is explained by the game's fitting into a middle-class mentality which demanded a relaxation from work suited to all ages and all seasons. It also possessed a practical relevance in that business contacts and deals could be pursued at play.[64] In reading golf club histories such as those of Richard Holt and John Bromhead,[65] little doubt remains that golf was a game in which class and status was a major consideration in every aspect of its organization, from the appointment of the right kind of person as the club secretary, to the admission of new members (where ethnic as well as class factors sometimes applied), right down to the proper dress code and the maintenance of a correct relationship between members and the club professional. Even famous international tournament pro's like the American Walter Hagen were refused entry to clubhouses in the 1920s because their very presence offended the spirit of amateurism. Golf was the only game which created separate clubs, or sections within clubs, for working people (or 'artisans' as they were quaintly described). The social tone of a place might be set by its golf course, which, as Lowerson has noted, was important in attracting the right class of visitor. This was especially so at seaside resorts. Southport's links at Birkdale, for example, quickly secured the cachet 'Royal' and the club became a key force in defining what was a very middle-class town. This emphasis on decorous behaviour probably retarded the development of golf as a competitive sport. Though professional golf in Britain did grow after the First World War, it never received the backing from the game in general that it did in America, whose golfers dominated the game's major tournaments thereafter.

McKibbin attributes the relative decline of British golf, as he does also the general decline of British sport during the twentieth century, to these essentially 'political' reasons: sport's 'excessive voluntarism and the social codes of those who governed it'.[66] In this he has no doubt touched a nerve that historians have probed only fleetingly in the past; namely, the relationship between sport and social status. Lowerson's comments on the leisure clubs that grew up around urban oligarchies in the early part of the century pinpoints both the 'clubbability' that these organizations offered for a middle class often unsure about its social role and position, and the difficulty historians have faced in plumbing the depths of social meaning contained in them. 'Their ostensible purpose was a particular sport. But often far more significant and far less easily reconstructed by historians was their role as instruments of relatively fine social differentiation and arbiters of public custom.'[67] In many cases their social role was probably more profoundly influenced than we so far realize by the presence of their female membership, as certainly happened in the rapidly developing sport of tennis in the inter-war years. The tennis club, usually less exclusive in either class or gender terms than its rugby and golfing equivalents, became a central feature of middle-class communities at this time. The part played by such clubs in the production of Wimbledon champions might have been minimal, but if nothing else, they fulfilled an important function in the marriage market.[68]

CONCLUSION: CLUBS AND HISTORIANS

The life of the club is one of the untold stories of modern British social history. Although the club is so clearly important in the provision of sport and leisure, its functions and effects have not been subjected to a great deal of scrutiny by historians. This is particularly suprising in the area of sport, where there are countless histories constantly being produced by enthusiastic secretaries and members of local sports clubs. Unfortunately, however, most are celebratory and uncritical, and do not raise the kinds of questions that historians should be asking. But the material from which they are drawn is usually freely available, and all it needs is an effort of will on the part of sports historians to turn their attention from commercial provision (which has tended to consume most of their energies) to the neglected field of voluntary association. What Holt and Mason describe as the 'open seas of high performance' have been charted with care, but the 'quiet harbours of casual exertion and sociability' still remain to be explored.[69]

The relative absence of detailed work, therefore, forbids us from reaching very firm conclusions about the relationship between sport and social behaviour. What the present chapter has sought to do is to look critically at the club principle, and to try to move away from a rosy notion of the club as the embodiment of social unity. Sociological studies, together with the rather heterodox views on clubs and leisure offered in Ross McKibbin's recent work, suggest that social exclusion and political partisanship might be the chief functions of many voluntary associations. But McKibbin's argument is strongest when he speaks of attitudes generated in clubs responsible for a rather higher level of sporting endeavour than that pursued in the neighbourhood. In the national amateur organizations such as the MCC and the FA, thinking remained hidebound for a long time; even the test of war appeared not to have been visited upon these institutions.[70] Gradually, however, the promotion of commercialism, as we have seen, had some effect.

But it was only towards the very end of the century that old attitudes were laid to rest. 'Amateurism', once an honourable principle of selfless service and enjoyment of sport for its own sake, disappeared from the leading club circles to be replaced by a more 'realist' attitude geared to making money through sponsorship and television. When this happened, as Holt and Mason note, 'amateur' lost its old meaning and became a synonym for 'incompetent'.[71] But had national attitudes remained fixed in a time warp for so long because at the base of the voluntary-association pyramid people continued to regard sport and leisure as a channel to social prestige rather than a training ground for competition and victory? And, at this level, do those attitudes still prevail? This is a question that historians of sport have still to tackle in a systematic way.

Key Reading ●

Frankenberg, R. *Communities in Britain: Social Life in Town and Country.* Harmondsworth: Penguin Books, 1966.

McKibbin, R. *Classes and Cultures: England, 1918–1951.* Oxford: Oxford University Press, 1998.

Meller, H. *Leisure and the Changing City, 1870–1914.* London: Routledge and Kegan Paul, 1976.

Stacey, M. *Tradition and Change: A Study of Banbury.* Oxford: Oxford University Press, 1960.

Williams, J. *Cricket and England: A Cultural and Social History of the Interwar Years.* London: Frank Cass, 1999.

Chronology of Events

1752 Formation of the Jockey Club.

1787 Formation of the MCC.

1863 Formation of the FA; establishment of the Working Men's Club and Institute Union (CIU) by Rev. Henry Solly.

1866 Formation of the National Hunt Committee.

1868 Formation of the All England Croquet Club, which added 'Lawn Tennis' to its title in 1877.

1871 Formation of the Rugby Football Union.

1880 Formation of the Amateur Athletics Association.

1883 Establishment of the Boys' Brigade.

1885 Establishment of the Mothers' Union; 583000 members by 1939.

1891 National Sporting Club began to stage professional boxing contests and to promote the sport, until overall control was vested in the British Boxing Board of Control in 1929; establishment of the Church Lads' Brigade.

1897 Royal and Ancient Golf Club established its Rules of Golf Committee, becoming the *de facto* governing body of the game outside North America.

1915 Women's Institute established; wartime controls imposed over public house opening times, and lasted until the 1980s.

1932 Formation of the Townswomen's Guild.

1946 Family Welfare Association formed (formerly the Charity Organization Society, founded in 1869).

1963 Formation of Help the Aged; abolition of the amateur/professional distinction in cricket.

1968 MCC lost its control over cricket with the establishment of the Test and County Cricket Board.

part three

Public policy: the role of the state

chapter 9

State and Politics in Sport and Leisure

In Britain the themes that form the focus of this chapter have not readily converged. On the face of it, both sport and leisure have customarily been regarded as activities best left to the voluntary efforts of individuals and groups. This can be illustrated in a number of ways. Politics, in the conventional sense of party political discourse, has rarely (except in the case of Northern Ireland, discussed in Chapter 10) bothered much with either sport or leisure. Neither has ever been a major issue in a general election, with the possible exception of that of 1970. The state, in the national sense of parliament, government, central administration and the law, has usually been hesitant of involving itself, though local government has often been more interventionist than national agencies, as we shall see in the next chapter. But even at the local level, there has been no counterpart of the extensive public involvement in sport seen, for example, in the erstwhile German Democratic Republic. The relationship between sport and national propaganda has also been generally muted. There is, for example, no British equivalent of the Nazi Olympics of 1936, nor even of the Los Angeles Games of 1932, which were not without their share of American myth making.[1] The 1948 Olympics, held in London, were appropriately low-key in ideology, as befitted the Attlee government of the day whose encouragement of them had been keen.[2] Only in exceptional and small cases has Britain produced that political culture of leisure so impressively seen in the socialist movements of Continental Europe, notably the German social democrats.[3] There have been British left-wingers who linked sport and politics in, for example, the Workers' Olympics,[4] but on the whole, for the British labour movement, sport and leisure were simply activities to be enjoyed in workers' spare time, not instruments of the class struggle.

Such features have produced a culture in which, it has often seemed, 'sport' and 'politics' have moved in quite different spheres. It has enabled many, including some leading sportspeople, to claim that sport and politics should *not* be mixed, that sport is a category peculiarly immune from the pressures of normal life. However, as much of our discussion so far has shown, neither sport nor leisure is unaffected by social, economic and political activity; and this activity is itself influenced ideologically by the practices and texts of sport and leisure. In this sense, sport and leisure can communicate broad political meanings, including, as we have seen in Chapter 1, what it means to be part of Britain.

THE STATE

Before moving on with this discussion, it will be worth considering briefly the changing conceptions of the functions of 'the state' in Britain over the course of the century. During this time three principal 'models' of state activity have prevailed, though from the outset we should be cautious of a rigid separation. A simple chronology might propose that from the Victorian period until the Second World War the dominant model was of a state with a limited interventionist role. Although the Victorian conception of the state as 'night-watchman', restricted to functions of collecting taxes, dispensing justice, and conducting national defence and foreign policy, is probably not historically valid for this period, especially after the experiences of 1914–18, it does none the less contain the features which continued to be regarded by many politicians as the 'ideal type' of state; interventionist experiments during wartime, or those associated with Lloyd George's 'New Liberalism' were seen by many as regrettable aberrations.[5] During and after the Second World War, however, such hankerings for minimalism were increasingly anachronistic as the state took on a new set of functions summed up in the term 'welfare state', which first came into common usage in the late 1940s to describe the measures in social security and public ownership introduced by the Labour governments of 1945–51.[6] Many, though not all, historians of the post-war period have subscribed to an idea of 'consensus' in British society at this time. The idea has been applied to different areas of society, and there has been disagreement over the time-scale for which it is relevant, but generally it has involved a recognition of a state with extended powers, especially with a responsibility for economic management at a macro level and the securing of a guaranteed minimum standard of life.[7] The third model came into fashion in the 1970s among so-called 'New Right' politicians around Margaret Thatcher and Keith Joseph, as a response to economic and social problems in a time of high price inflation. In some ways the new model sought to invoke the idea of a minimalist state. It rejected the claim that the state should exercise an economic role, arguing that 'the economy' was nothing more than the combined efforts of individual businessmen. But allied to this, and somewhat paradoxically, the new thinking also produced a state with strong powers of coercion which could be deployed to enforce political and economic strategies.[8] This mixture, which has been described by some commentators as 'post-Fordist',[9] was seen in action most clearly during the miner's lock-out of 1984–85.

It must be stressed, however, that these simple categories approximate only crudely to historical reality. In practice, for example, New Right statecraft was never as Simon-pure as its theorists imagined, while in the era of the 'big state' there was often little evidence of interventionism in the field of sport and leisure. None the less, these characterisations are helpful in reminding us that the state's role, or at least people's perception of it, is not static, and that the changes in it have been both the cause and the effect of political conflicts.

SPORT, LEISURE AND THE STATE: THE VICTORIAN LEGACY

'Until the 1960s', claim Coghlan and Webb, 'central government played little or no part in sport.'[10] It is certainly true that the interest evinced by government ministers in sport and leisure, while not completely absent, was minimal for much of the century. Such interest as did exist traditionally stemmed from two principal concerns.

One was the anxiety over the general health and fitness of the population. This was a sporadic concern, present at certain times, absent at others. The 'health' of the population did not always mean its physical health, and there were times when government intervened to safeguard people's moral well-being. This was the case, for example, with the development of the cinema where the desire to ensure that the masses were not led astray by unsuitable material on screen led to a persistent censoring of film content. For the most part, however, this was conducted either by the British Board of Film Censors (an industry body, in spite of its official-sounding title) or local authorities, rather than by central government. The latter's role was more noticeable in the legislative attempts to protect the British film industry against American competition in the 1920s and 1930s, an attempt which also bore witness to the concern over the 'dilution' of national culture.[11] As against moral concerns, physical health was more often a spur to government intervention, with military preparedness frequently a consideration. It fuelled fears at the beginning of the century, when the reverses of the Boer War aroused suspicions about the physical standard of recruits to the army, and prompted a debate about 'national efficiency'.[12] The Public Health Act of 1907, which permitted local authorities to spend money on games and recreations, was one outcome of this debate. Similarly, in the tense international climate of the late 1930s, the government of the day was persuaded to introduce the Physical Training and Recreation Act of 1937, which made available through the Ministry of Education modest amounts of public money to aid voluntary organizations in the provision of facilities 'for physical training and recreation, including . . . the provision and equipment of gymnasiums, playing fields, swimming baths, bathing places, holiday camps and camping sites'.

The motivation here was clearly a perceived need to equip the nation physically for war, and although the involvement fell far short of that to be found in regimes such as the Soviet Union and Fascist Italy, it nevertheless established a precedent for government action in the future. On the whole, however, government at the national level still preferred to work through independent voluntary organisations like the National Playing Fields Association (established in 1925) and the Central Council of Physical Recreation (established 1935). And with good reason: the importance attached to the principle of voluntarism. When the National Fitness Council was established by the 1937 Act it provoked opposition from those who saw it as a threat to the voluntary principle and a portent of militarism. Even in the heady days of 1945, when Labour swept to power with the most progressive manifesto seen in British politics up to that time, the principle of voluntarism remained in sport when elsewhere a strong leaning towards public ownership and initiative was evident. Labour leaders showed little inclination to extend ideas of state involvement into sport, strongly opposing a Ministry of Sport and even the Swedish model of state subsidy.[13] A case in point was the government's refusal to take up the recommendation of the Hughes Report into the crowd disaster at Bolton Wanderers' football ground in 1946, which urged that legislation be undertaken to ensure the safety of sports grounds.[14]

During the two world wars government had resorted to measures that affected the conduct of sport, though even in these circumstances the approach was tentative. During the 1914–18 war the initial 'business as usual' mentality ensured, for example, that the Football League and FA Cup competitions continued to be played into 1915, when they were eventually stopped, more because of moral pressure than as a result of government order. In the 1939–45 conflict emergency orders of various kinds, mainly affecting the availability of fuel and transport, caused considerable disruption to the sporting world. But political leaders were, to their credit, aware that sport was essential to the maintenance of civilian morale, and sought as far as possible to encourage it. Herbert Morrison, Home Secretary in Churchill's war cabinet, was strongly of the view that sport helped rather than hindered the war effort, and defended his position against some quite severe patriotic sentiment: 'we have taken the view that there must be, within reasonable limitations, recreation for the people'.[15] In the Second World War most civilians who wanted to participate in sport could do so, and even though changes and re-organization were inevitable, there was often plenty of activity. Jack Rollin's marvellously detailed *Soccer At War* is testimony to that activity in just one sport.[16]

For those in the armed services opportunities were varied. In contrast to the First World War, the armed services in the Second used professional sportsmen as a cadre of physical training instructors. Their job was to stimulate interest and organize games among the troops. The impact of this is, surprisingly, little known. Compared with the attention given by historians to the Army Bureau of Current Affairs (sometimes wrongly credited with having

laid the foundations for Labour's 1945 election victory), the equally important role of sport in the armed services has passed largely unnoticed. By 1941
there were well over two million men in the Army 'of whom an impressive
proportion', says Angus Calder, 'were "browned off" in camps in Britain'.[17]
Considering the Army's peacetime interest in sport, and the high quality of
wartime service teams, it is inconceivable that a great number of these men
did not participate in sports, voluntarily or by order. According to a survey
carried out in 1946 among soldiers in the Far East, sport was high on the list
of things they liked best about the army.[18]

The other main impulse forcing government to intervene in sport also had
to do with war, but in this case its prevention rather than its prosecution.
Martin Polley's researches have revealed a consistent involvement in sport by
Foreign Office officials from the late nineteenth century onwards. They were
specifically interested in the Olympic Games, and wanted to use sport as a
tool of diplomacy.[19] Such activity became especially acute in the 1930s, when
the aim of the Foreign Office was to prevent a diplomatic convergence of
powers whose interests were considered to be inimical to those of Great
Britain. Thus, as part of the policy of Appeasement, sporting contacts were
exploited to maintain friendly relations with countries such as Germany, Italy
and Japan, and Foreign Office officials were frequently in touch with the governing bodies of the sports concerned to urge accommodation with foreign
wishes. Several sporting events became the subject of such diplomacy. In relation to the Berlin Olympics of 1936, for example, the British government's aim
was to ensure that the Games went ahead, notwithstanding the attempts by
lobbies in the USA, Sweden and among left-wing organizations in Britain to
organize a boycott. Equally, in the bidding stage for the 1940 Olympics, the
Foreign Office sought to use its influence with the British Olympic Association to ensure that the Japanese bid to host the Games was favoured above
bids from Britain itself and Finland. In soccer, matches between England and
Germany attracted a similar *realpolitik*. The first match played between the
two countries following the installation of the Nazi regime, at Tottenham
Hotspur's ground in December 1935, had been the focus of a campaign by
the labour movement and Jewish groups to bring about its abandonment on
the grounds of the human rights abuses committed by the Nazis. But both
the Home Office and the Foreign Office resisted this pressure, the latter, in
particular, being sensitive to offending Germany. Vansittart, the Permanent
Secretary, wished to avoid any kind of diplomatic incident, a position supported by the Foreign Secretary himself, Sir Samuel Hoare, who retreated
into the conventional position that this was a matter for the private organizations which had arranged the match. Again, in 1938, when England played
Germany at soccer in Berlin, the Foreign Office prevailed upon the Football
Association to make sure that, prior to the kick-off, the English players honoured their guests by giving the Nazi salute.[20] Such diplomatic intrigue is to
be expected in the era of Appeasement, and indeed it continued into the phase
of the Cold War. At the time of the World Cup of 1966 in England, for example,
there was much Foreign Office interference in the competition because a

team from North Korea (a country that Great Britain did not recognize) had qualified.[21]

SPORT, LEISURE AND 'MODERNIZATION'

If, by the 1960s, there seemed to have emerged a wider and deeper involvement in sport and leisure by central government, this was not the result of any concerted evolutionary plan. Government responsibilities, though greater in number, were in their nature essentially what they had always been: a mixture of regulatory, paternalist, enabling and diplomatic functions. As Houlihan has pointed out: 'what makes the period from 1960 onwards distinctive is not so much that new issues or themes emerged to replace those of the past, rather it is the acceptance by government that sport was a legitimate governmental responsibility'.[22] In this context, and in contrast with the later years of the century, ideological considerations played little, if any, part. A measure of this is, as we have seen, the low level of interest displayed in sport by the Labour governments of 1945–51. Compared with the landmark activity in social insurance and health, Lewis Silkin's National Parks and Countryside Act of 1949, which owed its origins to the left-wing campaigns of the 1930s for access to the countryside, was a notable exception to the endeavours of a government which continued to believe that sport and leisure were matters for individuals to sort out for themselves. The Prime Minister, a keen sports-follower who once described himself as 'the government's centre-half' (perhaps thinking of the pre-1925 position, rather than the third-back 'stopper') embodied old-fashioned virtues on the relationship between state and sport. Asked by an MP in the House of Commons if he would consider appointing a minister of sport and physical culture, he replied simply: 'No, Sir.'[23] In many ways 1945 represented a return to normality in sport, as the old establishments reasserted themselves and any hint of change brought on by the war was snuffed out.[24] The Conservatives, returned to power in 1951, were no more predisposed than Labour had been to interfere in these areas.

Nor did the Conservatives interfere in any major way. In the General Election of 1959 both major parties, true to form, had opposed the creation of a Minister of Sport. When returned to office the Conservatives acted on the recommendations of the Wolfenden Report of 1960 in a half-hearted way, giving to Lord Hailsham, as Lord Privy Seal and Minister for Science, responsibility for sport. It was left to Harold Wilson's Labour administration elected in 1964 to give more solid substance to the idea of a national co-ordinating body for sport. The creation in the following year of the Sports Council in an advisory capacity was a major step forward, the first time there had been a body representing the whole of British sport. When elevated in 1972 by Edward Heath's government to the position of an executive body 'at arm's length' from its parent government department, the Sports Council was able to flex its muscles and disburse money. These developments were significant, representing not only a departure from tradition but becoming for some a cause for suspicion. What caused them?

There seems little doubt that the economic and social changes of the 1950s were largely responsible. To a degree the changes in leisure patterns at this time were more than adequately catered for by the voluntary and commercial sectors: the holiday boom, the rise of motor-car related leisure, the popularity of television, and the rich youth culture of rock n'roll all happened without anything but the most indirect stimulus from government. However, there were aspects of each of these developments, as well as other changes, which suggested a need for government involvement in leisure. Concerns arose, for example, over the behaviour of youth, especially the behaviour of young *men*. The fears they provoked were varied, and ranged from their apparent proneness to violence, as evident in the Teddy Boy movement or in the Mods and Rockers conflicts of the early 1960s, or over their seeming apathy, graphically and alarmingly portrayed by Richard Hoggart in *The Uses of Literacy* (1957). Further, the fashion for televison viewing, especially the new commercial channel to which many sets were permanently tuned in working-class households (perhaps at last feeling liberated from the BBC's overweaning *hauteur*), reawakened all those old fears among intellectuals of a nation of passive morons. These anxieties, which had a strong undercurrent of anti-Americanism, were reflected in a Labour Party manifesto of 1959, *Leisure For Living*, which evoked labour movement themes of former days about the proper uses of leisure: 'once full employment is again secured, the emphasis will increasingly be not on jobs for all but on leisure for all – leisure *and how to use it*'.[25] It was Resolution 42 at the TUC of the following year that triggered the creation of a new arts initiative – Centre 42 – through which Arnold Wesker and others sought to combat some of the perceived cultural evils of the affluent society.[26]

Alongside these developments were rather more straightforward concerns about sporting standards, especially in an international context. The 1950s brought a mixture of fortunes for British athletes. To set against the conquest of Everest and the recovery of the Ashes in 1953, Bannister's first sub-four-minute mile the following year, and the generally good performances of middle-distance runners, there was the dismal failure in the 1952 Olympics alongside the seemingly sudden decline of British soccer. This was illustrated in defeats at home for both Scotland and England at the feet of Hungary, and in the results of British teams in all three World Cup competitions during the decade: always mediocre, and on occasions – as in England's 1-0 defeat by the USA in 1950, or Scotland's losing 7-0 to Uruguay in 1954 – humiliating.[27]

In the face of such developments in sport and the wider field of leisure the Central Council of Physical Recreation (CCPR), especially concerned about youth in the likely event of the abolition of National Service, set up the Wolfenden Committee in 1957. It was to inquire into a broad area of sport, games and outdoor activities, and 'to make recommendations to the CCPR as to any practical measures which should be taken by statutory or voluntary bodies in order that these activities may play their full part in promoting the general welfare of the community'. Its report, published in 1960, was, as Houlihan comments, 'a watershed in the development of sport policy'.[28] Commentators on the Report, *Sport and the Community*,[29] have betrayed a certain

'Whiggishness' in seizing upon and emphasizing its main recommendation – for the setting up of a Sports Development Council, an idea which eventually came into being with the Sports Council and which has strongly influenced public policy on sport ever since. Important though this was, Wolfenden ranged over a number of other issues and its tone reveals much about the state of thinking on sport and leisure in the late 1950s.

The enquiries of the committee chaired by Sir John Wolfenden covered all sports, 'from cricket to climbing and from boxing to badminton'. None of its members was an 'expert' on sport; selection was dictated by considerations of interest and all-round experience. The central concern of the committee was 'the general welfare of the community', and thus it conformed to a well-established set of perspectives about the proper use of leisure. Wolfenden was informed by the familiar idea that leisure time had increased, but was not always being put to good use. In this context, the perceived needs of youth were prioritized. Much emphasis was placed on 'the Gap' (so-called), which occurred when young people left sports participation at school and did not immediately continue in adult sporting organizations. On this Wolfenden's concerns tied in closely with those explored by the Albemarle Committee,[30] and a link between the youth service and the various bodies responsible for sports and games was suggested. In other respects Wolfenden's position reflected many of the views about the function of sport in society that had emerged from the schools – especially the public schools: that sport was a basic human need, that it promoted health, that it encouraged admirable qualities of self-discipline, endurance, self-reliance and determination, and that it might also inculcate moral and aesthetic sensibilities through 'sportsmanship' and the appreciation of 'the poetry of motion'. Such attributes were not accepted uncritically by the committee, and, indeed, some attempt was made not to appear to seem old-fashioned. The committee's even-handedness of approach was apparent in its sympathy for ordinary football supporters – 'It is a mistake to suppose that the spectator at a first-class football match is merely passive' – and in its sceptical line on 'amateurism', which in some respects was regarded as an outmoded concept.

On the whole Wolfenden struck a modernizing note. Its view of the general interest and involvement of the British people in sport was less pessimistic than some contemporary criticisms, but it clearly felt that more was needed in the form of material support for the immense energy injected into sport through the voluntary sector. Responsibility was lain upon local authorities and Parliament to provide funds to sustain the various governing bodies in sport; and, contrary to the views of some of those governing bodies, the committee saw great possibilities in the new medium of television for enhancing public interest and awareness in sport. Moreover, it was in the pages of the Wolfenden Report that the idea of 'multi-sports centres', later to be a ubiquitous feature of the urban landscape, first made itself heard.

This was one of the main legacies of the Wolfenden Report, resulting from the committee's most innovative recommendation, its self-styled 'New Deal': the establishment of a Sports Development Council. Wolfenden had unhesitatingly rejected the idea of a ministry of sport: 'The notion of subjecting to ministerial and departmental management activities so diverse and so essentially spontaneous as those with which we are concerned is, we believe, foreign to the whole national attitude towards sport.'[31] Instead, the Committee envisaged a small body responsible for disbursing to the various governing bodies a sum of public money, made available by the Treasury. Such a Council would develop the 'synoptic' view of the overall needs of sport that none of the existing bodies was able to have, and would thus be at the centre of a web of information which could be used to lead British sport forward.

As a 'quango', on the lines of the Arts Council or the University Grants Committee, the Sports Council, as it became known when intially set up by the Labour government in 1965, has been responsible for some important improvements in sport and leisure provision since the 1970s by providing grant aid to voluntary associations and local authorities. Moral and financial encouragement from the Sports Council, together with its technical advice, has moved mountains. The 1970s was a time of immense growth in leisure provision. Because money previously hoarded by parsimonious local authorities was suddenly being released and spent in anticipation of local government reorganization, a whole rash of new leisure centres, swimming pools and golf courses appeared.[32] Mixed in with the concern to improve provision was also a political sensitivity which saw in sport and leisure a means of alleviating potential social problems such as crime, unemployment, violence and deprivation. Particular attention was paid by central government to what, in a new phrase, began to be referred to as the 'inner cities'. Important White Papers came out in the mid-1970s on this issue, principally *Sport and Recreation* (1975).[33] Following on from that was the Football and the Community scheme launched by Denis Howell, Labour's minister with responsibility for sport, to make money available to professional soccer clubs for developing their facilities for use by the local community. Much of this, as with the inner city focus of earlier schemes, was done with youth and the growing problem of soccer hooliganism in mind.[34] But not all the Sports Council's initiatives were of this kind. Much emphasis was placed upon the achievement of high standards in national and international competition through national centres administered by the Sports Council for elite training and coaching, to which were added later a series of 'centres of excellence' specializing in particular sports. Further notable initiatives have come on drug taking in sport, and the continuing attempt to make sport widely accessible in the community through the *Sport For All* campaign. Not all have been successful, the relationship between ministers and Sports Council officials has not always been harmonious, and lack of adequate finance has dogged the Council's tracks. John Coghlan's accounts of the body's activities, flavoured by his experiences as a former Acting Director, make all too clear the difficulties faced by those who have tried to lead this particular venture in shaping sport policy.[35] But for all its shortcomings, the Sports Council provides an excellent example of the state taking an interventionist role in sport and leisure, both to enhance the quality of life of its citizens and to eradicate as far as possible troublesome elements that might spill over into politics.

SPORT AND POLITICS: SOUTH AFRICA, MOSCOW AND HOOLIGANS

In all of the guises so far examined, the involvement of the state in sport and leisure could be described as 'politics' only in a relatively loose form. It has been to do with the perceived function of the central state in relation to the needs of the nation and population. In that sense, there has been a marked continuity of practice between the different political groupings in government. This is not to deny that such activity has given rise to 'political' debate and disagreement – such as that, for example, which accompanied the establishment of the Sports Council itself as an executive body in 1971.[36] Moreover, the tendency for the functions of the state (provision of leisure centres, for example) to converge with the attempted solution of social problems (such as unemployed young men) has increased the potential for sport and politics to intermix. But as an everyday topic of political discourse, sport has not attained the levels reached by subjects such as taxation, housing, education, employment and defence. There have, however, been exceptions, and these have generally related to high-profile sport.

Some of them came from outside British society. The most obvious case was that of South Africa and apartheid. Beginning with demonstrations by anti-apartheid groups against the South African cricket tour of 1960, the movement to boycott goods from South Africa and ban its sportspeople from international competition had reached significant proportions by the late 1960s. There were demonstrations, sometimes violent, during the South African rugby tour of Britain in the winter of 1969–70, and a concerted and successful campaign – 'Stop the Seventy Tour' – against the visit of the South African cricketers in 1970. The Labour government, mindful of its position on race relations, intervened to cancel the tour.[37] But the biggest and most controversial incident in the apartheid question arose in the late summer of 1968, a few months after Enoch Powell's notorious Birmingham speech on repatriation of black immigrants. It happened in cricket, where it produced, according to the writer and commentator Brian Johnston, an even bigger crisis than the Bodyline tour of the early 1930s.[38] It was the 'D'Oliveira Affair'.

Basil D'Oliveira was a dark-skinned South African cricketer. With the help of a group of cricketers and journalists, who included the writer and broadcaster John Arlott and John Kay of the *Manchester Evening News*, D'Oliveira had come to England in 1960 to play for Middleton in the Central Lancashire League.[39] In 1965 he moved into county cricket, playing for Worcestershire, and in the following year he became a member of the England team. Poor form during a tour of the West Indies in 1967–68 had put his test place in some jeopardy, but he was recalled following the illness of another player for the final match in the 1968 series against Australia. D'Oliveira scored 158, and thus made himself a strong candidate for selection for the England team to tour South Africa in the winter of 1968–69. However, well before this the South African authorities had made it known that D'Oliveira's selection would not be acceptable to them, a stance which both Denis Howell and the Foreign

Office had completely rejected. 'The one thing we must hope for', said a secret telegram from London to the British Ambassador in Pretoria, 'is that Mr D'Oliveira keeps his form and the MCC keep their nerve.'[40] Howell announced in the Commons that he had been given the assurance of the MCC that its touring party to South Africa for 1968–69 would be chosen on merit.[41] According to D'Oliveira, pressure was brought to bear on him from South African sources during the summer of 1968 not to participate in the tour, since his presence in South Africa would pose a severe embarrassment to the South African government.[42] He claims that he was offered very generous terms by a South African businessman to take a coaching appointment in the country so that he would not be available to play for England on the tour.

In the event, despite his big innings against Australia, D'Oliveira was not selected for the touring party, a decision which to many defied cricket logic and smacked of capitulation to the South African cause – 'truckling to apartheid', as Arlott phrased it.[43] Liberal opinion, with Arlott in *The Guardian* in full swing backed by such eminent figures as Learie Constantine and David Sheppard, mounted such an offensive that, when a player dropped out of the touring party through injury, D'Oliveira was quickly installed in his place. But the South African government cancelled the tour, claiming that the MCC team had been chosen under political pressure. The passions and conflicts generated by the affair ran on into the arguments conducted over the rugby tour and the 1970 visit of the South African cricket team. They exposed some deep rifts in British society. Those people, including some leading cricketers, who felt that the affair was bringing politics into sport and that sporting contacts with South Africa helped to 'build bridges', were suspected by their opponents of placing the interests of cricket above those of human rights. Arlott's decision not to broadcast for the BBC should the 1970 tour go ahead brought a rebarbative reply from Peter May, the former England captain and a revered member of the cricket establishment, who had been a member of the very selection committee which had omitted D'Oliveira in the first place.[44]

In spite of these developments, British rugby teams continued to tour South Africa in the 1970s, a policy which threatened to bring forth a general boycott on British athletes by countries now firmly distanced from any contact with the Nationalist regime in South Africa. To forestall such a boycott threatened for the 1978 Commonwealth Games in Canada, and to preserve some unity among members of the Commonwealth, the British government devised a position which was agreed by other Commonwealth heads of government meeting at the Gleneagles Hotel in Scotland in June 1977. The crux of the position was:

> the urgent duty of each of their Governments vigorously to combat the evil of apartheid by witholding any form of support for, and by taking every practical step to discourage, contact or competition by their nationals with sporting organizations, teams or sportsmen from South Africa or from any other country where sports are organized on the basis of race, colour or ethnic origin.

The 'Commonwealth Statement on Apartheid in Sport', as the pronouncement was known, concluded by saying: 'there were unlikely to be future sporting contacts of any significance between Commonwealth countries or their nationals and South Africa while that country continues to pursue the detestable policy of apartheid'.[45]

Whereas the South African issue was brought to British politics largely by events external to Britain, the other principal political matter to affect British sport in recent years owed much more to domestic developments. This was the attempted boycott of the Olympic Games of 1980, held in Moscow. Of course, the Olympic movement was no stranger to politics, in the form either of internal intrigue or public dissension. The Games of 1976, in Montreal, had provided ample evidence of both, with a boycott by black athletes protesting against New Zealand's rugby links with South Africa, and financial problems in Montreal itself over the cost of mounting the Games. The Moscow Games produced conflicts of a different kind. First of all, there was a call to remove the games from Moscow by the Women's Campaign for Soviet Jewry. Then, from a British point of view, there was the return in May 1979 of a new Conservative government, headed by Margaret Thatcher. This coincided with a hardening of international relations between East and West, in part caused by Thatcher herself, whose 'New Right' politics included an element of anti-Red bashing which earned her the nickname 'Iron Lady', and which soured the climate of *détente* that had prevailed since the Cuban missile crisis of 1962. Another, and bigger, contributory factor was the arrival of a new phase of nuclear strategy in which 'theatre' weapons began to be deployed, including cruise missiles stationed in western Europe. With the Soviet invasion of Afghanistan at Christmas 1979, however, Cold War relations reached a very heated stage indeed. Many feared for the prospects of peace in the 1980s. As one diplomatic ploy to put pressure on the Soviet Union to withdraw its forces from Afghanistan, the American President, Jimmy Carter, threatened an American boycott of the 1980 Olympics. The threat went unheeded in Moscow and, accordingly, the US Olympics Committee was prevailed upon not to send a team to the Games. As a gesture of support for the USA, Margaret Thatcher attempted the same tactic in Britain. Her case, however, was maladroitly put and she failed, as Carter failed internationally, to persuade political opinion that the Games should be used as a bargaining counter in the Cold War.[46] John Coghlan, scarcely a friendly witness of all this, noted: 'the majority of British people resent young athletes being pushed around by politicians'.[47] Although the government won the debates on this issue in the Commons, its entreaties were disregarded by the British Olympic Association (BOA), which sent to Moscow a team that enjoyed some success, winning five gold medals.

The Moscow case differed from the South African in a number of respects. In the D'Oliveira affair the government had not initially taken a leading role, and the South African regime could quite clearly be seen as the villain of the piece. Many British people, though perhaps less than liberal on race issues, could content themselves with the view that this was a case of injustice to an individual whose interest the government was concerned for. In 1980 the attempted boycott was a far less clear-cut issue. Its connection with party politics seemed close, the Opposition did not support it, and it was never made clear why sport should be the chosen instrument of diplomacy when trade and financial links with the Soviet union were left untouched. Whatever people's views over the Soviet intervention in Afghanistan, and most deplored it, the boycott looked too transparently like an opportunity for New Right politicians to win their spurs with some Cold War propaganda. Above all, unlike the D'Oliveira business, the Conservative government did not seem to have been drawn into the affair reluctantly. Thatcher and her colleagues waded in, doing themselves little credit in the process. The Moscow affair did nothing to enhance their prestige, already low as a consequence of increasing unemployment figures. By 1983, however, all seemed to have been forgotten in the aftermath of the Falklands/Malvinas War.[48]

The politics of the 1980 Olympic Games, however, introduced what was to be a recurring political involvement with sport for the remainder of the decade and beyond. South Africa and Moscow were both, in their different ways, fairly obvious set-piece political issues which were settled one way or the other quite quickly. But in other respects they differed significantly. The D'Oliveira affair was in some ways a chance happening, and related to British government policy at the time only in the sense that a programme of reform in race relations was being conducted which contrasted with the treatment being meted out to D'Oliveira by the South Africans. The attempted boycott of the Moscow Games, on the other hand, was intimately connected to government Cold War policy, and a clear manipulation of sport for diplomatic ends. It heralded a relationship betwen sport and politics that developed in the 1980s as sport became increasingly entangled with some of the new attitudes that flowed from Downing Street.

Much of the impetus for this stemmed from soccer 'hooliganism', a feature that began to be exhibited at soccer grounds in the 1960s and which by the late 1980s had produced many baneful effects. Academics of various disciplines who sought to understand it produced a range of interpretations with varying degrees of plausibility. They included the argument put forward by Ian Taylor that hooliganism was a reaction by supporters who wanted to reclaim their game in the face of the increased commercialization of soccer, and Peter Marsh's anthropological interpretation which saw it as ritualized aggression carried out in very specific and confined forms by young men identifying themselves through the control of territory.[49] It was not a social phenomenon easily comprehended. In political discourse, however, including that of the press, understanding was less the aim than condemnation. Soccer hooligans became part of a web of narratives about 'law and order' which articulated crime, unemployment, over-manning, trade unions and the welfare state into a composite picture of 'what had gone wrong' with Britain.[50] The inference drawn was that the social-democratic consensus, forged in the war years and maintained therafter by both Conservative and Labour politicians, its objective being to secure full employment and a decent minimum of social services, had produced by the 1960s a 'nanny state' in which individual responsibility had been sacrificed to a culture of 'dependency'. This vision was most clearly illustrated in the thinking of a group of Conservative backbenchers who, in 1990, produced a series of manifestos under the general heading 'No Turning Back'.[51] They out-Thatchered Thatcher in their desire to see a rolling back of the boundaries of the state, a restoration of family values, and a restriction of taxation levels. As in much of New Right thinking, there was a good deal of rhetoric – the Treasury, for example, never did embrace Milton Friedmann to the extent that Margaret Thatcher did – but rhetoric itself can be a powerful political weapon.

Sport provided an arena for some of these rhetorical flourishes. Soccer, a game for which the Prime Minister had no affection, was especially singled out for treatment. It was the site on which English *men* customarily disgraced themselves, frequently as visitors to matches played overseas, and the media images of violence associated with this behaviour provided fuel for the 'law and order' campaign that formed an important part of popular Toryism.[52] As Dave Russell has suggested, football may well have played an influential role during the course of the century in fashioning middle-class perceptions of the working class in Britain.[53] The attempts of soccer clubs, in company with the police, to deal with hooliganism were overlain with political rhetoric about the 'English disease'. Thus the separation of rival supporters, the installation of surveillance cameras, the erection of fences to prevent pitch invasions, and the searching of spectators on entry to grounds – all practical and helpful measures – were only part of the approach to the problem. Added to these was an element of political comment which seemed to be designed to generalize about the nature of the working class from the specific behaviour of the soccer hooligan. This reached a peak in the mid-1980s with two tragic occurrences – the fire at the stadium of Bradford City during a match in May 1985, in which 57 people died, and the deaths of 38 Italian supporters at the European Cup Final between Juventus and Liverpool in Brussels at the end of the same month. Ian Taylor has shown how these quite different and separate events became conflated in the popular press and media as manifestations of 'hooliganism'. In the Bradford fire, for example, fatalities occurred not as a result of hooligan behaviour, but because spectators were unable to escape through locked turnstiles at the back of the stand. This, however, was linked to the hooligan issue by the suggestion that the turnstiles had been locked to keep rival fans apart, the implication being that had it not been for hooliganism the deaths would not have occurred. Although the Popplewell enquiry, set up to investigate the Bradford fire, judiciously refrained from making such connections, right-wing elements of the media were not so cautious. Football, according to the *Sunday Times* was 'a slum sport played in slum stadiums and increasingly watched by slum people, who deter decent folk from turning up'. After Heysel, Liverpool and its people were demonized; according to Richard West in *The Spectator*, they displayed 'in their most disgusting form the open sores of the English disease that has made this country at first pitied abroad, then scorned and now detested'.[54]

CONCLUSION

The effect of this rhetoric is difficult, indeed impossible, fully to gauge. Such an image of football and the working class might have served to mobilize Conservative electoral support (much of it from working-class football supporters themselves) for the election victories of 1987 and 1992. In this way sport contributed to the political life of the country. What is more certain is that the politicians who addressed themselves to the problems of football violence, as Margaret Thatcher herself did by backing Luton Town's introduction in 1986–87 of a membership scheme prohibiting attendance at their stadium of all visiting supporters, had very little effect in bringing about changes. The apparent improvements that occurred during the 1990s were far more to do with business modernization in football than with political-legal impositions. If football's house has been put in order – and the aggressive, chauvinistic behaviour of English fans in the Low Countries during the Euro 2000 competition makes the idea seem a little premature – the initiative has come largely from within the game rather than from outside.[55]

Football's problems might have been in the forefront of public discussion in the last decade of the twentieth century, but they were not the only aspects drawing sport and leisure more fully into political discourse than at any other time in the century. The twin pressures of increasing commercialization and concerns about the standard of achievement in elite sport – seen most clearly in the general disappointment with the performance of British athletes in the 1996 Olympics at Atlanta – have forced late twentieth-century governments to take sport and leisure more seriously than their predecessors. As Holt and Mason point out, a situation in which the manager of the British Olympic team was called to 10 Downing Street to account for the poor performance of those in his charge, as happened after the 1996 Games, could scarcely have been envisaged in an earlier age. And whilst there might be a measure of political hyperbole in the statement made by Kate Hoey in April 2000, when she averred that sport would become a 'central tenet of government policy', there is no doubt that the subject has a far larger place in her political mind than it did in that of her predecessor Viscount Hailsham, when he was appointed the first minister with responsibility for sport in the early 1960s.

Key Reading •

Allison, L., ed. *The Changing Politics of Sport.* Manchester: Manchester University Press, 1993.

Coghlan, J. F., with Webb, I. *Sport and British Politics Since 1960.* London: Falmer Press, 1990.

Henry, I. *The Politics of Leisure Policy.* Basingstoke: Macmillan – now Palgrave, 1993.

Houlihan, B. *The Government and Politics of Sport.* London: Routledge, 1991.

Sugden, J., and Bairner, A. *Sport, Sectarianism and Society in a Divided Ireland.* Leicester: Leicester University Press, 1993.

Chronology of Events

1907 Public Health Act enabled local authorities to use the rates for making provision available for sports and recreation facilities.

1923 Foundation of British Workers' Sports Federation to promote sport for working people; complemented in 1930 by the National Workers' Sports Association, which was supported by the Labour Party.

1925 Establishment of the National Playing Fields Association, to secure space in urban areas for sport.

1935 Creation, following the initiatives of Phyllis Coulson, of the Central Council of Recreative Physical Training, which in 1944 became the Central Council of Physical Recreation (CCPR). Received grants-in-aid from the Board (later Ministry) of Education.

1937 Physical Training and Recreation Act provided public money for sporting facilities and set up the National Fitness Council.

1943 Trades Union Congress initiative 'Leisure For All' aimed at improving leisure opportunities and facilities after the war; linked with the Youth Advisory Council's plea for better sporting and leisure facilities for young people.

1944 Education Act made it a requirement for local authority schools to include sport in the educational curriculum.

1946 Backing from Foreign Office, especially Minister of State Philip Noel-Baker, for 1948 Olympic Games to be held in London; Foreign Secretary Ernest Bevin secured government financial support to help the Games.

1960 Wolfenden Report, *Sport in the Community*, commissioned by the CCPR in 1957, recommended the setting up of a Sports Development Council to disburse public money for the encouragement of sporting activity. Rejected the idea of a ministry of sport.

1962 Sport included among the departmental responsibilities of the Ministry of Education.

1965 New Labour government set up the Sports Council in an advisory capacity.

1971 Sports Council received Royal Charter and became a 'quango'.

1972 Launching in Britain by the Sports Council of the 'Sport For All' campaign, initiated by the Council of Europe.

1975 White Paper on Sport and Recreation pointed to sport as an antidote to frustration and aggression among urban youth; the 1970s generally saw an extensive programme of leisure centre building in Britain, with 770 such centres by the beginning of the 1980s (there had been 27 a decade earlier).

1980 Attempt by the Conservative government to stop British athletes competing in the Moscow Olympic Games; British Olympics Association refused to comply with government requests.

1981 Under a directive from the Department of Education and Science schools were required to sell off 'excess' playing field space.

1989–90 Interim and Final Reports of Lord Justice Taylor following the Hillsborough football crowd disaster of April 1989; the removal of standing areas from major football grounds and the creation of all-seat accommodation was one of Taylor's chief recommendations.

1994 Launch of National Lottery, some of the proceeds of which were directed to sport; swimming and football have especially benefited.

1995 Department of National Heritage policy statement *Sport: Raising the Game* brought about a reorganization of the Sports Council with the creation in 1997 of the UK Sports Council, and national Sports Councils (e.g. Sport England) funded through public and National Lottery money.

chapter 1

From 'Rational Recreation' to 'Sport for All': The Place of the Municipality in Sport and Leisure

CONTENTS

As we saw in the previous chapter, the state has been the least active 'sector' in the provision of sport and leisure in Britain. Compared with the voluntary and commercial sectors, its role has been slight and intermittent, and only in the final third of the century has it begun to play a more prominent part. But while in the main being a fair generalization of the state's role, to persist exclusively with this viewpoint might lead to some misunderstandings. The main distortion is its undervaluing of the role played by the various agencies that make up the state at a *local* level. In fact, at this level, through what we might term 'the municipality', the state has consistently performed an important function in the shaping and provision of leisure since the nineteenth century.

The municipality – a term which encompasses a wide variety of county, borough and municipal authorities, with similarly varying stocks of resources and inclinations to spend them[1] – seemed in many places the natural forum for action; especially when other sectors – the market for reasons of profit, or voluntary associations for reasons of resources – were unwilling or unable to take an initiative. From the 1840s, and in some cases earlier, municipal authorities were able to use permissive powers contained in a host of parliamentary statutes primarily aimed at ensuring basic standards of health to develop improved leisure amenities such as parks, wash-houses, libraries and museums. It produced a groundswell of opinion and action which, in spite of periodic financial stringencies caused by economic depression and fluctuations, had caused the principle of municipal leisure to become strongly established by the middle years of the twentieth century.[2] Even this, however, though it produced some dynamic ventures by local authorities seized by the idea of extending leisure to their citizens, did not create a uniform pattern of action. Municipal involvement in leisure was prompted by a mixture of motives – utilitarian, moral, political, financial and economic – and produced, therefore, a variety of responses across the country.

LEISURE AND CIVIC CULTURE: THE 'GOLDEN AGE'

An initial concern behind much municipal action was utilitarian: that is to say, it was bound up with the constellation of issues that accompanied the development of the new urban culture of nineteenth-century Britain. Many of these had to do with the severely practical matters of physical and moral health and safety. Attending these concerns, almost at every turn, were fears about the perceived threat posed by the urban masses. Dirt and disease, public order and crime (especially that relating to drunkenness, gambling and prostitution) were all primary concerns of those who sought to direct and police the new society, and all drew from those leaders measures of control instigated at the local level. The research of both Bernard Waites and Penny Summerfield has shown how many of these measures were present in the development of a leading Victorian leisure institution, the music hall.[3] A much-controlled and shaped leisure provision, the music hall was fundamentally a commercial enterprise, but which nevertheless owed its character to a series of state operations, through by-laws and police actions, designed to render it safe and respectable as a public activity. The history of the Victorian and Edwardian music hall is therefore in many respects a history of local state intervention seeking to transform it; to take this particular leisure form out of the disreputable condition from which it had emerged in the mid-nineteenth century, a low-life entertainment based on pubs whose denizens were often thieves, gamblers, prostitutes, drunks and the occasional 'oppositional' artiste, and translate it into something to which respectable men and women, if not their whole families, might safely be exposed. This involved the licensing of the halls, a function carried out in London by bodies such as the Metropolitan Board of Works and later the London County Council. It ensured both physical safety, with precautions required against the danger of fire, and moral propriety, as for example with the LCC order of 1914 prohibiting drinking in the auditorium. These were concerns with which music hall owners were often willing to comply, not only out of consideration for the law but in order to increase profits. Safe and orderly premises drew the audiences. Legal controls were therefore accompanied by a degree of self-regulation.[4]

The case of the music halls offers one example of a much broader process of using state powers of various kinds and to varying degrees to limit and direct popular leisure. The Street Betting Act of 1906, for example, attempted to deal with the problem of betting by driving it away from public places, a tactic which was only partially successful, but which placed a constant strain of vigilance on working-class gamblers, the social group against which the legislation had been primarily directed.[5] Other aspects of working-class leisure were, by contrast, lightly policed. Football crowds, for example, were regulated largely by the ground authorities, and it required a series of crowd disasters over the course of virtually the entire twentieth century to elicit positive action from the state.[6]

The impetus for municipal involvement in leisure, however, stemmed from more than just utilitarian concerns over health and safety, important though such matters were. In many instances of intervention there was a clear moral imperative. The control of people's leisure could never be entirely separated from the improvement of their minds, and the nineteenth-century crusade (the term is not too strong) for better leisure was intimately connected with perceptions of urban conditions that were completely novel, potentially or actually degrading, and in need of 'civilizing'. There was scarcely any venture in library or swimming-pool building that did not have an ideological link to the notion of encouraging the growth of a social citizenship that would engender a new urban life-style. In the most elevated cases it meant investing in the town the mark of the civilization of which it was believed the urban environment was the authentic expression. Leisure became therefore a part of a grander mission to build a new humane urban society of cultivated individuals. It was a mission enshrined in optimistic and grandiose civic architecture and in ideas such as Joseph Chamberlain's 'civic gospel' of Birmingham.[7]

Helen Meller's study of leisure development in Bristol brings all this into sharp focus. Exploiting opportunities provided in Victorian permissive legislation such as the Museums Act (1845) and the Public Libraries Acts (1850 and 1855), the governing elite of Bristol made available through municipal action a wide range of amenities for the city's population. This occurred whether the population wanted it or not. What Meller refers to as the 'municipalization' of cultural institutions resulted in the city's taking over at the end of the century a range of services – library, art gallery and museum – that had been created initially through voluntary endeavour. It led on to the building of branch libraries, public parks, wash-houses and swimming baths, all of which made available resources for leisure far beyond what municipalities were statutorily obliged to provide. The chief impetus for this strategy was, according to Meller, twofold: first, a concern about civilizing the population and setting standards not only of health but of mental recreation; and second, the competitive spirit that developed between towns and cities at this time in the provision of amenities, on which much 'municipal pride' rested. Municipal leisure became a test of civic worth. This dual purpose was neatly illustrated in Bristol with the opening in 1884 of Jacob's Well swimming bath, an impressive structure with the municipal coat of arms prominently displayed on its pedimented facade. It sustained both the health and the pride of Bristol's citizens.[8] The search for a civilized urban environment and the social citizens to grace it was expensive and usually under-resourced, and by the beginning of the twentieth century appeared to be waning in Bristol. But the idea was not confined to Bristol, and other towns continued to bear the traces of nineteenth-century idealism well into the middle years of the next century.

A moral imperative similar to that identified by Meller in Bristol was often found in much smaller communities. In Ashton-under-Lyne, for example, a textile town near Manchester with a population of some 60 000 in the interwar years, the idea of moral reform through leisure was a powerful force behind the local council's provision of baths and parks through the rates. Ashton's politics at this time was Conservative dominated and its councillors were not people inclined to throw money away. Financial caution always informed public spending. But the municipality, though not the major provider of leisure services in the borough, was responsible for some significant ventures, especially in areas of recreation that possessed a moral or 'rational' purpose. Thus, public parks and swimming baths were at the forefront of the council's leisure programme. The public baths took pride of place, housed in an imposing building which was said to look 'more like a church than a public bath', and with its large main pool and various supporting facilities it consumed high maintenance costs. But it stimulated a remarkable local interest in swimming, and accounted for a successful swimming club which produced several county and national swimmers, including the captain of England's water polo team in 1937–38. In the absence of a Football League, club swimming therefore helped to put Ashton-under-Lyne on the map. Moreover, being seen as a healthy sport, swimming carried a Victorian sense of moral purpose and was therefore a justifiable item of expenditure. Football and cricket, on the other hand, were not viewed as rational recreations and, consequently, there was always a dearth of public provision for them in Ashton-under-Lyne. The disciplined space of the public park, with its restrictions over use and movement, and its aim of promoting decorous public behaviour, seemed to evoke a more sympathetic response from local politicians than did the call for more football pitches.[9]

By this time, however, the moral purpose of municipal recreation, essentially a Victorian liberal creation, was being challenged and reinterpreted. The development of the labour movement into something that was more than just a loose alliance of trade union and socialist interests provided both a philosophical and, in places where the movement was electorally influential, a political counterpoint. Elements of the left in the labour movement had long been aware of leisure's ideological influence. Indeed, during its early years the Labour Party inherited from its various socialist associations an intellectual baggage which placed the question of leisure firmly into a political and, indeed, class context. In the 25 or so years before the First World War socialists were, as Chris Waters has shown, exceedingly sensitive to the influence of the various popular commercial leisure forms that had developed in Britain by this time – pubs, music halls, the popular press, sport and so on.[10] The hedonistic pleasures afforded by such agencies were felt to be a distraction from the serious business of improving the conditions, material and spiritual, of the working class. The aim of socialist movements like the Independent Labour Party (ILP) and the Social-Democratic Federation (SDF), and later the Communist Party of Great Britain (CPGB), was to generate a counter-culture informed by a sense of socialist fellowship. Popular commercial culture was not therefore something to be ignored; for the left-wing of the labour movement it was a battleground equal in importance to those of politics and industry, where the struggle to overcome the power of capitalism was to be waged. In these political circles leisure was to become a weapon in the class struggle. In other, more moderate, sections of the labour movement different perspectives prevailed. As Stephen Jones has pointed out, Labour leaders were generally more interested in securing the shorter hours and better pay that would enable workers to enjoy their leisure, but even so concern was shown for the content, purpose and use of leisure.[11] The Trades Union Congress (TUC), for example, launched an important enquiry into these matters during the Second World War.[12] When it came to the implementing of reforms, the municipality was an obvious battleground. Labour and socialist councillors campaigned on a number of issues, many of them practical and immediate, such as the call for more ample provision of sports fields.[13] But the vision could be more panoptic and incisive. The veteran socialist Dan Irving illustrated this in a planned strategy for municipal action on the eve of the First World War when he called for schools, libraries, theatres and a range of other services to be made available through the public purse for the 'comfort, convenience and healthful enjoyment' of the 'common people'. By including laundries and bakeries in his scheme, Irving went beyond the usual litany of municipal reform inherited from the Victorian period and showed sensitivity to specific class and gender issues. A labour force in which women and men might work in comparable roles was therefore one in which caring and domestic services needed to be made available by the state, not left by default to be vested in the 'women's sphere'.[14] Municipal reform of the environment and leisure could therefore be something that was attuned to the specific interests and conditions of working people rather than being projected as general 'provision'.

In places where the labour movement was able to achieve some electoral influence, and this did not usually happen before the 1920s, municipalities sometimes essayed changes of more than a piecemeal nature, although more often than not the impact was one of rhetoric rather than of substance. In 'Little Moscows' – industrial towns and villages where labour organizations were influenced by the Communist Party – efforts were often directed to achieving improvements in the educational system, either through reform of the curriculum or in the provision of school meals, and by electing socialist councillors to district education committees and school management committees.[15] In a broader sense the impact of socialist culture was often marginal. Though labour institutions such as miners' lodges and working-men's clubs were usually centres of oppositional ideas about leisure in communities of this kind, the electoral strength of the left was rarely great enough for the power of the municipality to be used as the agency for transforming the cultural life of the whole town.[16] In the Lancashire cotton town of Nelson, sometimes described as a 'Little Moscow' but in reality a left-wing Labour Party fiefdom where Labour dominated the local council from 1927 onwards, municipal resources were used alongside voluntary and commercial provisions to supplement working people's leisure experience. This most often occurred at times of unemployment or strike action. During the county-wide cotton lockouts of 1928 and 1931–32, for example, the town council of Nelson adopted a distinctive stance. Notwithstanding the arguments that had taken place during the General Strike of 1926 over the 'correct' position to be assumed by government in industrial conflicts, Nelson councillors made no attempt to remain neutral in the disputes, still less to take the part of 'authority' against the worker. They quite openly adopted a benevolent stance towards trade unionists and, through sub-committees of the council, worked with voluntary associations to promote the 'welfare of the townspeople', meaning that municipal resources would be mobilized to support striking cotton workers. A local chapel was reimbursed out of the rates to cover the costs of its keeping open a reading room for locked-out workers; admission charges to the public baths, tennis courts and bowling greens were reduced to half-price; and free concerts were staged in the local parks. These initiatives provided some succour to the labour movement in a time of difficulty. They also amounted to a statement of political support for the many people upon whose votes Labour depended to maintain its position in the council chamber.[17]

The range of motives for municipal involvement in leisure often included a naked economic one. This was most clearly evident in holiday resort towns, where leisure was the driving force of the local economy. Holiday-making, whether of a sustained weekly or fortnightly nature, or in the form of day excursions, was becoming big business by the late nineteenth century[18] and cut-throat competition between resort towns was a striking feature of the holiday trade. Business people with a property and retail interest in the developing of towns for tourist purposes frequently came to prominence, and dominance, on local councils, using their political power to steer the town's economy in a direction which suited the holiday interest. As Richard Roberts has pointed out, Bournemouth possessed no chamber of commerce for several years before the First World War. It did not need one: the council chamber served as 'the instrument of the resort's tradesmen'.[19] The role of the municipality as 'impresario' (Roberts' term) in providing a tourist infrastructure in the form of piers, promenades, pavilions and parks was in most cases crucial to the resort's success in attracting visitors. This plainly commercial trajectory could become a source of local friction between contending parties on a number of overlapping issues: the nature of the visitors to be attracted – 'better-off' or working class; the 'tone' of the resort;[20] and the benefits likely to accrue to residents, especially those not connected to the holiday trades. These considerations were balanced in all resorts, whether like Bournemouth and Eastbourne they retained an essentially 'better-class' image or, as in the case of Blackpool and Southend, they sought to attract a broader clientele. Usually the 'progressives' (as the tradesmen's party in Bournemouth styled itsef) prevailed. No resort was exclusively dedicated to a single class of visitors, and even the country's most successful working-class holiday resort, Blackpool, had a history of 'respectable' tourism, and a local interest group ready to promote it. It was in Blackpool that the relationship between municipal and commercial leisure development achieved its closest alignment, and where important features of the municipality's role in leisure are revealed.

John Walton's research has uncovered a fascinating local dynamic driving Blackpool's development towards a predominantly working-class resort with pockets of 'better-off' tourists. Its local government before and after incorporation in 1876 possessed a strong representation of the holiday and building trades, coalescing around two interest groups – one concerned to promote a more respectable form of tourism and the other, led by the Bickerstaffes and gaining the ascendancy in the 1890s, firmly committed to the creation of a working-class holiday industry. Among this group there was none of the 'high-minded motives' of philanthropic improvement which were present in Bristol, or even of the Nonconformist probity which shaped nearby South-port's quite different development as a seaside resort. In Blackpool an un-bridled commercialism was at work, to the extent even that considerations of the needs of the holiday trade outweighed those of local residents.[21] The moral imperative in the municipality's approach to leisure was nudged aside in favour of what Walton has called 'Blackpool's philistine pragmatism',[22] although some measure of seemliness was preserved in the controls exercised by the borough to ensure that the independent traders and hawkers, quacks and fraudsters who populated the South Shore were not allowed to detract from both the new mechanical and the indoor forms of entertainment. The town's attractions, notably its piers, promenade, Pleasure Beach, Tower and Winter Gardens, were vigorously advertised over a long period of time stretching well into the twentieth century, in the course of which Blackpool became a byword for innovation, pleasure, and modernity – 'a little America in Lancashire' as Tony Bennett has memorably described it.[23]

THE DECLINE OF THE MUNICIPALITY

Whether for reasons of health, morality, commerce or politics, municipal initiatives in leisure of the kinds described above have a characteristically Victorian stamp. They emerged in their different forms from a singular milieu, in which the problem of fashioning leisure to an urban environment occupied a central place in the minds of both civic leaders and those they led. In this respect Victorian approaches to leisure continued to exercise an influence long after the Victorian period had ended. We might therefore see the years between the 1860s and the Second World War as something of a 'golden age' of municipal leisure endeavour, if not of local government generally.[24] In spite of some flawed thinking and the practical failures that resulted from it, as the example of Bristol makes clear, there was at this time a distinctive sense that the local community could be improved through the application of local ideas and local energy.

As with much else in the Victorian legacy of local civic pride, its leisure traditions were gradually erased in the second half of the twentieth century. This process had a number of causes, ranging from changes in the social composition of local councils[25] to the acquisition by central government of extended powers in, for example, health and public utility provision. Even in 1935, in a volume celebrating a century of municipal government since the passing of the Municipal Corporations Act of 1835, William Robson warned that the idea of Britain as a country of 'local self-government' was fallacious.[26] The result of the gradual and seemingly ineluctable rise of central government was that in place of a multitude of local initiatives of a relatively independent nature, there developed a series of activities in local government which were increasingly constrained and sometimes shackled by central state influence. The chief feature of central–local relations in the Victorian period had been the imaginative use by municipalities of permissive powers contained in parliamentary legislation to do things the municipalities were not *required* to do and, indeed, which some felt were *ultra vires* in that they exceeded the municipalities' powers.[27] After the Second World War, and especially in the 1970s and 1980s, the influence of the central state over local initiatives was more pervasive, and the scope permitted to the municipality more circumscribed. Local government seemed no longer a partner of central government, more an agent carrying out its plans.

However, we must guard against an over-pessimistic view. Whilst it is certainly true that the economic problems of the late twentieth century, and the attempted political solutions to which they gave rise, forced a profound change in the relationship between central and local government, there was nevertheless scope for much municipal action, and much that could still be distinctive in that action.[28] Nick Hayes's case study of the building of the Nottingham Playhouse affords an excellent example of such municipal initiative, revealing as it does the subtle interplays of interest that emerged not only between the local and central governmental spheres, but also between the various 'sectors' of leisure provision. For all the political acrimony generated in Nottingham by the Playhouse project (acrimony which was never more apparent than on the very opening night of the new theatre in 1963), it remained a symbol of civic pride, an achievement which showed Nottingham as a national leader, and therefore something of which all local people, of whatever political persuasion, could feel proud.[29] A similar sentiment accompanied the city council's reconstruction programme in Coventry during the 15 or so years following the Second World War, when the building of a civic theatre – the Belgrade – yet again stood as a symbol of local resurgence, until overtaken in that role by the much grander symbol of Basil Spence's new cathedral in the early 1960s. In spite of this, however, the historian of Coventry's reconstruction is cautious about claiming too much for local initiative in this whole enterprise, noting that 'Whitehall domination' accounted for the gap between what local leaders had aspired to immediately after the war, and what had actually been achieved by the 1960s.[30]

None the less, there is plenty of evidence of local activity, especially in the provision of sports facilties. The pursuit of the objective of 'Sport For All', embraced by the Sports Council in the early 1970s, produced a quantitative leap in local leisure provision which resulted in the appearance in many British towns and cities of the leisure centre, a characteristically late twentieth-century social institution. From virtually none at the beginning of the 1970s, there were some 1200 such venues by the end of the following decade. Much of this, and of the parallel increase in the provision of swimming pools, was financed through local government. Houlihan has pointed out that by the end of the 1980s the Sports Council had a budget of some £45 million; local authorities by contrast were spending almost 20 times that amount on sport and leisure.[31] Moreover, there developed at the same time, as a consequence of the reorganization of local government in 1974, large leisure services departments to co-ordinate the provision at the local level of a wide range of services; and within them a cadre of leisure professionals skilled in the analysis of leisure needs and the administration of resources. Spurred on by the improved career opportunities that reorganization had created, they acquired an influential position in the formulation of leisure policy.[32] In addition, and stemming from the Education Act of 1944, local education authorities had become importantly involved in the development of sports and games through the school curriculum, a function previously associated mainly with private schools.

In general terms, however, central government's intervention in local affairs was becoming plainer; and nowhere more so than in Northern Ireland. In that part of the United Kingdom the district councils formed in the early 1970s to counteract sectarianism in local government were stripped of their responsibilties for leisure and recreational services. These were transferred to the Department of Education for Northern Ireland. The reasons for such an exceptional interventionist role relate, naturally, to the exceptional nature of Northern Irish politics and society. Economic backwardness over many years had resulted in poor recreational facilities in the province, and the dramatic upsurge of political violence in the late 1960s caused mainland political leaders to think that leisure might be a means of dampening sectarian hostilities; in particular the form this had often taken in the late 1960s and early 1970s, with large riotous assemblies of mainly young people taking to the streets for the 'Saturday night riot'. It was assumed that leisure centres would keep youths off the streets. As one official commented to a researcher: 'if you got them in there at ten in the morning and kept them there until late afternoon, they weren't dragging up stones to throw at the police at night'.[33]

The Northern Ireland Sports Council took an active part in the designing of a programme of extensive new facilities, backed by funds from central government, which endowed Belfast, in particular, with an assemblage of leisure centres far in excess of that enjoyed by similar sized cities in the United Kingdom. Ironically, however, a scheme intended to ease conflict actually served to intensify it. To begin with, it seems unlikely that the leisure centres, popular though they were, had the intended effects. By the time they were ready, the nature of political violence in the province was beginning to change, the presence of police and troops on the streets having served to eliminate riotous assemblies and bring about a different and more covert form of protest. Whether or not this would have happened, it is at best only debatable that the leisure centres would have had their desired effect. As it was, the new leisure centres themselves became the focus of sectarian hostilities. The siting of centres between areas of sectarian conflict does not seem to have been successful in overcoming divisions, for such centres (Maysfield in Belfast and the Brownlow leisure centre in Craigavon are clear examples) failed to draw people out of their 'safe' areas. By contrast, leisure centres placed in the heart of established communities with a strictly sectarian character were seen to flourish; and when in the early 1980s district council responsibility for leisure provision was restored, this process received an electoral impetus. Local politicians vied for funds to build leisure centres, which became a mark of party political achievement, often named after prominent local councillors and identified by the flying of partisan flags. Even over the apparently innocuous issue of Sunday opening tensions arose between Unionists and Nationalists: the former opposed it because the latter were in favour.[34]

The use of statutory powers allied to a political purpose was not confined to Northern Ireland. In other parts of Britain in the 1970s and 1980s local government leisure policy was deeply affected as a consequence of problems being visited upon central government. Some of these were of government's own making. Increasing levels of unemployment, and the perceived association of young people (especially black youths) with crime and disorder, led political leaders to 'target' these areas for sport and leisure provision, much in the way that leisure had been seen as a solution to political disorder in Northern Ireland. Such a manoeuvre was particularly noticeable in the aftermath of the urban riots of the early 1980s, when another recreational ploy – the disbursement of money for urban renewal including, with a whiff of Victorian 'rational recreation', the planting of public gardens – was also tried.[35] Much though this activity was related to current political problems, it was also fundamentally shaped by financial considerations arising from government policy and the economic depression that was partly caused by it. Throughout virtually the whole of the long period of Conservative government from 1979 to 1997, there was a concern to keep direct taxes as low as possible at a time when high levels of unemployment meant, in any case, a generally shrinking tax base. To maintain a strategy of retrenchment it was necessary to rein in the potential of local government, especially Labour-contolled authorities, to spend money. Various devices including rate-capping, the introduction of the 'poll tax' (Community Charge), and the system of compulsory competitive tendering that was required of local authorities in the Local Government Act of 1988 in an attempt to achieve cost effectiveness in the provision of municipal services, all ensured a diminution in the relative autonomy once enjoyed by the municipality. It was summed up in two contrasting images. First, and most dramatically, in the abolition in 1986 of the Greater London Council (GLC), a body which had been a vigorous opponent of central strategy and which in many ways was the epitome of local government autonomy; and second, far less dramatic but no less significant, in the enforced sale of their playing fields by many local schools in an attempt to make good shortfalls in their budgets brought about by reductions in central government grants for education.

These developments were closely linked with Conservative government policy, and indeed reached their apogee in the high summer of Thatcherism in the mid- to late 1980s. But the root cause was deeper than simply party politics and changes of government. It began with the erosion of the so-called 'social-democratic consensus', characterized by the objectives, to which all major parties more or less subscribed, of full employment, rising real wages, and social welfare achieved through Keynesian public spending (a regime sometimes described by commentators as 'Fordist'). With Britain's relative economic decline in the 1960s and the advent in the 1970s of high levels of inflation, precursors of the full-blown 'post-Fordist' strategies of the 1980s were encountered.[36] In fact, it was a Labour Secretary of State who introduced to Parliament in 1975 the White Paper which exemplified the emergence of new approaches in the area of sport and leisure. At precisely the point when local government was spending more on leisure provision than ever before, the White Paper *Sport and Recreation* cautioned:

> The Government accept [*sic*] that recreation should be regarded as 'one of the community's everyday needs' and that provision for it is 'part of the general fabric of the social services'. They recognise that if public provision were to keep pace with the increasing demand for facilities of all kinds this would necessitate a substantial increase (in real terms) of levels of expenditure by local authorities and central government agencies . . . It is . . . already clear that for some years to come local authorities may be obliged to spend less in total on a number of services including sport and recreation than in the recent past.[37]

The White Paper went on to outline the 'priorities' envisaged for recreation policy. These included: areas of special need ('inner urban areas which have suffered from environmental deprivation and have lagged behind particularly in recreational provision'[38]); the opening up for use by the public of major voluntary facilities, such as football clubs; the development of a youth sports programme; participation in sport by the disabled; and the allocating of funds to help gifted sportspeople.[39] The White Paper had echoes of the Wolfenden Report in its call for the strengthening of links between schools and local sports clubs in order to overcome 'the gap', and also in the idea of greater national co-ordination of recreational activity, now more possible through a network of agencies such as the Sports Council, the Countryside Commission and the Tourist Boards. It represented an important step in a process, which was to go farther under subsequent governments, of subordinating local government to national strategy, essentially through the discipline of financial controls.

The caging of local authority was not, however, a straightforward matter, and some municipalities struggled to be free of their bonds. The GLC was a celebrated example, its leisure policy designed in highly political terms, in the manner almost of the 'Little Moscows' of old, to help under-privileged groups in the community. But its success merely brought down on its head the wrath of central government, and the demise of the GLC was the consequence. Examples of towns and cities perpetuating socialist traditions, resisting control, and using their powers to promote counter-strategies, are rare. Sheffield enjoyed some limited success in the 1980s, but more typical of the response of local authorities operating in this climate is the example of 'Northville' (Leeds) described by Ian Henry. This was a large local authority controlled politically by a moderate Labour council which enjoyed harmonious, if not cordial, relations with central government. This was reflected in its guarded willingness to co-operate with a central government inspired Urban Development Corporation which restricted some of the local council's own powers. What is, however, more interesting about this case study is the fact that, in order to forestall the effects of the Urban Development Corporation, the council created its own company (the City Development Company) which in association with private capital embarked on a number of leisure initiatives. The irony of this manoeuvre was that the City Development Company came to adopt precisely the tactics and methods that it had been feared would attend the operations of the Urban Development Corporation: secrecy of planning, lack of co-operation with elected councillors, the selling of council real estate to assist private development, hostility and suspicion from local people, and so on. Further to this, central influence brought about a series of restrictions on expenditure, including compulsory competitive tendering, and had the effect of limiting new leisure and recreation schemes to those which were likely to attract commercial interest and capital rather than those which might have been perceived to be for the public good. Thus, the city council in 'Northville' was forced to conduct a series of manoeuvres in order to negotiate its position with that of central government and its quasi-public creatures such as the Urban Development Corporation. The scope for manoeuvre was, however, limited, even drawing a Labour authority into measures disliked by its own supporters. It is Henry's contention that, in the grander scheme of things, taking into account global movements of capital and the economic changes that accompany them, the contradictions inherent in the central–local relationships characterizing what he calls 'Right post-Fordism' will work against all left political parties, causing them further to do things that will alienate their supporters.[40]

CONCLUSION

The involvement of local government in sport and leisure therefore presents us with a kaleidoscopic image. There have been many different intitiatives undertaken at this level which have been influenced by various circumstances and motives. In this shifting process, however, some things stand out. One is the long-term trend which has seen local activity being brought more fully into national strategy. It is a change that has resulted not so much in lower levels of spending by the municipality as in a limitation of the scope for its initiative, a consequence seen in many areas other than sport and leisure. A second outcome of the changes in the state–leisure relationship at the local level provides, paradoxically, an element of continuity across the years. The emphasis on health in the rational recreation schemes of many municipalities in the Victorian period still has an echo in the modern leisure centre, the institution which for most people probably represents the embodiment of the local state's contribution to leisure. The leisure centre is now, at the beginning of the twenty-first century, not only a familiar feature of the landscape, but also something of a palimpsest upon which can be seen inscribed many of the features of contemporary social life. Less than half a mile from where these words are being written is situated just such a centre, which in its daily operations no doubt typifies several hundred similar places throughout the country. It enjoys a pleasant location, adjacent to a secondary school which uses many of its faciltities in the physical education curriculum. It offers a range of sporting and leisure activities – football, snooker, aerobics, fitness training, squash, badminton, tennis, indoor cricket, swimming and many others – to a range of clients who come from the immediate neighbourhood and also from farther afield. Use is by both the casual and the pre-booked club client. The centre's café and bar are popular venues for locals, especially when big sporting occasions are being shown on its large-screen television which receives the satellite broadcasts. The centre has also housed many popular musical concerts. In many ways it seems a natural centre for its community which, being semirural, has no other obvious focal point. It strives hard, in the spirit of Sport For All, to present itself as a unifying force. The walls of the leisure centre display various posters and advertisements which reveal an attempt to speak to many groups in the community: the parents of the very young, the elderly, the unemployed, women, youths. In some senses it might almost be the physical manifestation of the meeting place envisaged by reconstructionists years ago, who sought physical recreation and social solidarity under one roof. For all this, however, we know from surveys that the usage of such centres is limited, in both overall percentage terms and in relation to social class, age, gender and ethnicity. We are a long way from achieving 'sport for all'. Perhaps 'sport for some' is the best that can be claimed so far.[41] The local leisure centre none the less stands as a reminder of the continuing importance of the municipality in helping to shape and make available leisure activities.

Key Reading

Houlihan, B. *The Government and Politics of Sport.* London: Routledge, 1991.

Henry, I. *The Politics of Leisure Policy.* Basingstoke: Macmillan – now Palgrave, 1993.

Macintyre, S. *Little Moscows: Communism and Working Class Militance in Inter-War Britain.* London: Croom Helm, 1980.

Meller, H. *Leisure and the Changing City, 1870–1914.* London: Routledge and Kegan Paul, 1976.

Walton, J., and Walvin, J. *Leisure in Britain, 1780–1939.* Manchester: Manchester University Press, 1983.

Chronology of Events

1846–1870 Numerous acts of parliament empowered local government to provide leisure services: 1846 Public Baths and Workhouses Act; 1849 Museums Act; 1850 Libraries Act; 1852 Recreation Grounds Act; 1870 Education Act – introduced rudimentary physical education in the curriculum.

1925–33 Creation of over 1000 local recreation grounds following pressure from the National Playing Fields Association.

1936 Some 50 municipal golf courses had been established in England, mostly since the war of 1914–18.

1937 The Physical Training and Recreation Act conferred on local authorities powers to make provision for playing fields, gymnasiums, holiday camps, campsites and swimming baths.

1958 Extension to 1937 Act gave local authorities power to grant loans to voluntary organizations for the sport and leisure activities defined in the original Act.

1974 Reorganization of local government resulted in the creation of large leisure services departments amalgamating previously separate departments (e.g. parks and gardens).

1980 Local Government Planning and Land Act introduced the block grant system, with local government funding based upon central government's assessment of local authorities' needs; also introduced Compulsory Competitive Tendering (CCT), extended to sport and leisure services in 1989.

1982 Local Government Finance Act prevented local authorities from raising a supplementary rate.

1984 Rates Act introduced 'rate-capping' to limit rates set by local authorities.

1986 Abolition of the Greater London Council.

2000 Local authorities required to ensure that continuous improvements are made in the running of their leisure services, according to 'Best Value Performance' plans.

chapter 11

Conclusion: Describing Cyrano's Nose

Historians often refer to 'Cleopatra's nose' when talking about the problem of causation and accident in history: would the politics of the Mediterranean in Roman times have been different if Cleopatra's nose had been bigger, and Caesar and Marc Anthony had not been attracted to her? But concluding a study which has attempted such a broad span as the present one brings to mind another nose: that of Cyrano de Bergerac. This, it will be recalled, was a physical feature of some prominence, a description of which might bring forth a variety of metaphors from someone with 'un peu de lettres et d'esprit'[1]. In a similar way, depending upon one's predilections, there are various emphases and themes that might form the basis of a conclusion to a study of sport and leisure in the twentieth century. It might be done in any of the following ways:

Quantitatively: by showing the increase in participation in sport and leisure through the century. For despite the evident unevenness of participation rates, with white middle-class males being far more involved in sport and leisure than elderly women from ethnic communities, there has none the less been a long-term increase across the century in the numbers of people involved in leisure activity of various kinds.[2] As Holt and Mason note, the fears of those at the beginning of the century, who thought that spectatorism might soon outweigh active involvement, have proved groundless.[3]

Economically: by revealing the determinants that have shaped the development of sport and leisure. Whilst there is no straightforward relationship between economic circumstances and leisure activity, there is no doubt that periods of economic upturn have provided opportunities for development which were not present in times of mass unemployment and business depression. Thus, the 1950s contrasts with the 1930s in this respect, although not for all people in all parts of the country. Generally speaking, though, what explains the rise in participation is a general rise in material living standards, and a greater amount of time at an individual's disposal to devote to leisure.

Theoretically: by deploying the empirical evidence to prove or disprove the various theories on the role of sport and leisure. Such an activity, as is argued below, has its attractions but can often be as misleading as it is enlightening.

Semiotically: by showing how the 'signs' of sport and leisure create meanings in our lives. One of the major themes of this study has been the importance, perhaps hitherto neglected by historians, of the *ideological* influence of sport and leisure as communicated through a variety of cultural texts and practices in helping us to think not only about sport and leisure, but about many other aspects of our lives and relationships.

Heroically: by remembering the great moments of sport that live in people's thought and which become part of the popular memory. Contrary to much writing about sport, which has dwelt on the heroic, this book has tended to play it down; if only because it has been felt that other aspects should have attention directed to them. But this is not to underestimate the enormous importance attached by people who follow sport to the achievements of the 'stars'.

Whiggishly: by asserting the 'progress' of sport and leisure as we move through the century. This is an implicit theme in much popular discourse about sport, though one which the present study rejects. Its stance has been to acknowledge that though things do change, they do not necessarily improve.

Reverently: by assuming that sport and leisure are 'good things' that exist for the health of society. This book holds no brief for sport or leisure one way or the other. Just as historians of war do not wish for conflict, though analyse its significance when it happens, so historians of sport and leisure should take their cue from the fact that they are activities which involve many people, and are therefore worth studying for that reason; whether or not the historian happens to *like* sport or leisure is neither here nor there.

Chronologically: by examining the continuities and changes in sport and leisure practice and organization across the century.

And so on: the list, especially if wrought with Cyranoesque eloquence and wit, could be an extensive one.

THE 'SECTORS' REVISITED

To a degree these themes are encompassed in the organizing framework of this book, which has been that of the three 'sectors' of sport and leisure provision: the commercial, the voluntary and the state. The commercial has grown to a great size, so that it is now common for people to refer to the 'leisure industry'. There are many ways in which British people purchase leisure through the market, which itself has come to occupy an important place in the late twentieth-century national and international economy, far more important than ever it was in 1900, or even in 1950. It is exceedingly difficult to quantify exactly how much all this involvement in sport and leisure amounts to. John Benson's attempts to estimate expenditure on three aspects of leisure – sport, tourism and shopping – show significant though variable increases over the period between 1860 and 1980.[4] Any number of random indicators can be cited to express the volume of the sport and leisure business as it currently stands. By the end of the twentieth century football alone, for example, was said to account internationally for some £150 billion.[5] At the same time sport and leisure in Britain made up £10 billion of consumer expenditure annually, employed three-quarters of a million workers, and produced £3.5 billion in tax revenue.[6] In 1900 Britain was the most commercially developed of the European countries in terms of sport and leisure. It no longer holds this exceptional position, but there is no doubt that the commercial sector continues to fulfil an important fuction in the provision of sport and leisure to many millions of British people.

Whether it is the *most* important sector depends on one's judgement of what is important. The voluntary sector might be seen as the one which is most distinctively British, in that it was through the activities of clubs and other leisure organizations that a peculiarly British 'amateur' ethos of self-help and improvement developed, some might say to the detriment of British competitiveness in the world at large.[7] Be that as it may, a great deal of 'social capital' was invested in voluntary associations, where people did things because they wanted to, and in so doing formed bonds and networks which made up so much of the country's social fabric. Towards the end of the twentieth century there were indications that some of these bonds and networks seemed less secure than once they had been. A. H. Halsey, writing in the early 1970s, noted that there was an 'Americanization' of Britain taking place which reduced the social homogeneity of the population and had led to an increased sense of impersonality. A decline of involvement in religious organizations and the development of racial tensions resulting from immigration were identified by Halsey as key aspects of this process.[8] These features scarcely diminished in the last 30 years of the century, although there was perhaps a need to guard against undue pessimism. Some voluntary activities were notably losing support. In the larger women's associations, for example, there was an almost unrelieved decline of membership between 1971 and 1991, with that of the Mothers' Union and the National Union of Townswomen's Guilds falling by almost half. By contrast, however, membership of various organizations for young people had held up quite well, with some – the Cub Scouts, Brownie Guides, National Association of Boys' Clubs, and participation in the Duke of Edinburgh's Award scheme – actually showing an increase.[9] None the less, the trend of decline seemed sufficiently clear by the end of the century for British commentators to be giving at least some consideration to the ideas of the American social scientist Robert Putnam, whose concerns about the decline of social capital in the USA were felt to have relevance to Britain.[10]

One of Putnam's stopping-off points on a recent visit to London was 10 Downing Street. In spite of the professed wish of the Conservative administrations of the years between 1979 and 1997 to 'roll back' the boundaries of the state, the voice of government continued to be heard in many quarters. The Labour government of Tony Blair is little different in this respect. It reminds us that the state sector has played an increasingly active part in the area of sport and leisure, in a number of different central and local guises. The former achieve a high profile in the media, and the government's clear association with the English bid to host the 2006 World Cup was just one indication of this, so is the feeling in press and public that the government should also intervene to sort out the mess that has developed around the scheme to rebuild Wembley Stadium.[11] It should, however, be remembered that the relationship between the state and leisure is closest at the local level, where a far greater amount of public money changes hands between municipal authorities and organizations involved in promoting sport and leisure, and always has done.

GRAND NARRATIVES AND SOCIAL CONTROL

Such a summary of developments, however, serves only to point up the polymorphous nature of sport and leisure in twentieth-century Britain. The secular profusion of developments and experiences in this huge field makes for a constantly changing and varied picture. It is also one which, for the most part, evades the analyst's attempts to impose order and to set patterns. This being so, there is a strong temptation to dispense with a conclusion which attempts to tie everything together in a neat and tidy ending. The danger of attempting this lies in forcing events into a constraining pigeonhole, trying to extract a universal meaning from what is, in fact, a diverse field of activity which yields many meanings and trends, and which possesses no overarching shape. Imposing order can simply result in distortion. To suggest this is also to prompt some heretical thoughts which take us beyond the bounds of conventional history. It implies that there are no particular directions in which sport and leisure have been heading over the past hundred years. It might also suggest that, even if the nature of British society itself in the twentieth century can be apprehended in a totalizing way, sport and leisure have played no particular role in general social developments; that they stand aside from political, economic, social and cultural developments as mere entertainments. Such thoughts can be quickly banished. It is emphatically not the intention of this conclusion either to produce an academic version of Stephen Blackpool's 'it's aw a muddle', or to relegate sport and leisure to the substitute's bench of history. It has been a principal point of contention in the foregoing analysis that sport and leisure can be examined according to certain regularities, and that both play an important part in the development of British social relations.

However, there is a strong sense in which the enquiry undertaken in the present study gives some sustenance to the idea of the end of the grand, or 'meta', narrative: the attempt to compress into a single unifying explanation or theory an entire canvas of human activity. The rejection of such omniscient perspectives in favour of a smaller focus is, of course, a hallmark of some (though not all) postmodern historiographical practice. 'Truth claims' are the central issue here, though I must be careful of arrogating too much episte-mological importance to what has been offered in this book. There is an immense chasm between the attempts of a frustrated historian, despairing of making sense of a confusion of developments, and Lyotard's well-known assault on those explanatory narratives – Marxism, or the largely non-Marxist 'modernization theory' being prime examples – which attempt to appropri-ate to themselves the 'truth' about a society and its development. Lyotard, perhaps the philosopher *par excellence* of postmodernism, was concerned with the relative nature of the various discursive practices through which 'truth' was reached.[12] The present volume has not explicitly sought to issue any epis-temological challenges to anyone, nor has it embraced any particular school or trend of thought; indeed, it conforms in many respects to a fairly traditional empirical approach to its subject matter. Yet there are some links, tenuous perhaps, between the two projects – between the historian seeking under-standing and the philosopher looking for 'truth'. The chief one is in the way the whole field of sport and leisure is conceived in this book to be essentially an *ideological* one. That is to say, in addition to its being a field in which many activities occur – notably struggles to influence the ways in which people spend their free time, as well as attempts to make money out of their enjoy-ment of sport and leisure – it is primarily a field in which *meaning* is produced and contested. Sport and leisure therefore are themselves something through which 'truth' and 'reality' are constituted. This process, involving many medi-ations, takes places in multifarious forms and in relation to a variety of iden-tities. The operation of sport and leisure as social activity forms a part of the discourses and ideologies that make up Lyotard's 'little narratives'. To put it in another way, sport and leisure are not a passive 'object' which can be scru-tinized and understood by the social analyst; they are processes which actively contribute to our understanding of the world, and thus to the analyst's view of it. They are, moreover, quantitatively large processes in contemporary society, with a powerful embrace. As Richard Holt has reminded us, 'there is no escaping sport'.[13]

It is this very omnipresence of sport and leisure that registers them as important for the social historian, and which at the same time has drawn them into the grand narrative. In much contemporary writing, especially of sociologists and historians writing from a theoretical perspective – John Hargreaves is a good example – sport is regarded as a pivotal process which has a key function in the social structure.[14] 'Social control', a concept which has been taken up by some historians, is never far away from the study of sport and leisure in one form or another, implicitly or explicitly. It occupies a central place in many a grand narrative, which becomes a story about the development of the captalist system and its ethic, an edifice which sport and leisure, along with other social processes, serve to render as 'normal' to the population at large. The idea of social control is thus premissed upon an aberration that needs to be explained: why, for example, 'the system' maintains itself, or why 'the people' or 'the working class' do not rise up against it. It represents a particular kind of problematic. The controlling function sought might be found either as agency or structure. As, for example, a series of campaigns for the moral improvement of working-class men and women through rational recreation, a movement to be seen in some profusion in the earlier years of the century.[15] Or as a structural process that ensures the continuance of the capitalist system, with sport, a process emphasizing competition and team work, seen as reinforcing ideas of work discipline. Leisure activities as diverse as tourism and aerobics both create concerns about the body, and thus help to perpetuate gender stereotypes as well as stimulating the demand for the products of leisure consumption. The erotic element in sports, as a further example, has been seen as one of the primary fuels of modern commercial advertising. Economic imperatives and the social habits needed to recognize them are thus satisfied at one and the same time.[16] This whole process, especially in its structural forms, is most clearly, perhaps exaggeratedly, foregrounded in the work of the French theorist Jean-Marie Brohm.[17]

Seeing sport and leisure as having a disciplining function in modern society is especially noticeable when discussion is directed to the most recent of what economic historians like to call the 'leisure climacaterics'. There have been three over the course of the nineteenth and twentieth centuries. The first was that associated with the change from 'traditional' to 'modern' society and which, in Britain, involved the impact on leisure habits of the whole process of industrialization, a process that had possibly less impact than was once supposed. The second was that which produced the rise of mass culture in the late nineteenth and early twentieth centuries, establishing an extensive commercially based popular culture. During both of these phases leisure was a secondary concomitant of work, which claimed the primary social disciplining function. The third climacteric occurred during the final quarter of the twentieth century and is characterized by increasing levels of *un*employment, and the attempts by political authorities to casualize labour markets through the undermining of trade union power. Some significant changes in the nature of work resulted, including an increase in part-time female work, often on an outwork basis, the engagement of labour on short-term contracts, the release of older workers through early retirement schemes, and an increasing emphasis in the employment that remained on servicing the leisure needs of the community, especially through various forms of entertainment.[18] In this context, the relative decline of work as the structuring force in individuals' lives has caused some commentators to throw more emphasis on leisure as a focus of activity and identity, thus making it a yet more critical area of social concern. The perception of subversive leisure – or Rojek's 'abnormal leisure' – is no less present in these circumstances than it was during either of the two previous climacterics; it is perhaps even more acute, making the 'problem' of leisure a matter for yet greater concern.[19]

In the three 'sectors' investigated in this study there has been ample illustration of the concerns over sport and leisure, and the attempts to direct and regulate 'free time' so as to render it both safe and socially constructive. This is possibly the most abiding theme to emerge from the period studied: that leisure, though often regarded as a residual category in relation to work, is never 'innocent' activity. It has required constant attention to ensure its proper development. There is even a temptation to regard the 'providers' of leisure, whether commercial or statist, as being engaged in a conspiracy to produce something that will keep the population mollified, a notion fictionalized in Aldous Huxley's dystopian novel *Brave New World* (1932). Thus the immense growth since the end of the nineteenth century of commercial sport and leisure – examined here in terms of sporting practices and organization, the media that inform about them, the rise of the cinema, and the growth of mass tourism – could be seen in a reassuring light from the perspective of social control. In spite of the doubts that all these forms provoked in some people's minds about passive spectatorism and other non-active habits, they none the less kept millions of people amused and happy (a point often lost sight of by critics emphasizing alienation of the 'real self') while communicating essentially conservative images about society. British cultural and political elites have worried to an extent that might surprise and amuse citizens of the early twenty-first century that the content of leisure was, for example, unduly American and thus likely to undermine the common national culture and to loosen the bonds that tied society together. For critics like T. S. Eliot (if there ever was anyone quite like him), the 'democratization' of culture implicit in American imports challenged the organic community of both the upper and lower classes which had ensured political and social stability and continuity.[20] Similar issues bothered the members of the Pilkington Committee on broadcasting in the 1950s and 1960s. Forty years on, in a globalized culture, these concerns have a quaintly old-fashioned air about them. Who now worries about such matters? And in any case, the influence of American cultural imperialism has always been weakest in British sport whose main game – football – has conquered the world largely without American help. With or without American influence, commercial sport and leisure has certainly become an established feature of the modern economy, though only recently in sport has it begun to display the business characteristics evident much earlier in, say, the cinema. Whether it exercises a significant *controlling* function in our lives remains, however, questionable.

Its influence is not all-consuming. Many of those millions who enjoy commercial popular culture are also creating their own leisure forms through clubs, societies and home-based hobbies. Such activity is not of course as 'free' as it might seem; hobbies gave working men (they were usually male pursuits) a certain amount of freedom and autonomy from the routines of the workplace (not to mention the routines of the home), but they were often themselves enmeshed in a commercial market. George Orwell observed part of this on the shelves of high-street newsagents, where magazines and papers dealing in hobbies were evident in great profusion. They might even have been inspired by the culture of the workshop: 'the hobby of many carpenters and painters was carpentry and painting'.[21] In some senses therefore, the disciplines of work extended into the home. But it is difficult to avoid seeing much of this voluntary activity as a natural expression of people's everyday lives. J. B. Priestley summed it up well when he recalled from his youth the men who met in pubs to sing: '[they] were not being humbugged by any elaborate publicity scheme on the part of either music publishers or brewers . . . they were singing glees over their beer because they liked to sing glees over their beer'.[22] This kind of thing is especially so of women, who in the later part of the century had populated the voluntary domestic area of leisure in greater numbers than men.[23] Only an unnecessarily convoluted vision of social activity would make us want to see this as something 'engineered', either by representatives of authority or by 'the system'. It is not conflict free, it is often very partisan and divisive, but is it social control?

The answer is provided if we look at the most popular leisure form of the entire century, the activity that might be claimed to have introduced the single most qualitative improvement in many people's lives: watching television. It is one of the most private of leisure forms, something which has helped to secure the home as a social institution for all the family. From the outset, there has never been any sense in which individual families had any formal control over the medium. Moreover, inherited from its pre-existence as radio, the development of television was attended by a quite intrusive concern to ensure that what people watched in their own homes was 'suitable'. The relationship between voluntary activity and state involvement therefore became very close in the case of broadcasting, and was fairly soon joined by a commercial interest. Thus all three 'sectors' of leisure were present in the medium. It did not take long after the advent of commercial television for viewers to begin deserting the BBC and its paternalist culture in large numbers. Television's potential for social control was thus undermined by the presence of a leisure market in broadcasting, which gave people the opportunity to vote with their feet, or at least with their index fingers. What they voted for, of course, might only have been a different set of ideological emphases: game shows might be more 'popular' than 'educational' programmes, but if both operate according to similar conventional notions of gender relations, if each talks down to working-class viewers, or communicates an essentially white Anglo-Saxon view of the world, and if one adds to all this an emphasis through its advertisements on consumerism, then there is perhaps no real choice available. It would be nonsensical to suggest that broadcasting in either its statist or commercial form has *no* influence on people, and to this extent the idea of social control has some validity. But influential though television has been in providing people with visions of themselves, offering them a language through which to think about the world, it has never, for all its popularity, been the *only* discourse available. The inventory of social influences is a long one and, what is more, a contradictory one. To put it very simply, a viewer of *Coronation Street* might also be a trade unionist on strike.

Sport and leisure, through their very pervasiveness, contain many of these contradictions. Herein lies both their importance, and their intangibility. They are sites in which a whole series of meanings are created, contested and fashioned. Geertz showed this process at work through his observations of the Balinese cockfight.[24] This seems to me the principal reason for studying them. If it is not to be so, if our study of sport and leisure does not attempt to tease out the meaning of what we do in our 'free time', and to place it in some context of contestation and negotiation, it seems to me *not* to be a very significant aspect of our lives. There are others of greater importance. I would go along with the sentiments expressed on popular culture by Stuart Hall, and say that if the study of sport and leisure is not 'political' in the broadest sense of that term, then it isn't worth a damn.[25]

And yet, for all that, there is something peculiarly existential about sport and leisure, which an academic reckoning cannot quite account for. Sometimes the creative writer captures it better. In Howard Jacobson's novel *The Mighty Walzer*, the hero, a table-tennis player of some note in his youth, but now long past playing and regrettably coming to the realisation that he had only been 'so-so', wanders into the Ninth World Veterans' Championship at the Manchester G-Mex Centre.

> Why, there were men here, playing in the over-eighties' competition, wearing knee supports and elastic hose and bandages round every joint, so arthritic that they required the assistance of a third party to retrieve any ball for them that didn't finish up in the net . . . Could *their* imaginations still be rioting in futurity, looking forward to the day when they'd be world beaters?[26]

For Jacobson's veterans – men and women – sport made up a still-important element in their lives, capable of providing them with dreams and conflicts that drove them on, made life worth living. For the Mighty Walzer himself it defined a time in his life when achievement, subsequently unrealized, had seemed possible. Because we are thus intimately defined through our leisure it remains a subject of central importance to the historian, to be understood as best we might.

Key Reading •

Holt, R., and Mason, T. *Sport in Britain, 1945–2000*. Oxford: Blackwell, 2000.

Lyotard, J.-F. *The Postmodern Condition: A Report on Knowledge*. Manchester: Manchester University Press, 1984.

Rojek, C. *Leisure and Culture*. Basingstoke: Macmillan – now Palgrave, 2000.

Notes

1 INTRODUCTION: 'FREE TIME' IN THE TWENTIETH CENTURY

1. See R. W. Cox, *Sport in Britain: A Bibliography of Historical Publications 1800–1988* (Manchester: Manchester University Press, 1991) and his regular updates of publications in *International Journal of the History of Sport* and *The Sports Historian*.
2. *Social Trends* and the *Annual Abstract of Statistics*, produced by the Office for National Statistics (London: Stationery Office), are valuable repositories of this information.
3. Peter J. Beck notes in his recent *Scoring For Britain: International Football and International Politics, 1900–1939* (London: Frank Cass, 1999) that 'whereas previously I included a whole chapter justifying the historical study of sport, today such a rationale seems superfluous, even if my experience of service on the history panels for the 1992 and 1996 Research Assessment Exercises as well as for the Humanities Research Board . . . leads me to believe that the history of sport has yet to be fully accepted by all academic historians (p. vii). Andrew Blake, *The Body Language: The Meaning of Modern Sport* (London: Lawrence and Wishart, 1996) mounts a spirited offensive on cultural studies for its neglect of sport.
4. It is surprising, for example, that the leading journal of social and cultural history, *Past and Present*, has published very little on the subject of sport. The same is true of other leading journals. Perhaps sports historians do not submit work to them.
5. A. Marwick, *British Society Since 1945* (London: Penguin Books, 1996 edn). This is rectified to some extent in Marwick's more recent *A History of the Modern British Isles, 1914–1999: Circumstances, Events and Outcomes* (Oxford: Blackwell, 2000).
6. A notable exception to this trend is Ross McKibbin's admirable *Classes and Cultures: England 1918–1951* (Oxford: Oxford University Press, 1998) which brings many aspects of sport and leisure directly into prominence.
7. This is, perhaps, a slightly unfair comment on sports history. See J. Hill, 'British Sports History: A Post-Modern Future?', *Journal of Sport History*, 23, 1 (1996) 1–19.
8. This is essentially the approach adopted in the first truly academic study of British football, James Walvin's *The People's Game: A Social History of British Football* (London: Allen Lane, 1975).

9. T. Veblen, *The Theory of the Leisure Class* (Mineola, NY: Dover Publications, 1994 edn).

10. See R. Barthes, *Mythologies* (Paris: Seuil, 1957); P. Bourdieu and J.-C. Passeron, *Reproduction in Education, Society and Culture*, trans. R. Nice (London: Sage, 1977); J. Derrida, *Of Grammatology*, trans. G. Spivak (Baltimore, MD: Johns Hopkins University Press, 1976); and J. Baudrillard, *Selected Writings*, ed. M. Poster (Cambridge: Polity Press, 1988). None offers an especially accessible read, and first-timers might dip in at the shallow end by consulting E. Cashmore and C. Rojek, *Dictionary of Cultural Theorists* (London: Arnold, 1999).

11. Geertz's prose is more accessible, though still rather elliptical. See C. Geertz, *The Interpretation of Cultures: Selected Essays* (New York: Basic Books, 1973). Of the essays collected there 'Thick Description: Toward an Interpretive Theory of Culture' and 'Deep Play: Notes on the Balinese Cockfight' have much to say for historians. For a useful critique, see R. G. Walters, 'Signs of the Times: Clifford Geertz and Historians', *Social Research*, 47 (1980) 537–56.

12. *Interpretation of Cultures*, p. 5.

13. For a very interesting and lucid discussion of these matters in relation to sport and leisure, see C. M. Parratt, 'About Turns: Reflecting on Sport History in the 1990s', *Sport History Review*, 29, 1 (1998) 4–17.

14. See G. Turner, *British Cultural Studies* (London: Routledge, 1996 edn).

15. The problem with Gramsci, however, is that he did not always separate the two spheres, and he frequently operates with a large and fluid concept of 'the state'. See J. Femia, *Gramsci's Political Thought: Hegemony, Consciousness and the Revolutionary Process* (Oxford: Clarendon Press, 1981) pp. 26–9.

16. See the 'classic' collection of Gramsci's writings: G. Nowell Smith and Q. Hoare, eds, *Selections From the Prison Notebooks* (London: Lawrence and Wishart, 1971).

17. J. Hargreaves, *Sport, Power and Culture: A Social and Historical Analysis of Popular Sports in Britain* (Cambridge: Polity Press, 1986).

18. See Anne Showstack Sassoon, *Gramsci's Politics* (London: Croom Helm, 1980).

19. M. Polley, *Moving the Goalposts: A History of Sport and Society Since 1945* (London: Routledge, 1998); R. Holt, *Sport and the British: A Modern History* (Oxford: Oxford University Press, 1989); D. Birley, *Land of Sport and Glory: Sport and British Society, 1887–1910* (Manchester: Manchester University Press, 1995); D. Brailsford, *Sport, Time, and Society* (London: Routledge, 1991); N. Wigglesworth, *The Evolution of English Sport* (London: Frank Cass, 1996).

20. It was joined just at the point when this book was being prepared for the press by Richard Holt and Tony Mason, *Sport in Britain, 1945–2000* (Oxford: Blackwell, 2000).

21. See S. G. Jones, *Workers At Play: A Social and Economic History of Leisure, 1918–1939* (London: Routledge and Kegan Paul, 1986) and *Sport, Politics and the Working Class: Organised Labour and Sport in Interwar Britain* (Manchester: Manchester University Press, 1988).

22. On company paternalism, see: R. Fitzgerald, *British Labour Management and Industrial Welfare 1846–1975* (London: Croom Helm, 1988); R. Waller, *The Dukeries Transformed* (Oxford: Clarendon Press, 1983); S. Chapman, *Jesse Boots of Boots the Chemists* (London: Hodder and Stoughton, 1974); I. Campbell-Bradley, *Enlightened Entrepreneurs* (London: Weidenfeld and Nicholson, 1987); Catriona M. Parratt,

'"The Making of the Healthy and the Happy Home": Recreation, Education, and the Production of Working-Class Womanhood at the Rowntree Cocoa Works, York, c.1898–1914', in J. Hill and J. Williams, eds, *Sport and Identity in the North of England* (Keele: Keele University Press, 1996), pp. 53–83; John Bromhead, 'George Cadbury's Contribution to Sport', *The Sports Historian*, 20, 1 (2000) 97–117; Helen Jones, 'Employers' Welfare Schemes and Industrial Relations in Inter-War Britain', *Business History*, 25, 1 (1983) 61–75. In the early 1970s it was estimated that there were some 1500 industrial sports clubs in Britain. (*Second Report from the Select Committee of the House of Lords on Sport and Leisure* (London: HMSO, 1974) p. xxvii.).

23. A. Marwick, *War and Social Change in the Twentieth Century: A Comparative Study of Britain, France, Germany, Russia and the United States* (London: Macmillan, 1974) p. 13.

24. An interesting discussion of collecting, with some valuable thoughts on the nature of leisure, was provided by B. Rogan in a paper 'Collecting of Postal History Through 150 Years' given at the Third European Social Science History Conference, Amsterdam, 12–15 April 2000.

25. See, for example, D. Slater, 'Work/Leisure', in C. Jenks, ed., *Core Sociological Dichotomies* (London: Sage Publications, 1998) pp. 391–404.

26. See K. Roberts, *Leisure* (London: Longman, 1970); S. Parker, *The Future of Work and Leisure* (London: MacGibbon and Kee, 1971); *Leisure and Work* (London: Macmillan, 1983).

27. See C. Rojek, *Leisure and Culture* (Basingstoke: Macmillan – now Palgrave, 2000) pp. 19–20.

28. José Ortega y Gasset, *The Revolt of the Masses* (London: George Allen and Unwin, 1951 edn) p. 7.

29. See Stefan Collini, 'An Abiding Sense of the Demonic', *London Review of Books*, 20 January 2000, 32–4.

30. A point well brought out by Simon Gunn, 'Questions of Class and Identity: Conceptualising the Middle Class in Northern England, 1840–1914', paper given at the Third European Social Science History Conference, Amsterdam, 12–15 April 2000.

31. 'When Work Is Over', *Picture Post*, 4 January 1941, p. 39.

32. J. K. Galbraith, *The Affluent Society* (London: Andre Deutsch, 1997 edn) p. 261.

33. Jennifer Hargreaves, *Sporting Females: Critical Issues in the History and Sociology of Women's Sport* (London: Routledge, 1994) is a fine example of this writing.

34. E. Green, S. Hebron and D. Woodward, *Women's Leisure, What Leisure?* (Basingstoke: Macmillan – now Palgrave, 1990). See also the equally important work of M. Talbot, *Women and Leisure* (London: The Sports Council, 1979), and E. Wimbush and M. Talbot, *Relative Freedoms – Women and Leisure* (Milton Keynes: Open University Press, 1988). In the field of sport, the most important and comprehensive British contribution to these issues is Jennifer Hargreaves's *Sporting Females: Critical Issues in the History and Sociology of Women's Sports* (London: Routledge, 1994).

35. See, for example, T. Mason, 'Sport and Recreation', in P. Johnson, ed., *Twentieth Century Britain: Economic, Social and Cultural Change* (London: Longman, 1994) pp. 111–26; H. Cunningham, 'Leisure', in F. Leventhal, ed. *Twentieth Century Britain: An Encyclopedia* (New York: Garland Publishing, 1995) pp. 450–52.

36. Green, Hebron and Woodward, *Women's Leisure*, p. 5 and ch. 1 *passim*.

37. C. M. Parratt, 'Little Means or Time: Working Class Women and Leisure in Late Victorian and Edwardian England', *International Journal of the History of Sport*, 15, 2 (1998) 22–53; see also 'Making Leisure Work: Women's Rational Recreation in Late Victorian and Edwardian England', *Journal of Sport History*, 26, 3 (1999) 471–87.

38. E. Ross, 'Survival Networks: Women's Neighbourhood Sharing in London Before World War 1', *History Workshop: A Journal of Socialist and Feminist Historians*, 15 (1983) 4–27. Related to this is the work of Melanie Tebbutt, especially *Women's Talk: A Social History of 'Gossip' in Working-Class Neighbourhoods 1880–1960* (London: Scolar Press, 1995).

39. N. Hart, 'Gender and the Rise and Fall of Class Politics', *New Left Review*, 1989, 19–47.

40. An important contribution on this theme is G. Jarvie, ed., *Sport, Racism and Ethnicity* (London: Falmer Press, 1991).

41. H. Zaman, 'Islam, Well-being and Physical Activity: Perceptions of Muslim Young Women', in G. Clarke and B. Humberstone, eds, *Researching Women and Sport* (Basingstoke: Macmillan – now Palgrave, 1997) pp. 50–67.

42. Zaman, 'Islam, Well-being and Physical Activity', p. 61.

43. T. Mason, ed., *Sport in Britain: A Social History* (Cambridge: Cambridge University Press, 1989) pp. 4–5.

44. See Chapter 3 for a further discussion of some of these points.

45. R. Taylor, *Football and Its Fans* (Leicester: Leicester University Press, 1992) makes a bold, though not entirely successful, attempt to direct attention to the 'ordinary' fan.

46. M. Huggins, 'Second-Class Citizens? English Middle-Class Culture and Sport, 1850–1910: A Reconsideration', *International Journal of the History of Sport*, 17, 1 (2000) 1–34.

47. See, for example, G. Ryan, 'Cricket and the Moral Curriculum of the New Zealand Elite Secondary Schools, *c*.1860–*c*.1920', *Sports Historian*, 19, 2 (1999) 61–79.

48. This sentiment was strongly present in the Department of National Heritage's *Sport: Raising the Game* (London: Department of National Heritage, 1995), with a rather moralistic foreword by John Major.

49. R. Holt, *Sport and the British*, pp. 89–92, 172–4.

50. Francis Mulhearn, 'Notes on Culture and Cultural Struggle', *Screen Education*, 34 (1980) 31–5.

51. E. Hobsbawm, *Age of Extremes: The Short Twentieth Century, 1914–1991* (London: Abacus, 1994) ix.

52. See J. Benson, *The Rise of Consumer Society in Britain, 1880–1980* (London: Longman, 1994) ch. 1; P. Butson, *The Financing of Sport in the United Kingdom* (London: The Sports Council, 1983).

53. 'In his baggy shorts and heavy boots, he was a true hero to legions of flat-capped fans – and earned little more than they did' (*The Sun*, 24 February 2000).

54. T. Mason, 'Sport', in F. Leventhal, ed., *Twentieth Century Britain*, p. 739.

55. L. Colley, *Britons: Forging the Nation, 1707–1837* (London: Pimlico, 1994) p. 162.

56. D. Smith and G. Williams, *Fields of Praise: the Official History of the Welsh Rugby Union, 1881–1981* (Cardiff: University of Wales Press/Welsh Rugby Union, 1980).

57. Smith and Williams, *Fields of Praise*, esp. chs 5–7. See also G. Williams, *1905 And All That: Essays on Rugby Football, Sport and Welsh Society* (Llandysul: Gomer Press,

1991); 'From Grand Slam to Great Slump: Economy, Society and Rugby Football in Wales During the Depression', *Welsh History Review*, 11 (1993) 339–57.

58. D. Smith, 'Focal Heroes: A Welsh Fighting Class', in R. Holt, ed, *Sport and the Working Class in Modern Britain* (Manchester: Manchester University Press, 1990) p. 199.

59. G. Williams, 'The Road to Wigan Pier Revisited: The Migration of Welsh Rugby Talent Since 1918', in J. Bale and J. Maguire, eds, *The Global Sports Arena: Athletic Talent Migration in an Interdependent World* (London: Frank Cass, 1994) pp. 25–8.

60. Among H. F. Moorhouse's many articles on this theme are: 'Repressed Nationalism and Professional Football: Scotland versus England', in J. Mangan and R. Small, eds, *Sport, Culture, Society: International Historical and Sociological Perspectives* (London: E. and F. N. Spon, 1986) pp. 52–9; 'Shooting Stars: Footballers and Working-Class Culture in Twentieth-Century Scotland', in Holt, *Sport and the Working Class*, pp. 179–97; 'Blue Bonnets Over the Border: Scotland and the Migration of Footballers', in Bale and Maguire, *Global Sports Arena*, pp. 78–96; 'One State, Several Countries: Soccer and Nationality in a "United" Kingdom', *International Journal of the History of Sport*, 12, 2 (1995) 55–74.

61. See R. Holt, 'King Across the Border: Denis Law and Scottish Football', in G. Jarvie and G. Walker, eds, *Scottish Sport in the Making of a Nation: Ninety Minute Patriots?* (Leicester: Leicester University Press, 1994) pp. 58–74. All the obituaries and commemorative pieces on Jim Baxter, who died in 2001, made this point. See David Lacey's in the *Guardian*, 21 April 2001.

62. See B. Murray, *The Old Firm in the New Age: Celtic and Rangers Since the Souness Revolution* (Edinburgh: Mainstream Publishing, 1999).

63. See Jarvie and Walker, *Ninety Minute Patriots?*, ch. 1.

64. See James Knowlson, *Damned To Fame: The Life of Samuel Beckett* (London: Bloomsbury, 1997) p. 62. However, Philip Noel Baker, the Labour politician, also got a Nobel prize (though not for literature) and figured in athletics records.

65. M. Cronin, 'Defenders of the Nation? The Gaelic Athletic Association and Irish National Identity', *Irish Political Studies*, 11 (1996) 1–19; 'Sport and a Sense of Irishness', *Irish Studies Review*, 9 (1994) 13–18; 'Which Nation, Which Flag?: Boxing and National Identities in Ireland', *International Review for the Sociology of Sport*, 32, 2 (1997) 131–46. Holt, *Sport and the British*, pp. 239–42. See also M. Cronin and D. Mayall, *Sporting Nationalisms: Identity, Ethnicity, Immigration and Assimilation* (London: Frank Cass, 1998).

66. M. Cronin, 'Enshrined in Blood: The naming of Gaelic Athletic Association Grounds and Clubs', *Sports Historian*, 18, 1 (1998) 93.

67. J. Sugden and A. Bairner, *Sport, Sectarianism and Society in a Divided Ireland* (Leicester: Leicester University Press, 1993) pp. 70–91.

68. See C. Williams, *Bradman: An Australian Hero* (London: Abacus, 1997).

69. Tariq Ali, 'Anyone for Gulli-Danda?', *London Review of Books*, 15 July 1999, 30–1.

70. B. Stoddart, 'Cricket and Colonialism in the English-Speaking Caribbean to 1914: Towards a Cultural Analysis', in H. McD. Beckles and B. Stoddart, *Liberation Cricket: West Indies Cricket Culture* (Manchester: Manchester University Press, 1995) pp. 9–32.

71. L. N. Constantine, *Cricket and I* (London: Philip Allan, 1933) ch. 9.

72. C. L. R. James, *Beyond a Boundary* (London: Stanley Paul, 1969 edn) ch. 18.

73. B. Stoddart, 'Caribbean Cricket: The Role of Sport in Emerging Small-Nation Politics', in Beckles and Stoddart, *Liberation Cricket*, ch. 15.

74. Arnold Toynbee, 'The Dwarfing of Europe', in *Civilization on Trial* (Oxford: Oxford University Press, 1948) ch. 6.

75. See J. Williams, *Cricket and England: A Cultural and Social History of the Inter-War Years* (London: Frank Cass, 1999) esp. chs 1 and 6.

PART ONE: COMMERCIAL SPORT AND LEISURE

2 THE 'PECULIAR ECONOMICS' OF THE PEOPLE'S GAMES

1. See *Guardian*, 10 April 1999; Matthew Horsman, 'Sky Blues', *Media Guardian*, 12 April 1999. Also Stefan Szymanski and Tim Kuypers, *Winners and Losers* (Harmondsworth: Penguin Books, 2000) ch. 8.

2. Arnold Bennett, *The Card: A Story of Adventure in the Five Towns* (London: Penguin Books, 1975 edn) p. 211.

3. See C. Korr, *West Ham United: The Making of a Football Club* (London: Duckworth, 1986) pp. 17–18.

4. See S. Inglis, *The Football Grounds of Britain* (London: CollinsWillow, 1996 edn) pp. 16–29; T. Mason, *Association Football and English Society, 1863–1915* (Brighton: Harvester, 1981 edn) pp. 34–5; P. Soar and M. Tyler, *Centenary History* (London: Hamlyn, 1986). In the 1980s and 1990s there were proposals to move clubs to new locations: the projected move of Wimbledon F.C. (south London) to Dublin was probably the best-known example, though nothing has, as yet, come of it.

5. R. Holt, *Sport and the British: A Modern History* (Oxford: Oxford University Press, 1990 edn) p. 165.

6. W. Vamplew, *Pay Up and Play the Game: Professional Sport in Britain, 1875–1914* (Cambridge: Cambridge University Press, 1988).

7. Vamplew, *Pay Up*, p. 13 and ch. 8. For a rather more 'revisionist' argument, based on the development of football, see S. G. Jones, 'The Economic Aspect of Association Football in England, 1918–39', *British Journal Sports History*, 1, 3 (1984) 286–99.

8. The work of John Toulson reminds us, however, that the national organization of horse-racing was extensive, even before the coming of the railways. See his paper – 'The Movement of Race Horses in the First Two Decades of the Railway Age' – presented to the British Society of Sports History, Lancaster, April 2001.

9. See C. M. Parratt, 'Working Class Women and Leisure in Late Victorian and Edwardian England', *International Journal of the History of Sport*, 15, 2 (1998) 22–53.

10. See Chapter 4.

11. See T. Collins, *Rugby's Great Split: Class, Culture and the Origins of Rugby League Football* (London: Frank Cass, 1998).

12. Mason, *Association Football*, ch. 8; A. King, *The End of the Terraces: The Transformation of English Football in the 1990s* (Leicester: Leicester University Press, 1998).

13. J. Hill, 'League Cricket in the North and Midlands', in R. Holt, ed., *Sport and the Working Class in Modern Britain* (Manchester: Manchester University Press, 1990) pp. 121–41; '"First Class" Cricket and the Leagues: Some Notes on the

Development of English Cricket, 1900–1940', *International Journal of the History of Sport*, 4, 1 (1987) 68–81.

14. N. Tranter, *Sport, Economy and Society in Britain, 1750–1914* (Cambridge: Cambridge University Press, 1998) p. 1.

15. Mason, *Association Football*, esp. chs 1 and 2.

16. See K. Warsop (assisted by P. Wain), *The Magpies: The Story of Notts County Football Club* (Buckingham: Sporting and Leisure Press, 1984) pp. 15–36.

17. Vamplew, *Pay Up*, ch. 10.

18. Mason, *Association Football*, p. 38.

19. Mason, *Association Football*, p. 40.

20. Vamplew, *Pay Up*, p. 159.

21. Korr, *West Ham United*, pp. 10–16. See also A. J. Arnold, *A Game That Would Pay: A Business History of Professional Football in Bradford* (London: Duckworth, 1988); in 1910 over 80 per cent of Bradford Park Avenue's shares were held by one family (pp. 59–60).

22. Mason, *Association Football*, p. 99.

23. N. Varley, *Golden Boy: A Biography of Wilf Mannion* (London: Aurum Press, 1997) ch. 7.

24. D. Russell, *Football and the English: A Social History of Association Football in England, 1863–1995* (Preston: Carnegie Publishing, 1997) pp. 50–1.

25. The editor of the magazine *When Saturday Comes*, speaking at the annual conference of the British Society of Sports History, Nottingham, 1992. See also the views of Stanley Matthews about his relationships with the management of Stoke City in the 1930s. S. Matthews, *The Way It Was: My Autobiography* (London: Headline, 2000) pp. 69–70, 165–6, 192.

26. The pioneering work in this field, often using oral evidence, is by Gavin Mellor: see, for example, 'The Social and Geographical Make-Up of Football Crowds in the North-West of England, 1946–1962', *The Sports Historian*, 19, 2 (1999) 25–42.

27. See A. Davies, *Leisure, Gender and Poverty: Working Class Culture in Salford and Manchester, 1900–1939* (Buckingham: Open University Press, 1992) pp. 38–9. The cost of transport for those who lived on the new council estates on the edge of the city was also a factor preventing their attendance at United or City games. Davies suggests that people often played for or watched local club teams.

28. See D. Robins, 'Sport and Youth Culture', in Jennifer Hargreaves, ed., *Sport, Culture and Ideology* (London: Routledge and Kegan Paul, 1982) pp. 145–50.

29. See T. Mason, *Sport in Britain* (London: Faber and Faber, 1988) pp. 26–7; R. Lewis, 'Football Hooliganism in England Before 1914: A Critique of the Dunning Thesis', *International Journal of the History of Sport*, 13, 3 (1996) 310–39; P. Murphy, E. Dunning and J. Maguire, 'Football Spectator Violence and Disorder Before the First World War: A Reply to R. W. Lewis', *International Journal of the History of Sport*, 15, 1 (1998) 141–62.

30. R. Taylor, *Football and Its Fans: Supporters and Their Relations With the Game, 1885–1985* (Leicester: Leicester University Press, 1992).

31. Inglis, *Football Grounds of Britain*; also *The Football Grounds of Europe* (London: Willow Books, 1990).

32. Russell, *Football and the English*, pp. 144–51; J. Hill, *Striking For Soccer* (London: Sportsman's Book Club, 1963).

33. Football League, *Report of the Committee of Enquiry into Structure and Finance* (The Chester Report), (Lytham St Annes: Football League, 1982).

34. B. Glanville, *Football Memories* (London: Virgin Publishing, 1999) p. 268.

35. Often, it seemed, unnecessarily so: positions like goalkeeper and centre-half, once filled capably by home-grown players, were now taken up by expensive imports.

36. These developments are well covered in Stefan Szymanski and Tim Kuypers, *Winners and Losers* (Harmondsworth: Penguin Books, 2000) ch. 3.

37. See King, *End of the Terraces*, pt IV. For a recent statement of the 'embourgeoise-ment thesis', see Glanville, *Football Memories*, p. 269.

38. See J. Hill, 'Rite of Spring: Cup Finals and Community in the North of England', in J. Hill and J. Williams, eds, *Sport and Identity in the North of England* (Keele: Keele University Press, 1996) pp. 85–111.

39. See Chas Critcher, 'Football Since the War', in J. Clarke, C. Critcher and R. Johnson, *Working Class Culture: Studies in History and Theory* (London: Hutchinson, 1979) pp. 161–84.

40. N. Hornby, *Fever Pitch* (London: Gollancz, 1992).

41. One of the first of the genre was Hunter Davies, *The Glory Game* (London: Sphere Books, 1973). The first, and still the best, of the 'realist' school of players' autobi-ographies is Eamon Dunphy, *Only a Game?* (London: Peacock Books, 1977). Among the more interesting of the newer publications are Harry Pearson, *The Far Corner: A Mazy Dribble Through North-East Football* (London: Warner Books, 1995 edn) and Colin Shindler, *Manchester United Ruined My Life* (London: Headline, 1998). Shelley Webb, *Footballers' Wives* (London: Yellow Jersey Press, 1998) is an illuminating study by a footballer's wife.

42. See Chapter 9.

43. Home Office, *The Hillsborough Stadium Disaster, 15 April 1989; Inquiry By the Rt. Hon. Lord Justice Taylor, Final Report, Jan. 1990* (The Taylor Report) cm 962, (London: HMSO, 1990).

44. Taylor Report, p. 6.

45. Quoted in I. Taylor, 'Putting the Boot Into a Working-Class Sport: British Soccer After Bradford and Brussels', *Sociology of Sport Journal*, 4, 1 (1987) 182. See also A. King, 'New Directors, Customers, and Fans: The Transformation of English Football in the 1990s', *Sociology of Sport Journal*, 14 (1997) 224–40.

46. See J. Hill, '"First Class" Cricket and the Leagues: Some Notes on the Develop-ment of English Cricket, 1900–1940', *International Journal of the History of Sport*, 4, 1 (1987) 68–81.

47. S. Rae, *W. G. Grace: A Life* (London: Faber and Faber, 1998).

48. K. Sandiford and W. Vamplew, 'The Peculiar Economics of English Cricket Be-fore 1914', *British Journal of Sports History*, 3, 3 (1986) 311. J. Williams, *Cricket and England: A Cultural and Social History of the Inter-War Years* (London: Frank Cass, 1999) ch. 8.

49. Williams, *Cricket and England*, esp. chs 4, 6 and 8. On the alleged failure of the bour-geois revolution in Britain, see Perry Anderson's provocative 'Origins of the Present Crisis', in P. Anderson et al., *Towards Socialism* (London: Fontana, 1965) pp. 11–52.

50. Quoted in J. Kay, *A History of County Cricket: Lancashire* (London: Barker, 1972) p. 43.

51. See J. Williams, 'Recreational Cricket in the Bolton Area Between the Wars', in R. Holt, ed., *Sport and the Working Class in Modern Britain* (Manchester: Manchester University Press, 1990) pp. 101–20.

52. On league cricket, see: R. Genders, *League Cricket in England* (London: T. Werner Laurie, 1952); J. Hill, 'League Cricket in the North and Midlands, 1900–1940', in Holt, *Sport and the Working Class*, pp. 121–41; 'The Development of Professionalism in English League Cricket *c*.1900–1940', in J. A. Mangan and R. B. Small, eds, *Sport, Culture, Society: International Historical and Sociological Perspectives* (London: E. & F. N. Spon, 1986) pp. 109–16; G. Howat, *Learie Constantine* (London: George Allen and Unwin, 1975).

53. J. Lowerson, 'Golf', in Mason, *Sport in Britain*, p. 203.

54. Lowerson, 'Golf', p. 209.

55. See H. Walker, 'Lawn Tennis', in Mason, *Sport in Britain*, pp. 245–75; R. Holt, 'Heroes of the North: Sport and the Shaping of Regional Identity', in J. Hill and J. Williams, *Sport and Identity*, pp. 137–64.

56. J. Crump, 'Athletics', in Mason, *Sport in Britain*, p. 52.

57. Crump, 'Athletics', p. 55.

58. M. Polley, 'Before the Bonanza: Amateurism and Professionalism in British Athletics from the 1940s to 1970s', paper presented to the annual conference of the British Society of Sports History, Liverpool, April 2000.

59. J. Williams, '"A Wild Orgy of Speed": Responses to Speedway in Britain Before the Second World War', *Sports Historian*, 19, 1 (1999) 3.

60. Williams, 'A Wild Orgy of Speed'. See also D. Robins, 'Sport and Youth Culture', in Hargreaves, *Sport, Culture and Ideology*, pp. 138–40; G. Fraser, 'Speedway' in R. Cox, G. Jarvie and W. Vamplew, eds, *Encyclopedia of British Sport* (Oxford: ABC-Clio, 2000) pp. 360–65. The history of the sport is being developed by *The Speedway Researcher: Promoting Research Into the History of Speedway and Dirt Track Racing*, from 1998.

61. T. Collins, *Rugby's Great Split: Class, Culture and the Origins of Rugby League Football* (London: Frank Cass, 1998); also '"Noa Mutton, Noa Laaking": The Origins of Payment for Play in Rugby Football', *International Journal of the History of Sport*, 12, 1 (1995) 33–50.

62. See Chapter 3.

63. W. Vamplew, 'Horse Racing', in Mason, *Sport in Britain*, p. 215. See also M. Huggins, *Flat Racing and British Society 1790–1914: A Social and Economic History* (London: Frank Cass, 2000) ch. 4; R. Munting, *An Economic and Social History of Gambling in Britain and the USA* (Manchester: Manchester University Press, 1996).

64. R. McKibbin, *Classes and Cultures: England, 1918–1951* (Oxford: Oxford University Press, 1998) p. 371. See also the same author's 'Working-Class Gambling in Britain, 1880–1939', *Past and Present*, 82 (1979) 147–78.

65. C. Chinn, *Better Betting With a Decent Feller: Bookmaking, Betting and the British Working Class, 1750–1990* (London: Harvester/Wheatsheaf, 1991); M. Clapson, *A Bit of a Flutter: Popular Gambling and English Society, c.1823–1961* (Manchester: Manchester University Press, 1992).

66. McKibbin, *Classes and Cultures*, p. 376.

67. See G. Williams and G. Jarvie, 'Rugby Union', in Cox, Jarvie and Vamplew, *Encyclopedia of British Sport*, pp. 339–45.

3 SPORT AND THE MEDIA

1. Editor's foreword to T. Collins, *Rugby's Great Split: Class, Culture and the Origins of Rugby League Football* (London: Frank Cass, 1998) ix.
2. *Daily Express*, 23 June 1947.
3. See J. Hill, 'The Legend of Denis Compton', *Sports Historian*, 18, 2 (1998) 19–33.
4. J. W. Hobson and H. Henry, *Hulton Readership Survey* (London: Hulton Publishing, 1947).
5. See T. Mason, *Association Football and English Society 1863–1915* (Brighton: Harvester, 1981 edn) ch. 6; 'All the Winners and the Half Times', *Sports Historian*, 13 (1993) 3–13.
6. *Bury Times*, 25 April 1900; 22 April 1903.
7. See W. Harper, *How You Played the Game: The Life of Grantland Rice* (Columbia, MO: University of Missouri Press, 1998).
8. R. Holt, *Sport and the British: A Modern History* (Oxford: Oxford University Press, 1990 edn) pp. 307–11. See also H. Cudlipp, *Publish and Be Damned!* (London: Andrew Dakers, 1953); G. Green, *Pardon Me For Living* (London: George Allen and Unwin, 1985); M. Pugh, 'The *Daily Mirror* and the Revival of Labour 1935–45', *Twentieth Century British History*, 9, 3 (1998) 420–38.
9. Women's cricket was reported in some sections of the national press, though sometimes rather condescendingly. See J. Williams, *Cricket and England: A Cultural and Social History of the Inter-War Years* (London: Frank Cass, 1998) pp. 98–106.
10. W. Meisl, *Soccer Revolution* (London: Phoenix Sports Books, 1955) p. 12.
11. Central Council of Physical Recreation, *Sport and the Community* (The Wolfenden Report) (London: CCPR, 1960) pp. 80–1.
12. See J. Williams, 'Postcolonial Tensions and Racism in England-Pakistan Cricket', paper delivered to the conference 'Sport, Postcolonialism and the Body', De Montfort University, Leicester, July 1999.
13. T. Mason, *Sport in Britain* (London: Faber and Faber, 1988) p. 49.
14. *The Times*, 27 April 1914.
15. London: Secker and Warburg, 1962. David Storey's novel about rugby league, *This Sporting Life* (London: Longmans, 1960) surpasses it. On Cardus, see: Neville Cardus, *Autobiography* (London: William Collins, 1947); Christopher Brookes, *His Own Man: The Life of Neville Cardus* (London: Methuen, 1985); and the selection of his cricket writings included in N. Cardus, *Good Days* (London: Rupert Hart-Davis, 1949).
16. A fuller dicussion of the BBC's approach to broadcasting follows in Chapter 6.
17. A. Briggs, *The History of Broadcasting in the United Kingdom: vol. 1 The Birth of Broadcasting* (London: Oxford University Press, 1961) pp. 164–83; P. Scannell and D. Cardiff, *A Social History of British Broadcasting: vol. 1 1922–1939, Serving the Nation* (Oxford: Basil Blackwell, 1991) ch. 1.
18. G. Whannel, *Fields in Vision: Television Sport and Cultural Transformation* (London: Routledge, 1992) p. 29; ch. 2 provides a good summary of the development of sports coverage at the BBC from the 1920s to the 1950s.
19. BBC Written Archives, Reading. File SA 1953–54, T 14/93/15, 1 December 1953. It was a commentator brought up in the 'Lobby' school – Kenneth Wolstenholme –

who delivered probably the most memorable wisecrack of all, at the close of the 1966 football World Cup Final: 'some people are coming on to the pitch – they think it's all over. [Hurst scores]. It is now.'

20. A. Briggs, *The History of Broadcasting in the United Kingdom; vol. IV – Sound and Vision* (Oxford: Oxford University Press, 1979) p. 854.
21. See the study of listening habits conducted in a working-class neighbourhood of Bristol in the later 1930s: H. Jennings and W. Gill, *Broadcasting in Everyday Life: A Survey of the Social Effects of the Coming of Broadcasting* (London: BBC, n.d.) pp. 37–9.
22. P. Scannell and D. Cardiff, 'Serving the Nation: Public Service Broadcasting Before the War', in B. Waites, T. Bennett and G. Martin, eds, *Popular Culture: Past and Present* (London: Croom Helm/Open University Press, 1982) pp. 161–88. Briggs, *History of Broadcasting*, I, pp. 327–47.
23. Briggs, *History of Broadcasting*, IV, p. 854.
24. A. Briggs, *The History of Broadcasting in the United Kingdom – vol. II The Golden Age of the Wireless* (Oxford: Oxford University Press, 1965) p. 315.
25. Mason, *Sport in Britain*, p. 53.
26. See S. Chadwick, 'The Will of the North', *Rugby League Review*, 13 May 1954, written after the largest attendance for a Rugby League final had been recorded at Bradford in 1954; the event, according to Chadwick, 'demonstrated to the rulers of the Rugby Football League in a clear and unmistakable manner that [people] desired the final of the game's major trophy to be played in their midst'.
27. Briggs, *History of Broadcasting*, IV, p. 854.
28. See D. Russell, *Football and the English: A Social History of Association Football in England, 1863–1995* (Preston: Carnegie Publishing, 1997) pp. 188–9; R. Haynes, 'A Pageant of Sound and Vision: Football's Relationship with Television, 1936–60', *International Journal of the History of Sport*, 15, 1 (1998) 211–26.
29. Whannel, *Fields in Vision*, p. 34.
30. See G. Moorhouse, *At The George: And Other Essays of Rugby League* (London: Sceptre, 1990) pp. 44–5.
31. B. Rader, *In Its Own Image: How Television Has Transformed Sports* (London: Collier Macmillan, 1984).
32. A. and J. Clarke, ' "Highlights and Action Replays", – Ideology, Sport and the Media', in Jennifer Hargreaves, ed., *Sport, Culure and Ideology* (London: Routledge and Kegan Paul, 1982) pp. 62–87.
33. British radio and television contrasts with that of the USA, where female sports presenters have been quite numerous and successful, though having encountered much male prejudice and hostility. One newspaper reporter, Lisa Olsen of the *Boston Herald*, was subjected to blatant and orchestrated sexual harassment by professional footballers, who appear to have been supported by both their club owner and their fans. See David F. Salter, *Crashing the Old Boys' Network: The Tragedies and Triumphs of Girls and Women in Sports* (Wesport, CT: Praeger, 1996) ch. 8. I am grateful to Catriona Parratt for drawing my attention to this case. See also Allen Guttmann, *The Erotic in Sports* (New York: Columbia University Press, 1996) pp. 80–90.
34. On Donna Symmonds, see: *The Guardian*, 26 August 2000.
35. See B. Glanville, *Soccer Nemesis* (London: Secker and Warburg, 1955).
36. J. A. Mangan, *Athleticism in the Victorian and Edwardian Public School: The Emergence*

and Consolidation of an Educational Ideology (Cambridge: Cambridge University Press, 1981) esp. ch. 8; *The Games Ethic and Imperialism: Aspects of the Diffusion of an Ideal* (Harmondsworth: Viking, 1986).

37. Quoted in Mangan, *Athleticism in the Victorian and Edwardian Public School*, p. 188.

38. J. Richards, *Happiest Days: The Public Schools in English Fiction* (Manchester: Manchester University Press, 1988) p. 136.

39. M. Cadogan and P. Craig, *'You're a Brick Angela!': A New Look for Girls' Fiction, 1839–1975* (London: Victor Gollancz, 1976) esp. ch. xiii.

40. For example: E. M. Brent-Dyer, *The Chalet School Wins the Trick* (London: Armada, 1985 edn); B. Bryant, *Show Horse* (London: Bantam Books, 1993).

41. Williams, *Cricket and England*, ch. 1.

42. A. G. MacDonnell, *England Their England* (London: Macmillan 1964 edn) The book was first published in 1933.

43. See J. Arlott, *Basingstoke Boy: The Autobiography* (London: Fontana, 1992 edn)

44. N. Cardus, *Good Days* (London: Rupert Hart-Davis, 1949) p. 40.

45. Williams, *Cricket and England*, pp. 69–70.

46. Russell, *Football and the English*, pp. 110–11.

47. For example: M. Hardcastle, *Soccer Special* (London: Dean, 1992); 'Goalkeeping? Easy!', in W. Cooling, ed., *Go For Goal* (London: Dolphin, 1997) pp. 31–45.

48. See H. Carpenter and M. Prichard, *The Oxford Companion to Children's Literature* (Oxford: Oxford University Press, 1984) p. 573. Also B. Green, *Spectator*, 26 December 1970.

49. A. Melling, '"Ray of the Rovers": The Working-Class Heroine in Popular Football Fiction, 1915–25', *International Journal of the History of Sport*, 15, 1 (1998) 98.

4 GOING TO THE PICTURES: AMERICA AND THE CINEMA

1. *The New Survey of London Life and Labour: vol. IX, Life and Leisure* (London: P. S. King and Son, Ltd, 1935) p. 43.

2. A. J. P. Taylor, *English History, 1914–1945* (Oxford: Clarendon Press, 1965) p. 313. In the early 1950s one estimate of annual cinema admissions made them 14 times greater than those of either of the next most popular forms of commercial leisure (theatres and music halls, and football); the gross takings of cinemas were estimated as six times greater. (A.H. Halsey, ed., *Trends in British Society since 1900: A Guide to the Changing Social Structure of Britain* (London: Macmillan, 1972) p. 558, (table 16.18).

3. R. McKibbin, *Classes and Cultures: England, 1918–1951* (Oxford: Oxford University Press, 1998) p. 419.

4. See J. Chapman, 'Film and Flea-Pits: *The Smallest Show On Earth*', in A. Burton, T. O'Sullivan and P. Wells, eds, *Liberal Directions: Basil Dearden and Postwar British Film Culture* (Trowbridge: Flick Books, 1997) pp. 194–202.

5. D. Mayall, 'Palaces for Entertainment and Instruction: A Study of the Early Cinema in Birmingham, 1908–18', *Midland History*, X (1985) 98.

6. N. Hiley, ' "Let's Go To the Pictures": The British Cinema Audience in the 1920s and 1930s', *Journal of Popular British Cinema* 2 (1999) 48.

7. I. Thomas, *The Bandsman's Daughter: An Autobiography* (London: Futura Publications, 1980) p. 23.

8. McKibbin, *Classes and Cultures*, p. 423.

9. M. O'Brien and A. Eyles, *Enter the Dream House: Memories of Cinemas in South London from the Twenties to the Sixties* (London: British Film Institute, 1993).

10. See also A. Eyles, *Gaumont British Cinemas* (London: Cinema Theatre Association/ British Film Institute, 1996).

11. Hiley, 'British Cinema Audience', p. 49.

12. Taylor, *English History*, p. 313.

13. D. Caradog Jones, ed., *Social Survey of Merseyside*, 3 vols (Liverpool: University of Liverpool Press, 1934); S. Rowson, 'A Statistical Survey of the Cinema Industry in Great Britain in 1934', *Journal of the Royal Statistical Society*, xcix (1936) 67–129; *The New Survey of London Life and Labour*, IX, p. 45.

14. Open University, *The Historical Development of Popular Culture in Britain (2)* (Milton Keynes: Open University Press, 1981) p. 6.

15. See Claire Langhamer, *Women's Leisure in England, 1920–60* (Manchester: Manchester University Press, 2000) pp. 58–63.

16. McKibbin, *Classes and Cultures*, p. 419.

17. S. Harper and V. Porter, 'Cinema Audience tastes in 1950s Britain', *Journal of Popular British Cinema*, 2 (1999) 66–82.

18. Hiley, 'British Cinema Audience'.

19. There were similar protests from other leisure industries. The tax lasted until 1957.

20. Hiley, 'British Cinema Audience', p. 43.

21. Hiley, 'British Cinema Audience'; Mayall, 'Palaces For Entertainment'.

22. Mayall, 'Palaces of Entertainment'.

23. J. Richards, *The Age of the Dream Palace: Cinema and Society in Britain, 1930–39* (London: Routledge, 1989 edn) part II. Also A. Kuhn, *Cinema, Censorship and Sexuality, 1909–25* (London: Routledge, 1989 edn) ch. 2.

24. Open University, *Historical Development of Popular Culture (2)* p. 12.

25. Open University, *Supplementary Material U203 Block 2 – Offprints Booklet 2* (Milton Keynes: Open University Press, 1981) p. 10.

26. McKibbin, *Classes and Cultures*, p. 431.

27. See, for example, J. Hay, *Popular Film Culture in Fascist Italy: The Passing of the Rex* (Bloomington, IN: Indiana University Press, 1987) ch. 2.

28. See A. Medhurst 'Music Hall and British Cinema', in C. Barr, ed., *All Our Yesterdays: 90 Years of British Cinema* (London: British Film Institute, 1986) pp. 168–88.

29. P. Joyce, *Visions of the People: Industrial England and the Question of Class, 1848–1914* (Cambridge: Cambridge University Press, 1991) pp. 317–21.

30. Joyce, *Visions of the People*, p. 307.

31. See Richards, *Age of the Dream Palace*, pp. 181–3; *Stars in Our Eyes: Lancashire Stars of Stage, Screen and Radio* (Preston: Lancashire County Books, 1994) pp. 12–29.

32. Hiley, 'British Cinema Audience', p. 49; J. Chapman, 'British Cinema and "The People's War"', in N. Hayes and J. Hill, eds, ' "Millions Like Us?": British Culture in the Second World War* (Liverpool: Liverpool University Press, 1999) pp. 33–61.

33. Quoted in Chapman, 'British Cinema and "The People's War"', p. 33.

34. A. Aldgate and J. Richards, *Britain Can Take It: The British Cinema in the Second World War* (Edinburgh: Edinburgh University Press, 1994 edn) p. 14. P. Stead, *Film and the Working Class: The Feature Film in British and American Society* (London: Routledge, 1991 edn) pp. 127–9.

35. Chapman, 'British Cinema and "The People's War"', pp. 56–9; Aldgate and Richards, *Britain Can take It*, p. 14; Stead, *Film and the Working Class*, pp. 133–4.
36. Aldgate and Richards, *Britain Can Take It*, p. 158.
37. See J. Ramsden, 'Re-focusing "The People's War": British War Films of the 1950s', *Journal of Contemporary History*, 33, 1 (1998) 35–63. Also N. Rattigan, 'The Last Gasp of the Middle Class; British War Films of the 1950s', in W. W. Dixon, ed., *Reviewing British Cinema, 1900–1992: Essays and Interviews* (Albany, NY: State University of New York Press, 1994) pp. 143–53.
38. Harper and Porter, 'Cinema Audience Tastes in 1950s Britain'.
39. See V. Porter and S. Harper, 'Throbbing Hearts and Smart Repartee: The Reception of American Films in 1950s Britain', *Media History*, 4, 2 (1998) 175–89.
40. C. Geraghty, 'Women and Sixties British Cinema: The Development of the "Darling Girl"', in R. Murphy, ed., *The British Cinema Book* (London: British Film Institute, 1997) p. 161.
41. B. Pimlott, *Harold Wilson* (London: HarperCollins, 1993 edn) p. 118.
42. Account based on: M. Dickinson and S. Street, *Cinema and State: The Film Industry and the Government, 1927–84* (London: British Film Institute, 1985); R. Murphy, 'Under the Shadow of Hollywood', in Barr, *All Our Yesterdays*, pp. 47–69; I. Christie, review of R. Low, *The History of British Film* in *Journal of Popular British Cinema*, 2 (1999) 136–40.
43. See Office of National Statistics, *Social Trends, 30* (London: Stationery Office, 2000) p. 215, table 13.12.
44. See A. Eyles, 'Exhibition and the Cinemagoing Experience', in Murphy, *British Cinema Book*, pp. 217–25.
45. See *Social Trends, 30*, p. 215, table 13.12.
46. See George Perry, *The Great British Picture Show: From the Nineties to the Seventies* (London: Paladin, 1975).
47. For a local example of this, see Jeff Hill, 'Leisure', in John Beckett, ed., *A Centenary History of Nottingham* (Manchester: Manchester University Press, 1997) ch. 22.
48. The quotation is from Perry, *The Great British Picture Show*, p. 11.
49. See Tony Aldgate, 'The British Cinema in the 1930s', in The Open University, *Popular Culture: The Historical Development of Popular Culture in Britain (2)*, unit 7 (Milton Keynes: The Open University Press, 1981) p. 28.

5 'GETTING AWAY FROM IT ALL': THE HOLIDAY SPIRIT

1. J. A. R. Pimlott, *The Englishman's Holiday: A Social History* (Hassocks: Harvester Press, 1976 edn) p. 238.
2. It is worth remembering that in 1979, for example, 41 per cent of the population took no holiday at all. (The Open University, *Popular Culture and Everyday Life (2)*, unit 11, Milton Keynes: Open University Press, 1981, p. 17).
3. Office of National Statistics, *Social Trends, 30* (London: Stationery Office, 2000) p. 209.
4. Cited in A. H. Halsey, ed., *Trends in British Society Since 1900: A Guide to the Changing Social Structure of Britain* (London: Macmillan, 1972) p. 549, table 16.6.

5. See John Urry, *The Tourist Gaze: Leisure and Travel in Contemporary Societies* (London: Sage Publications, 1990) pp. 5–7.

6. See Pimlott, *The Englishman's Holiday*, ch. IV; Fred Inglis, *The Delicious History of the Holiday* (London: Routledge, 2000) ch. 2.

7. E. S. Turner, 'Morality in the Oxygen', *London Review of Books*, 14 December 2000, p. 28.

8. Inglis, *Delicious History of the Holiday*, ch. 2. Richard Holt, 'An Englishman in the Alps: Arnold Lunn, Amateurism and the Invention of Alpine Ski Racing', *International Journal of the History of Sport*, 9 (December, 1992) 421–32.

9. On this and many other aspects of the seaside resort see John Walton, *The British Seaside: Holidays and Resorts in the Twentieth Century* (Manchester: Manchester University Press, 2000); *The English Seaside Resort: A Social History* (Leicester: Leicester University Press, 1983); James Walvin, *Beside the Seaside: A Social History of the Popular Seaside Holiday* (London; Allen Lane, 1978).

10. Pimlott, *The Englishman's Holiday*, p. 214.

11. *The New Survey of London Life and Labour, IX – Life and Leisure* (London: P. S. King and Son Ltd, 1935) p. 78.

12. *New Survey of London Life and Labour*, IX, p. 87. See also Robert Poole, *The Lancashire Wakes Holidays* (Preston: Lancashire County Books, 1994).

13. See Su Barton, ' "Why Should Working Men Visit the Exhibition?": Workers and the Great Exhibition and the Ethos of Industrialisation', in Ian Inkster, ed., *The Golden Age: Essays in British Social and Economic History 1850–1870* (Aldershot: Ashgate, 2000) pp. 146–63. See also Harold Perkin's masterly chapter on the railways and the seaside in Harold Perkin, *The Age of the Railway* (London: Panther Books, 1970) ch. 8.

14. Walton, *The British Seaside*, p. 143.

15. Walton, *The British Seaside*, pp. 45–6. See also John K. Walton, 'The Seaside Resorts of England and Wales, 1900–1950: Growth, Diffusion and the Emergence of New Forms of Coastal Tourism', in G. Shaw and A. Williams, eds, *The Rise and Fall of British Coastal Resorts: Cultural and Economic Perspectives* (London: Mansell, 1997) pp. 21–48.

16. Pimlott, *The Englishman's Holiday*, p. 240.

17. See John Walton, *Blackpool* (Edinburgh: Keele University Press, 1998); Tony Bennett, 'Hegemony, Ideology, Pleasure: Blackpool', in T. Bennett, C. Mercer, and J. Woollacott, eds, *Popular Culture and Social Relations* (Milton Keynes: Open University Press, 1986) pp. 135–54.

18. A. J. P. Taylor, *A Personal History* (London: Hamish Hamilton, 1983), ch. 1. Also Kathleen Burk, *Troublemaker: The Life and History of A. J. P. Taylor* (London: Yale University Press, 2000) ch. 1.

19. See Peter Fleetwood-Hesketh, *Murray's Lancashire Architectural Guide* (London: John Murray, 1955) pp. 172–3; A. J. P. Taylor, 'A Southport Childhood', *Spectator*, 20 September 1980, pp. 15–16.

20. Between 1948 and 1958 the number of motor licences issued for private cars and vans increased from 1.3 million to 4.5 million; it then more than doubled in the next decade (to 10.8 million). (A. H. Halsey, *Trends in British Society Since 1900: A Guide to the Changing Social Structure of Britain* (Basingstoke: Macmillan, 1972) p. 280.)

21. Walton, *The British Seaside*, p. 65.

22. See Arthur Marwick, *British Society Since 1945* (Harmondsworth: Penguin Books, 1996 edn) p. 71.

23. The period from 1950 until 1974 has been described by Julian Demetriadi as 'the golden years' of the English seaside resort. 'The Golden Years: English Seaside Resorts, 1950–1974', in Shaw and Williams, *The Rise and Fall of British Coastal Resorts*, pp. 49–75.

24. *Social Trends*, 30, p. 209.

25. See Walton, *The British Seaside*, pp. 66–7.

26. *Social Trends*, 21 (1991) and 30 (2000). Nevertheless Blackpool's decline as a resort is worrying – visitor numbers dropped by 30 per cent between 1995 and 2001. Unemployment in some central wards is 10–12 per cent. A plan to revive the economy through the building of a 'Las Vegas-style' casino, however, has been opposed by small-business people, who fear that the attempt to attract gamblers will squeeze out the many small hotels and gift shops (*Guardian*, 10 April 2001).

27. See Walton, *The British Seaside*, chs 1 and 7.

28. *Observer*, 25 February 2001.

29. Welsh National Tourist Board, *Meirionnydd in the Snowdonia National Park* (Cardiff, 1995).

30. J. B. Priestley, 'When Work Is Over', *Picture Post*, 4 January 1941, pp. 39–40.

31. Stephen G. Jones, *Sport, Politics and the Working Class: Organised Labour and Sport in Interwar Britain* (Manchester: Manchester University Press, 1988) esp. pp. 138–46. Also Richard Holt, *Sport and the British: A Modern History* (Oxford: Oxford University Press, 1990 edn) pp. 194–202.

32. Cited in Open University, *Popular Culture and Everyday Life (2)*, p. 16.

33. Pimlott, *The Englishman's Holiday*, pp. 257–8.

34. See Robert Hewison, *The Heritage Industry: Britain in a Climate of Decline* (London: Methuen, 1987). Hewison noted that by the mid-1980s the number of museums in Britain had doubled since 1960 (p. 82).

35. Pimlott, *The Englishman's Holiday* p. 258.

36. Central Statistical Office, *Social Trends*, 21 (London: HMSO, 1991) p. 180.

37. Figures from *Social Trends* (21, 1991, p. 189; 30, 2000, p. 209).

38. *Social Trends*, 30, p. 217.

39. Urry, *Tourist Gaze*, p. 12.

40. See L. Turner and J. Ash, *The Golden Hordes* (London: Constable, 1975).

41. Urry, *Tourist Gaze*, p. 1–2.

42. See V. Turner and E. Turner, *Image and Pilgrimage in Christian Culture: Anthropological Perspectives* (Oxford: Basil Blackwell, 1978).

43. Cited in Richard Hoggart, *The Uses of Literacy: Aspects of Working Class Life with Special Reference to Publications and Entertainments* (Harmondsworth: Pelican Books, 1958) p. 50.

44. See D. J. Boorstin, *The Image, A Guide to Pseudo-Events in America* (New York: Harper and Row, 1964); D. MacCannell, *The Tourist: A New Theory of the Leisure Class* (London: Macmillan, 1976).

45. Saga Holiday Brochure, 1997.

46. For example, Gerald Brenan, *The Spanish Labyrinth* (Cambridge: Cambridge University Press, 1990 edn); *The Face of Spain* (London, 1950); Laurie Lee, *As I Walked Out*

One Midsummer Morning (Harmondsworth: Penguin Books, 1971); Chris Stewart, *Driving Over Lemons: An Optimist in Andalucia* (London: Sort of Books, 1999).

47. See John Urry, *Consuming Places* (London: Routledge, 1995) pp. 132–3.

48. See Eric Dunning, 'Figurational Sociology and its Critics', in E. Dunning and C. Rojek, eds, *Sport and Leisure in the Civilizing Process* (Basingstoke: Macmillan – now Palgrave, 1992) pp. 221–84.

49. John Benson, *The Rise of Consumer Society in Britain 1880–1980* (London: Longman, 1994) p. 97.

50. Claire Langhamer, *Women's Leisure in England, 1920–1960* (Manchester: Manchester University Press, 2000) pp. 36–9.

PART TWO: LEISURE, THE HOME AND VOLUNTARY ACTIVITY

6 LEISURE, THE HOME, RADIO AND TELEVISION

1. H. Cunningham, *Leisure in the Industrial Revolution c.1780–c.1880* (London: Croom Helm, 1980) esp. ch. 3.

2. P. Bailey, *Leisure and Class in Victorian England* (London: Routledge and Kegan Paul, 1978) pp. 59–61, 170.

3. G. Stedman Jones, *Languages of Class: Studies in English Working Class History, 1832–1982* (Cambridge: Cambridge University Press, 1983) ch. 4.

4. Stedman Jones, *Languages of Class*, pp. 234–5.

5. R. Williams, *Television, Technology and Cultural Forms* (London: Routledge, 1990 edn) provides a valuable discussion of the convergence of interests in the formation of public broadcasting at this time.

6. M. Pegg, *Broadcasting and Society, 1918–1939* (London: Croom Helm, 1983) p. 7.

7. P. Scannell and D. Cardiff, *A Social History of British Broadcasting – vol. 1 1922–1939, Serving the Nation* (Oxford: Basil Blackwell, 1991) pp. 357–9. Hilda Jennings' and Winifred Gill's survey of Bristol in the late 1930s suggested that 'control' of the radio had become more democratic, with all family members having a say in the choice of programmes, even though 'father' still exercised the major influence: *Broadcasting in Everyday Life: A Survey of the Social Effects of the Coming of Broadcasting* (BBC: London, n.d.) pp. 21–3.

8. R. McKibbin, *Classes and Cultures: England, 1918–1951* (Oxford: Oxford University Press, 1998) p. 460.

9. McKibbin, *Classes and Cultures*, p. 462.

10. A. Briggs, *The History of Broadcasting in the United Kingdom: vol. II – The Golden Age of the Wireless* (Oxford: Oxford University Press, 1965) pp. 260–5, 315–20; Pegg, *Broadcasting and Society*, pp. 105–6.

11. Asa Briggs has commented of Reith in the 1930s that he 'frequently set out deliberately to move against the currents of the times rather than with them'. ('Broadcasting Retrospect', *New Society*, 15 November 1962.) In a work commissioned by the BBC Jennings and Gill found evidence of listeners' interest in and affection for radio, and they were warmly supportive in their conclusions of the social and educational benefits bestowed by broadcasting. Their stance contrasted sharply with some of the more pessimistic attitudes towards broadcasting, especially that

of commercial television, to be found 20 years later. See *Broadcasting in Everyday Life*, esp. pp. 39–40.

12. Scannell and Cardiff, *Social History of British Broadcasting* pp. 230, 295.
13. Scannell and Cardiff, *Social History of British Broadcasting*, chs 4 and 5; Pegg, *Broadcasting and Society*, ch. 7.
14. P. Scannell and D. Cardiff, 'Radio in World War 2', *The Historical Development of Popular Culture in Britain* (Milton Keynes: The Open University Press, 1981) pp 31–78; 'Serving the Nation: Public Service Broadcasting Before the War', in B. Waites, T. Bennett, and G. Martin, eds, *Popular Culture: Past and Present* (London: Croom Helm, 1981) pp. 161–88.
15. Scannell and Cardiff, 'Radio in World War 2', p. 45.
16. Quoted in Scannell and Cardiff, 'Radio in World War 2', p. 39.
17. Scannell and Cardiff, 'Radio in World War 2', p. 61.
18. See S. Nicholas, *Echo of War: Home Front Propaganda and the Wartime BBC 1939–45* (Manchester: Manchester University Press, 1996); 'The People's Radio: The BBC and Its Audience 1939–1945', in N. Hayes and J. Hill, eds, '"Millions Like Us?": British Culture in the Second World War* (Liverpool: Liverpool University Press, 1999) pp. 62–92.
19. Nicholas, 'The BBC and Its Audience', pp. 83–4.
20. Scannell and Cardiff, 'Radio in World War 2', p. 69.
21. Nicholas, 'The BBC and Its Audience', p. 91.
22. Exactly how young is a little difficult to say. The habit of radio listening remained relatively stable in the later part of the century, with the 35–64 age group providing most male listeners, and the over 64s most female listeners. (*Social Trends*, 30, London; Stationery Office, 2000, p. 212.)
23. A. Briggs, *A History of Broadcasting in the United Kingdom: vol V. – Competition, 1955–74* (Oxford: Oxford University Press, 1995) ch. 8.
24. On radio developments, see: A. Crisell, *An Introductory of British Broadcasting* (London: Routledge, 1997) pp. 142–5. A. J. P. Taylor, *English History, 1914–1945* (Oxford: Clarendon Press, 1965) p. 52 n. 3.
25. H. Perkin, *The Rise of Professional Society: England Since 1880* (London: Routledge, 1989) p. 421.
26. A. Marwick, *British Society Since 1945* (London: Penguin Books, 1996 edn) p. 246.
27. H. C. Debs, 5s, vol. 525 (1953–54) col. 1462 (London: HMSO, 1954).
28. Quoted in J. Curran and J. Seaton, *Power Without Responsibility: The Press and Broadcasting in Britain* (London: Routledge, 1997 edn) p. 191.
29. HC Debs, 5s, vol. 525, col. 1446. This principle was, of course, forgotten in the 1990s by governments keen to court the big broadcasting companies, and sporting organizations desperate to sell 'exclusive' rights for large amounts of money.
30. Seaton and Curran, *Power Without Responsibility*, p. 192.
31. See P. Clarke, *Hope and Glory: Britain, 1900–1990* (London: Penguin Books, 1997) ch. 8.
32. Seaton and Curran, *Power Without Responsibility*, ch. 12.
33. *Daily Express*, 26, 27, 30 November; 3 December 1953. The criticisms of television mainly came from a series of interviews conducted by the paper's reporter Bob Pennington with soccer referees.

34. *Report of the Committee on Broadcasting, 1960* (The Pilkington Report) (London: HMSO, Cmnd 1753, 1962). Ferdynand Zweig, a well-known academic observer of the working class, held television to be responsible for the decline of the 'traditional realism and common-sense of the working class'; these were being weakened by the working-class person's constantly being drawn into a 'world of illusion and make believe'. F. Zweig, *The Worker in an Affluent Society: Family Life and Industry* (London: Heinemann, 1961) pp. 108–11.

35. V. Packard, *The Hidden Persuaders* (Harmondsworth: Penguin Books, 1960); see also C. Lodziak, *The Power of Television: A Critical Appraisal* (London: Frances Pinter, 1986) ch. 1. Perhaps the most influential of such approaches has been M. McLuhan, *Understanding Media* (London: Routledge and Kegan Paul, 1964).

36. B. Sendall, *Independent Television in Britain – vol. 2: Expansion and Change 1958–68* (London: Macmillan, 1983) parts II and III.

37. Pilkington Report, p. 67.

38. Pilkington Report, pp. 292–3.

39. Briggs, *History of Broadcasting*, vol. V, p. 303.

40. Crisell, *Introductory History*, p. 112.

41. Briggs, *History of Broadcasting*, vol. V, p. 201.

42. See Briggs, *History of Broadcasting*, vol V, pp. 294–303.

43. D. Morley, *The Nationwide Audience: Structure and Decoding* (London: British Film Institute, 1980). See also D. Morley *Cultural Studies and Communications* (London: Edward Arnold, 1996). For a study carried out in the Morley tradition but arriving at slightly different conclusions, see J. Roscoe, H. Marshall and K. Gleeson, 'The Television Audience: A Reconstruction of the Taken-for-Granted Terms "Active", "Social" and "Critical"', *European Journal of Communication*, 10, 1 (1995) 87–108.

44. See J. Roscoe, H. Marshall and K. Gleeson, 'The Television Audience', *European Journal of Communications*, 10, 1 (1995) 87–108.

45. C. Lodziak, *The Power of Television* (London: Frances Pinter, 1986).

46. T. Harrisson, *Britain Revisited* (London: Victor Gollancz, 1961) p. 207. See also P. Johnson, *Twentieth Century Britain: Economic, Social and Cultural Change* (London: Longman, 1994) p. 11, who argues that television made people better informed.

47. R. Silverstone, *Television and Everyday Life* (London: Routledge, 1994) notes the 'serious gap in . . . research' on these aspects of media reception, and the tendency in the research that has been conducted to 'abstract the dynamics of media reception from the social environment in which it takes place' (pp. 2–3). See also Jennings and Gill, *Broadcasting in Everyday Life*.

48. T. O'Sullivan, 'Television memories and Cultures of Viewing 1950–65', in J. Corner, ed, *Popular Television in Britain: Studies in Cultural History* (London: British Film Institute, 1991) p. 164.

49. O'Sullivan, 'Television Memories', p. 171.

50. See D. Morley and D. Silverstone, 'Domestic Communications – Technologies and Meanings', *Media, Culture and Society*, 12 (1991) 31–55.

51. See C. Rojek, *Decentring Leisure* (London: Sage Publications, 1995) p. 7.

52. Home Office, *Report of the Committee on the Future of Broadcasting* (The Annan Committee, cmnd 6753) (London: HMSO, 1977) pp. 29, 473.

7 YOUTH, AGE AND THE PROBLEM OF LEISURE

1. See G. Pearson, *Hooligan: A History of Respectable Fears* (London: Macmillan, 1983).
2. See M. Brake, *Comparative Youth Culture: The Sociology of Youth Cultures in America, Britain and Canada* (London: Routledge, 1985) ch. 2.
3. See T. H. Eriksen, *Small Places, Large Issues: An Introduction to Social and Cultural Anthropology* (London: Pluto Press, 1995) pp. 121–8; C. Rojek, *Leisure and Culture* (Basingstoke: Macmillan – now Palgrave, 2000) pp. 147–50.
4. A. McRobbie, *Feminism and Youth Culture: From 'Jackie' to 'Just Seventeen'* (Basingstoke: Macmillan – now Palgrave, 1991) ch. 2.
5. M. Abrams, *The Teenage Consumer* (London: London Press Exchange, 1959).
6. D. Fowler, *The First Teenagers: The Lifestyle of Young Wage-Earners in Interwar Britain* (London: Woburn Press, 1995) p. 169.
7. A. Marwick, *British Society Since 1945* (London: Penguin Books, 1996 edn) p. 71.
8. Abrams, *Teenage Consumer*, pp. 13–14.
9. F. Zweig, *Labour, Life and Poverty* (Wakefield: E.P. Publishing, 1975 edn); *The Worker in an Affluent Society: Family Life and Industry* (London: Heinemann, 1961).
10. J. Benson, *The Rise of Consumer Society in Britain, 1880–1980* (London: Longman, 1994) ch. 7.
11. Benson, *Rise of Consumer Society*, p. 175.
12. S. Cohen, *Folk Devils and Moral Panics: The Creation of the Mods and Rockers* (London: MacGibbon and Kee, 1972). Such youth groups, Cohen claimed, were used as a model of how not to behave: 'visible reminders of what we should not be' (p. 10).
13. There is a good discussion of these attitudes in Brake, *Comparative Youth Culture*, ch. 2.
14. The classic study of this movement of opinion is S. Hall, C. Critcher, T. Jefferson and B. Roberts, *Policing the Crisis* (London: Macmillan, 1978).
15. R. Hoggart, *The Uses of Literacy: Aspects of Working-Class Life with Special Reference to Publications and Entertainments* (London: Chatto and Windus, 1957). See esp. ch. 8 (a).
16. Hoggart, *Uses of Literacy*, p. 248.
17. Hoggart, *Uses of Literacy*, p. 248.
18. Hoggart, *Uses of Literacy*, p. 340.
19. D. Thompson, ed., *Discrimination and Popular Culture* (Harmondsworth: Penguin Books, 1964)
20. K. O. Morgan, *The People's Peace: British History, 1945–1990* (Oxford: Oxford University Press, 1992) pp. 108–9.
21. D. Butler and A. King, *The British General Election of 1964* (London: Macmillan, 1965) p. 30. A spate of critical studies appeared around this time, including Andrew Shonfield's *British Economic Policy Since the War* and Anthony Sampson's *Anatomy of Britain*. On the Left, the collection of essays *Towards Socialism* (London: Fontana, 1965), which included Perry Anderson's 'Origins of the Present Crisis', was very influential.
22. Harmondsworth: Penguin Books, 1961.
23. Central Council of Physical Recreation, *Sport and the Community* (London: CCPR, 1960). Known after its Chairman, Sir John Wolfenden, as the 'Wolfenden Report';

a report on homosexuality and prostitution by a committee chaired by Wolfenden in 1957 is confusingly also known by the same name.

24. Ministry of Education, *The Youth Service in England and Wales: Report of the Committee Appointed by the Minister of Education in November 1958* (London: HMSO, 1960).

25. Albemarle Report, p. 1.

26. See Albemarle Report, ch. 10 'Recommendations and Priorities'.

27. T. R. Fyvel, *The Insecure Offenders: Rebellious Youth in the Welfare State* (Harmondsworth: Penguin Books, 1963 edn) p. 255.

28. See D. Hebdige, *Subculture: The Meaning of Style* (London: Methuen, 1979); K. Leech, *Youthquake: the Growth of a Counter-Culture Through Two Decades* (London: Sheldon Press, 1973).

29. R. Gosling, *Lady Albemarle's Boys* (London: Fabian Society, 1961).

30. See B. Berger, 'On the Youthfulness of Youth Culture', *Social Research*, 30, 3 (1963) 319–432.

31. See *Guardian*, 31 May 2000.

32. Hebdige, *Subculture* is an excellent book which nevertheless reflects this male-centredness very markedly.

33. C. Dyhouse, *Girls Growing Up in Late Victorian and Edwardian England* (London: Routledge and Kegan Paul, 1981) pp. 111–14.

34. See C. M. Parratt, ' "The Making of the Healthy and the Happy Home": Recreation, Education, and the Production of Working-Class Womanhood at the Rowntree Cocoa Works, York, *c.*1898–1914', in J. Hill and J. Williams, eds, *Sport and Identity in the North of England* (Keele: Keele University Press, 1996) pp. 53–83.

35. A. McRobbie, '*Jackie*: An Ideology of Adolescent Femininity', in B. Waites, T. Bennett and G. Martin, eds, *Popular Culture: Past and Present* (London: Croom Helm/Open University Press, 1982) pp. 263–83.

36. See A. McRobbie, *Feminism and Youth Culture*, chs 5 and 6: J. Winship, *Inside Women's Magazines* (London: Pandora, 1987) esp. ch. 4.

37. S. Scraton, ' "Boys Muscle In Where Angels Fear To Tread" – Girls' Sub-Cultures and Physical Activities', in C. Critcher, P. Bramham and A. Tomlinson, eds, *Sociology of Leisure: A Reader* (London: E. & F. N. Spon, 1995) pp. 117–29.

38. Marwick, *British Society Since 1945*, p. 152.

39. P. Jephcott, *Rising Twenty: Notes on Some Ordinary Girls* (London: Faber and Faber, 1948) p. 158; see also the same author's *Girls Growing Up* (London: Faber and Faber, 1942).

40. G. Gorer, *Exploring English Character* (London: Cresset Press, 1955) pp. 86–7, 115, 125, 138, 161.

41. K. Wellings, J. Field, A. Johnson and J. Wadsworth (with S. Bradshaw), *Sexual Behaviour in Britain: The National Survey of Sexual Attitudes and Lifestyles* (Harmondsworth: Penguin Books, 1994) pp. 84, 133, 173–5, 226–7, 271.

42. McRobbie, *Feminism and Youth Culture*, p. 227.

43. Marwick, *British Society Since 1945*, p. 142.

44. Some of these statements, conventional wisdoms of anthropology, are questioned in Pat Thane's *Old Age in English History: Past Experiences, Present Issues* (Oxford: Oxford University Press, 2000), which appeared just as this book was going to press.

45. Office for National Statistics, *Annual Abstract of Statistics* (London: Stationery Office, 1999) p. 28.
46. J. Benson, *Prime Time: A History of the Middle Aged in Twentieth Century Britain* (London: Longman, 1997).
47. Quoted in P. Thompson, C. Itzin and M. Abendstern, *I Don't Feel Old: The Experience of Later Life* (Oxford: Oxford University Press, 1991) p. 157.
48. See M. Abrams, 'Leisure Time Use by the Elderly and Leisure Provision for the Elderly', in Critcher, Bramham and Tomlinson, *Sociology of Leisure*, pp. 78–87.
49. Thompson, Itzin and Abenstern, *I Don't Feel Old.*

8 THE CLUB PRINCIPLE

1. P. Clark, *British Clubs and Societies, 1580–1800: The Origins of an Associational World* (Oxford: Oxford University Press, 2000). See also Roy Porter's review of this book, which includes the Goncourt brothers' quip: 'The Need for Buddies', *London Review of Books*, 22 June 2000, 30–1.
2. These rather general figures are quoted on the website of the NCVO, which estimated that the largest proportion of voluntary activity was devoted to social care. (See www.communities.org.uk/articles/vol.html)
3. *Second Report from the Select Committee of the House of Lords on Sport and Leisure* (London: HMSO, 1974) p. xxvi.
4. Open University, *Popular Culture and Everyday Life* (Milton Keynes: Open University Press, 1981) p. 42.
5. J. Bishop and P. Hoggett, 'Mutual Aid in Leisure', in C. Critcher, P. Bramham and A. Tomlinson, eds, *Sociology of Leisure: A Reader* (London: E & F. N. Spon, 1995) p. 197.
6. Bishop and Hoggett, 'Mutual Aid in Leisure', pp. 197–8. There is a very good explanation of the various types of clubs operating in the London area in the 1930s to be found in *The New Survey of London Life and Labour: volume IX – Life and Leisure* (London: P. S. King and Son Ltd, 1935) ch. vi. For a useful summary of the constitutional and legal aspects of club activity, see Valerie Collins, *Recreation and the Law* (London: E. and F. N. Spon, 1993 edn) ch. 5.
7. On the MCC, see: J. Williams, *Cricket and England: A Cultural and Social History of the Inter-War Years* (London: Frank Cass, 1999) pp. 20–5.
8. P. Willmott and M. Young, *Family and Class in a London Suburb* (London: Routledge and Kegan Paul, 1960) p. 91.
9. Willmott and Young, *Family and Class*, p. 87.
10. M. Young and P. Willmott, *Family and Kinship in East London* (London: Routledge and Kegan Paul, 1957) pp. 84–5, 92–3.
11. A recent account of the famous pub crawl up Tottenham Court Road by Marx, Bauer and Liebknecht can be found in Francis Wheen, *Karl Marx* (London: Fourth Estate, 1999) pp. 256–7.
12. In *The New Survey of London Life and Labour* it was noted that, although clubs had increased in relation to pubs throughout the London area since the 1914–18 War, the ratio of pubs to clubs was highest in working-class areas (IX, pp. 123–4).

13. A. Davies, *Leisure, Gender and Poverty: Working Class Culture in Salford and Manchester, 1900–1939* (Buckingham: Open University Press, 1992) esp. ch. 3.

14. For example B. Harrison, *Drink and the Victorians: The Temperance Question in England, 1815–72* (Keele: Keele University Press, 1994 edn).

15. Mass-Observation, *The Pub and the People: A Worktown Study* (London: Victor Gollancz, 1943). The fieldwork was carried out just before the outbreak of war.

16. M-O, *Pub and the People*, p. 17.

17. M-O, *Pub and the People*, pp. 76–8.

18. See Young and Willmott, *Family and Kinship*, pp. 126–7; R. McKibbin, *Classes and Cultures: England, 1918–1951* (Oxford: Oxford University Press, 1998) pp. 183–4.

19. B. Jackson, *Working Class Community: Some General Notions Raised by a Series of Studies in Northern England* (London: Routledge and Kegan Paul, 1968) p. 40.

20. McKibbin, *Classes and Cultures*, p. 184.

21. Quoted in J. Hill, ' "When Work is Over": Labour, Leisure and Culture in Wartime Britain', in N. Hayes and J. Hill, eds, *'Millions Like Us?': British Culture in the Second World War* (Liverpool: Liverpool University Press, 1999) p. 250. See also J. Crump, 'Recreation in Coventry Between the Wars', in B. Lancaster and T. Mason, eds, *Life and Labour in a Twentieth Century City: The Experience of Coventry* (Coventry: University of Warwick/Cryfield Press, n.d.), who emphasizes the educational work carried out by the clubs in Coventry between the wars. *The New Survey of London Life and Labour*, however, presents a pessimistic view of the effectiveness of such activities in the CIU clubs in London (IX, pp. 126–30).

22. B. Jackson, *Working Class Community*, p. 63; also N. Dennis, F. Henriques and C. Slaughter, *Coal Is Our Life: An Analysis of a Yorkshire Mining Community* (London: Eyre and Spottiswoode, 1956) pp. 142–54.

23. See N. Baker, 'The Amateur Ideal in a Society of Equality: Change and Continuity in Post-Second World War British Sport, 1945–48', *International Journal of the History of Sport*, 12, 1 (1995) 99–126.

24. Open University, *Popular Culture and Everyday Life*, p. 42; K. Newton, *Second City Politics: Democratic Processes and Decision-Making in Birmingham* (Oxford: Clarendon Press, 1976) pp. 256–8.

25. K. Sillitoe, *Planning For Leisure* (London: HMSO, 1969); Bishop and Hoggett, 'Mutual Aid in Leisure', pp. 201–2.

26. H. Meller, *Leisure and the Changing City, 1870–1914* (London: Routledge and Kegan Paul, 1976) p. 236.

27. See R. Frankenberg, *Communities in Britain: Social Life in Town and Country* (Harmondsworth: Penguin Books, 1966) ch. 4.

28. Dennis, Henriques and Slaughter, *Coal Is Our Life*.

29. A. Birch, *Small Town Politics* (Oxford: Oxford University Press, 1959).

30. Birch, *Small Town Politics*, p. 195.

31. *Neighbourhood and Community: An Enquiry Into Social Relationships on Housing Estates in Liverpool and Sheffield* (Liverpool: University of Liverpool Press, 1954).

32. *Neighbourhood and Community*, pp. 27–39.

33. Frankenberg, *Communities in Britain*, pp. 201–14.

34. M. Stacey, *Tradition and Change: A Study of Banbury* (Oxford: Oxford University Press, 1960).

35. Stacey, *Tradition and Change*, p. 75.

36. Stacey, *Tradition and Change*, pp. 75, 82–3.

37. R. D. Putnam, 'Bowling Alone: America's Declining Social Capital', *Journal of Democracy*, 6, 1 (1995) 65–78. Putnam's concern that the decline of bowling leagues and clubs bodes ill for America's civil society has not yet been extended to Britain. His appearance, however, on BBC Radio 4's programme *Start The Week* (26th March 2001) was clearly intended to provoke debate on the relevance of the issue to Britain.

38. C. L. R. James, *Beyond a Boundary* (London: Stanley Paul, 1969 edn) pp. 55–6.

39. B. Stoddart, 'Cricket and Colonialism in the English-Speaking Caribbean to 1914: Towards a Cultural Analysis', in H. Beckles and B. Stoddart, *Liberation Cricket: West Indies Cricket Culture* (Manchester: Manchester University Press, 1995) p. 19.

40. Dennis, Henriques and Slaughter, *Coal Is Our Life*, p. 163.

41. Dennis, Henriques and Slaughter, *Coal Is Our Life*, pp. 158, 170.

42. Frankenberg, *Communities in Britain*, pp. 96–101.

43. Birch, *Small Town Politics*, pp. 38–40, 182–3, 195.

44. J. Hill, *Nelson: Politics, Economy, Community* (Edinburgh: Keele University Press, 1997) ch.7.

45. Hill, *Nelson*, p. 141.

46. J. Williams, 'South Asians and Cricket in Bolton', *Sports Historian*, 14 (1994) 56–65. R. Glass (with H. Pollins), *Newcomers: The First West Indians in London* (London: George Allen and Unwin, 1960).

47. Stacey, *Tradition and Change*, p. 88.

48. Stacey, *Tradition and Change*, pp. 87–9.

49. McKibbin, *Classes and Cultures*, pp. 84–98.

50. As, for example, in Nelson: Hill, *Nelson*, pp. 103–5.

51. McKibbin, *Classes and Cultures*, p. 96.

52. See P. Williamson, *Stanley Baldwin: Conservative Leadership and National Values* (Cambridge: Cambridge University Press, 1999).

53. McKibbin, *Classes and Cultures*, pp. 377–85.

54. See Jack Williams, *Cricket and England: A Cultural and Social History of the Inter-War Years* (London: Frank Cass, 1999) pp. 114–31.

55. Recounted by Ian Hall, a former Derbyshire county cricketer, in a paper given at the annual conference of the British Society of Sports History, Manchester, 1993. See also Ian Hall, 'County Cricket and League Football As Occupations in the 1960s: An Insider's View', *The Sports Historian*, 14 (1994) 38–44.

56. See K. A. P. Sandiford, 'The Professionalization of Modern Cricket', *British Journal of Sports History* 2, 3 (1985) 270–89.

57. *Daily Mail*, 26 November 1953.

58. *Daily Mirror*, 26 November 1953.

59. See A. Hardaker, *Hardaker of the League* (London: Pelham Books, 1977) pp. 57–8, 114, 149.

60. Hardaker, *Hardaker of the League*, p. 68.

61. See T. Collins, *Rugby's Great Split: Class, Culture and the Origins of Rugby League Football* (London: Frank Cass, 1998).

62. See G. Williams, 'Rugby Union', in T. Mason, ed., *Sport In Britain: A Social History* (Cambridge: Cambridge University Press, 1989) p. 324.

63. McKibbin, *Classes and Cultures*, p. 361.

64. J. Lowerson, *Sport and the English Middle Classes, 1870–1914* (Manchester: Manchester University Press, 1993) chs 4 and 5.

65. R. Holt, *Stanmore Golf Club, 1893–1993: A Social History* (London: Stanmore Golf Club, 1993); J. Bromhead, *Droitwich Golf Club, 1897–1997* (Droitwich: Grant Books, 1996).

66. McKibbin, *Classes and Cultures*, p. 380.

67. Lowerson, *Sport and the English Middle Classes*, p. 98.

68. See Richard Holt and Tony Mason, *Sport in Britain, 1945–2000* (Oxford: Blackwell, 2000) pp. 53–8.

69. Holt and Mason, *Sport in Britain*, p. 38.

70. See N. Baker, 'A More Even Playing Field? Sport During and After the War', in N. Hayes and J. Hill, eds, *'Millions Like Us?': British Culture in the Second World War* (Liverpool: Liverpool University Press, 1999) pp. 125–55.

71. Holt and Mason, *Sport in Britain*, p. 62.

PART THREE: PUBLIC POLICY: THE ROLE OF THE STATE

9 STATE AND POLITICS IN SPORT AND LEISURE

1. M. Dyreson, 'Marketing National Identity: The Olympic Games of 1932 and American Culture', North American Society for Sport History, *Proceedings* (1995) 64–5. On the 1936 Olympic Games, see: B. Murray, 'Berlin in 1936: Old and New Work on the Nazi Olympics', *International Journal of the History of Sport*, 9, 1 (1992) 29–49; Richard D. Mandell, *The Nazi Olympics* (London: Souvenir Press, 1972).

2. A. Bullock, *The Life and Times of Ernest Bevin, vol. 3 Foreign Secretary 1945–51* (London: Heinemann, 1983) p. 230; Richard Holt and Tony Mason, *Sport in Britain 1945–2000* (Oxford: Blackwell, 2000) ch. 2.

3. See W. L. Guttsman, *The German Social Democratic Party, 1875–1933: From Ghetto to Government* (London: George Allen and Unwin, 1981); S. G. Jones, *Sport, Politics and the Working Class: Organised Labour and Sport in Interwar Britain* (Manchester: Manchester University Press, 1988); A. Kruger and J. Riordan, eds, *The Story of Worker Sport* (Champaign, IL.: Human Kinetics, 1996).

4. J. Riordan, 'The Workers' Olympics', in A. Tomlinson and G. Whannel, eds, *Five-Ring Circus: Money, Power and Politics at the Olympic Games* (London: Pluto Press, 1984) pp. 98–112.

5. In 1918 'Nearly everyone, Labour and Conservative alike', says A. J. P. Taylor, 'regarded the wartime controls and direction as evils which should be got rid of as soon as possible.' A. J. P. Taylor, *English History, 1914–1945* (Oxford: Clarendon Press, 1965) p. 139.

6. R. Lowe, *The Welfare State in Britain Since 1945* (Basingstoke: Macmillan – now Palgrave, 1993) ch. 2.

7. See K. O. Morgan, *The People's Peace: British History, 1945–1990* (Oxford: Oxford University Press, 1990) ch. 4; Paul Addison, *The Road to 1945: British Politics and the Second World War* (London: Pimlico revised edn, 1994) pp. 279–92; 'Consensus

Revisited', *Twentieth Century British History*, 4 (1993) 91–4; D. Kavanagh, 'The Postwar Consensus', *Twentieth Century British History*, 3 (1992) 175–90.

8. A. Gamble, *The Free Economy and the Strong State: The Politics of Thatcherism* (Basingstoke: Macmillan, 1988).

9. I. P. Henry, *The Politics of Leisure Policy* (Basingstoke: Macmillan – now Palgrave, 1993) pp. 172–83; Anthony King, *The End of the Terraces: The Transformation of English Football in the 1990s* (Leicester: Leicester University Press, 1998) ch. 3.

10. J. F. Coghlan with I. Webb, *Sport and British Politics Since 1960* (London: Falmer Press, 1990) p. 5.

11. On censorship, see: Annette Kuhn, *Cinema, Censorship and Sexuality, 1909–25* (London: Routledge, 1989 edn) esp. ch. 2; Jeffrey Richards, *The Age of the Dream Palace: Cinema and Society in Britain, 1930–1939* (London: Routledge, 1989 edn) part II. There is a relatively small literature on local authority censorship, but see Sian Lewis, 'The Town Hall Film Censor: Developing a Social and Legal Consensus for the Cultural Regulation of the Cinema' (paper presented to the Social History Society conference, Belfast, January 2001).

12. G. R. Searle, *The Quest for National Efficiency, 1899–1914* (Oxford: Basil Blackwell, 1971).

13. See N. Baker, 'A More Even Playing Field? Sport During and After the War', in N. Hayes and J. Hill, eds, *'Millions Like Us?':British Culture in the Second World War* (Liverpool: Liverpool University Press, 1999) pp. 125–55.

14. Home Office, *Enquiry into the Disaster at the Bolton Wanderers Football Ground, 9 March 1946* (The Hughes Report) (London: HMSO, 1946); N. Baker, 'Have They Forgotten Bolton?', *Sports Historian*, 18 (1998) 120–51.

15. Quoted in Baker, 'A More Even Playing Field?', p. 131.

16. J. Rollin, *Soccer At War* (London: Willow Books, 1985). See also A. Calder, *The People's War: Britain, 1939–45* (London: Panther, 1971) pp. 431–5.

17. Calder, *People's War*, p. 287.

18. T. Mason, ed., *Sport in Britain: A Social History* (Cambridge: Cambridge University Press, 1989) p. 1. This was based on a survey of 'other ranks' of the South East Asia Command carried out in early 1946 among 'young' (mostly under 25) and 'old' (over 25) troops. The 'old' soldiers replied more positively about sport, and also had far fewer negative responses on army life than their younger counterparts. See E. W. Browne, W. B. Coates and A. F. Wells, *The Soldier and the Army: Opinions on Some Aspects of Army Life* (No. 1 Special Research Section, RAMC, SEAC: 1946) esp. pp. 38–40. I am grateful to Tony Mason for drawing my attention to this source.

19. M. Polley, 'Olympic Diplomacy: The British Government and the Projected 1940 Olympic Games', *International Journal of the History of Sport*, 9, 2 (1992) 169–87; 'The British Government and the Olympic Games in the 1930s', *Sports Historian*, 17, 1 (1997) 30–40.

20. Accounts from P. J. Beck, *Scoring for Britain: International Football and International Politics, 1900–1939* (London: Frank Cass, 1999) chs 7–9; 'England v. Germany, 1938', *History Today*, June 1982, 29–34; R. Holt and T. Mason, 'Le Football, le Fascisme et la Politique Etrangere Britannique: L'Angleterre, L'Italie et l'Allemagne 1934–35', in P. Arnaud and A. Wahl, eds, *Sport et Relations Internationales* (Metz: Université de Metz, 1994) pp. 73–96; S. G. Jones, *Sport, Politics and the Working Class* (Manchester: Manchester University Press, 1988) pp. 181–6.

21. M. Polley, 'The Diplomatic Background to the 1966 Football World Cup', *Sports Historian*, 18, 2 (1998) 1–19; D. Howell, *Made in Birmingham: The Memoirs of Denis Howell* (London: Queen Anne Press, 1990) pp. 160–3.
22. B. Houlihan, *The Government and Politics of Sport* (London: Routledge, 1991) p. 27.
23. Quoted in Richard Holt and Tony Mason, *Sport in Britain 1945–2000* (Oxford: Blackwell, 2000) p. 26.
24. See N. Baker, 'A More Even Playing Field? Sport During and After the War', in Hayes and Hill, *'Millions Like Us?'*, pp. 125–55; 'The Amateur Ideal in a Society of Equality', *International Journal of the History of Sport*, 12 (1995) 99–126.
25. Labour Party, *Leisure For Living* (London: Labour Party, 1959) p. 5.
26. See TUC, *Annual Congress Report*, 1960, p. 435; 1961, pp. 453–5.
27. The exception was the remarkable performance in the 1958 World Cup of Northern Ireland, with an unusually good side built around Blanchflower, McIlroy and MacParland.
28. Houlihan, *Government and Politics of Sport*, p. 87.
29. Central Council of Physical Recreation, *Sport and the Community* (The Report of the Wolfenden Committee on Sport) (London: CCPR, 1960).
30. Ministry of Education, *The Youth Service in England and Wales* (London: HMSO, 1960).
31. Wolfenden Report, p. 97.
32. See also Chapter 10.
33. Department of the Environment, *Sport and Recreation* (London: HMSO, 1975). See also the same Department's *Recreation and Deprivation in Inner Urban Areas* (London: HMSO, 1977).
34. J. Hargreaves, *Sport, Power and Culture: A Social and Historical Analysis of Popular Sports in Britain* (Cambridge: Polity Press, 1986) p. 190.
35. Coghlan with Webb, *Sport and British Politics*; see also Howell, *Made in Birmingham*, esp. pp. 155–60, 231–43.
36. Howell, *Made in Birmingham*, pp. 214–15, 231.
37. M. Polley, *Moving the Goalposts: A History of Sport and Society Since 1945* (London: Routledge, 1998) p. 31.
38. B. Johnston, *It's Been a Piece of Cake: A Tribute to My Favourite Test Cricketers* (London: Mandarin, 1990) p. 174.
39. See B. D'Oliveira, *Time to Declare: An Autobiography* (London: J. M. Dent, 1980) ch. 2.
40. Quoted in the *Guardian*, 8 February 1999.
41. See Howell, *Made in Birmingham*, pp. 200–9; also *Guardian*, 8 February 1999.
42. *Time To Declare*, pp. 61–70.
43. Quoted in T. Heald, *The Authorized Biography of the Incomparable Denis Compton* (London: Pavilion Books, 1996) p. 213.
44. See P. May, *A Game Enjoyed: An Autobiography* (London: Stanley Paul, 1985) pp. 190–1. Also T. Arlott, *John Arlott: A Memoir* (London: Pan Books, 1994) p. 168.
45. Full text quoted in Coghlan with Webb, *Sport and British Politics*, pp. 298–9.
46. Account from: N. Macfarlane, *Sport and Politics: A World Divided* (London: Willow Books, 1986) ch. 11; E. Hobsbawm, *Age of Extremes: The Short Twentieth Century, 1914–1991* (London: Abacus, 1995) ch. 8.
47. Coghlan with Webb, *Sport and British Politics*, p. 245.

48. K. O. Morgan, *The People's Peace: British History, 1945–1990* (Oxford: Oxford University Press, 1992) pp. 458–63.

49. See I. Taylor, 'Soccer Consciousness and Soccer Hooliganism', in S. Cohen, ed., *Images of Deviance* (Harmondsworth: Penguin, 1971) pp. 134–64; 'On the Sports Violence Question: Soccer Hooliganism Revisited', in Jennifer Hargreaves, ed., *Sport, Culture and Ideology* (London: Routledge and Kegan Paul, 1982) pp. 152–96; 'Football Mad: A Speculative Sociology of Football Hooliganism', in E. Dunning, ed., *The Sociology of Sport: A Collection of Readings* (London: Frank Cass, 1971) pp. 352–7; P. Marsh, E. Rosser and R. Harré, *The Rules of Disorder* (London: Routledge and Kegan Paul, 1978); J. Maguire, 'The Emergence of Football Spectating As a Social Problem, 1880–1985: A Figurational and Developmental Perspective', *Sociology of Sport Journal*, 3 (1986) 217–44. On the historical dimensions see E. Dunning, P. Murphy and J. Williams, *The Roots of Football Hooliganism: An Historical and Sociological Study* (London: Routledge and Kegan Paul, 1988); J. Williams, E. Dunning and P. Murphy, *Hooligans Abroad: The Behaviour and Control of English Fans in Continental Europe* (London: Routledge, 1989); W. Vamplew, 'Ungentlemanly Conduct: The Control of Soccer Crowd Behaviour in England, 1888–1914', in T. C. Smout, ed., *The Search for Wealth and Stability* (London: Macmillan, 1980); and the debate in the *International Journal of the History of Sport*, between R. W. Lewis, 'Football Hooliganism in England Before 1914: A Critique of the Dunning Thesis', 13, 3 (1996) 310–39, and P. Murphy, E. Dunning and J. Maguire, 'Football Spectator Violence ad Disorder before the First World War: A Reply to R. W. Lewis', 15, 1 (1998) 141–62.

50. For a good general discussion of these overlapping issues, see: A. Marwick, *British Society Since 1945* (London: Penguin Books, 1996 edn) ch. 21.

51. See for example: *Choice and Responsibilty: The Enabling State* (London: Conservative Political Centre, n.d. [c.1990]).

52. See J. Williams, E. Dunning and P. Murphy, *Hooligans Abroad*. Also S. Hall and M. Jacques, *The Politics of Thatcherism* (London: Lawrence and Wishart, 1983).

53. D. Russell, *Football and the English: A Social History of Association Football in England, 1863–1995* (Preston: Carnegie Publishing, 1997) p. 237.

54. I. Taylor, 'Putting the Boot into a Working-Class Sport: British Soccer After Bradford and Brussels', *Sociology of Sport Journal*, 4 (1987) 171–91.

55. On business developments in the 1990s, see: A. King, *The End of the Terraces: The Transformation of English Football in the 1990s* (Leicester: Leicester University Press, 1998) esp. part IV.

10 FROM 'RATIONAL RECREATION' TO 'SPORT FOR ALL': THE PLACE OF THE MUNICIPALITY IN SPORT AND LEISURE

1. See R. A. W. Rhodes, *Beyond Westminster: The Sub-Central Governments of Britain* (London: Unwin Hyman, 1988) sec. 3.6.

2. See Stephen G. Jones, *Workers At Play: A Social and Economic History of Leisure, 1918–1939* (London: Routledge and Kegan Paul, 1986) ch. 4.

3. P. Summerfield, 'The Effingham Arms and the Empire: Deliberate Selection in the Evolution of Music Hall in London', in E. Yeo and S. Yeo, eds, *Popular Culture and*

Class Conflict, 1590–1914 (Brighton: Harvester Press, 1981); B. Waites, 'The Music Hall', in Open University, *Popular Culture*, Block 2, unit 5 (Milton Keynes: Open University Press, 1981) pp. 43–76.

4. Summerfield, 'Effingham Arms'; Waites, 'Music Hall'; P. Bailey, *Leisure and Class in Victorian Britain: Rational Recreation and the Contest for Control, 1830–1885* (London: Routledge and Kegan Paul, 1978) p. 168; *Popular Culture and Performance in the Victorian City* (Cambridge: Cambridge University Press, 1998) ch. 1; Dave Russell, *Popular Music in England, 1840–1914* (Montreal: McGill-Queens's University Press, 1987) chs 1–3.

5. M. Clapson, *A Bit of a Flutter: Popular Gambling and English Society, c.1823–1961* (Manchester: Manchester University Press, 1992); C. Chinn, *Better Betting With a Decent Feller: Bookmaking, Betting and the British Working Class, 1750–1990* (London: Harvester, 1991) pp. 222–3.

6. See, for example, *Report of the Departmental Committee on Crowds* (The Shortt Report) cmd. 2088 (London: HMSO, 1924). This report was commissioned following the crowd scenes at the new Wembley Stadium during the Cup Final of 1923.

7. See A. Briggs, *Victorian Cities* (Harmondsworth: Penguin Books, 1968) ch. 5; E. P. Hennock, *Fit and Proper Persons: Ideal and Reality in 19th Century Urban Government* (London: Edward Arnold, 1973) esp. ch. 5.

8. Helen Meller, *Leisure and the Changing City, 1870–1914* (London: Routledge and Kegan Paul, 1976) p. 115 and ch. 5.

9. David Bowker, 'Parks and Baths: Recreation and municipal government in Ashton-under-Lyne between the wars' in Richard Holt ed., *Sport and the Working Class in Modern Britain* (Manchester: Manchester University Press, 1990) pp. 84–100. Stephen Jones none the less sees this period as one of increasing municipalization of leisure. See Stephen G. Jones, *Workers At Play: A Social and Economic History of Leisure, 1918–1939* (London: Routledge and Kegan Paul, 1986) p. 94.

10. Chris Waters, *British Socialists and the Politics of Popular Culture* (Manchester: Manchester University Press, 1990) esp. ch. 6.

11. Jones, *Workers At Play*, ch. 6.

12. See J. Hill, '"When Work Is Over": Labour Leisure and Culture in Wartime Britain', in N. Hayes and J. Hill, eds, *'Millions Like Us?': British Culture in the Second World War* (Liverpool: Liverpool University Press, 1999) p. 236–60.

13. S. G. Jones, *Sport, Politics and the Working Class: Organised Labour and Sport in Inter-War Britain* (Manchester: Manchester University Press, 1988) pp. 146–64.

14. D. Irving, *The Municipality From A Worker's Point of View* (London: Twentieth Century Press, n.d.) p. 15.

15. S. Macintyre, *Little Moscows: Communism and Working Class Militance in Inter-War Britain* (London: Croom Helm, 1980) pp. 164–6.

16. Macintyre, *Little Moscows*, ch. 8.

17. J. Hill, *Nelson: Politics, Economy, Community* (Edinburgh: Keele University Press, 1997) pp. 92–3.

18. See J. Lowerson and J. Myerscough, *Time to Spare in Victorian England* (Hassocks: Harvester, 1977). See also ch. 5.

19. R. Roberts, 'The Corporation as Impresario: The Municipal Provision of Entertainment in Victorian and Edwardian Bournemouth', in J. Walton and J. Walvin, eds, *Leisure in Britain 1780–1939* (Manchester: Manchester University Press, 1983) p. 142.

20. See A. J. Durie and M. J. Huggins, 'Sport, Social Tone and the Seaside Resorts of Great Britain, c.1850–1914', *International Journal of the History of Sport*, I (1998) 173–87.

21. J. Walton, 'Municipal Government and the Holiday Industry in Blackpool, 1876–1914', in Walton and Walvin, *Leisure in Britain*, pp. 160–85.

22. Walton, 'Municipal Government in Blackpool', p. 182.

23. T. Bennett, 'Hegemony, Ideology, Pleasure: Blackpool', in T. Bennett, C. Mercer and J. Wollacott, *Popular Culture and Social Relations* (Milton Keynes: Open University Press, 1986) p. 142.

24. J. Stevenson, *British Society, 1914–45* (Harmondsworth: Penguin, 1984) pp. 307–9.

25. See J. M. Lee, *Social Leaders and Public Persons: A Study of County Government in Cheshire Since 1888* (Oxford: Clarendon Press, 1963).

26. H. Laski, W. Jennings and W. Robson, *A Century of Municipal Progress, 1835–1935* (London: George Allen and Unwin, 1935) p. 430.

27. R. Roberts, 'The Corporation as Impresario', pp. 138–9.

28. Rhodes, *Beyond Westminster*, argues this forcefully (pp. 194, 206–7).

29. N. Hayes, *Consensus and Controversy: City Politics in Nottingham, 1945–66* (Liverpool: Liverpool University Press, 1996) ch. 8.

30. N. Tiratsoo, *Reconstruction, Affluence and Labour Politics: Coventry, 1945–60* (London: Routledge, 1990) pp. 85, 102.

31. B. Houlihan, *The Government and Politics of Sport* (London: Routledge, 1991) pp. 51–2.

32. Houlihan, *Government and Politics of Sport*, pp. 54–64; I. Henry and P. Bramham, 'Leisure, the Local State and Social Order', *Leisure Studies*, 5 (1986) 189–210. The professional experts of local government have been seen as one source of the loss of council chamber influence in the post-war years. See Rhodes, *Beyond Westminster*, pp. 187–8.

33. Quoted in J. Sugden and A. Bairner, *Sport, Sectarianism and Society in a Divided Ireland* (Leicester: Leicester University Press, 1993) p. 115.

34. J. Sugden and A. Bairner, *Sport, Sectarianism and Society*, ch. 6; 'Northern Ireland: The Politics of Leisure in a Divided Society', *Leisure Studies*, 5 (1986); Houlihan, *Government and Politics of Sport*, pp. 65–7. The Sports Council for Northern Ireland has continued to try and overcome sectarian allegiances through the promotion of equality in sport; see, for example, *Sport in the Community: A Policy for the Sports Council of Northern Ireland* (Belfast: Sports Council for Northern Ireland, n.d. [c.2000]).

35. See J. Hargreaves, *Sport, Power and Culture: A Social and Historical Analysis of Popular Sports in Britain* (Cambridge: Polity Press, 1986) pp. 188–9.

36. See I. P. Henry, *The Politics of Leisure Policy* (Basingstoke: Macmillan – now Palgrave, 1993) ch. 7.

37. Department of the Environment, *Sport and Recreation* (London: HMSO, 1975) pp. 1–2.

38. Department of Environment, *Sport and Recreation*, p. 16.

39. Department of Environment, *Sport and Recreation*, pp. 56–63.
40. Henry, *Politics of Leisure Policy*, pp. 190–203.
41. See, for example: C. Brackenridge and D. Woodward, 'Gender Inequalities in Leisure and Sport in Post-War Britain', in J. Obelkevich and P. Catterall, eds, *Understanding Post-War British Society* (London: Routledge, 1994) pp. 192–203; A. Phelps, 'Recreation', in S. Brazier and others, *A New Geography of Nottingham* (Nottingham: Trent Polytechnic, 1988 edn) pp. 91–102.

11 CONCLUSION: DESCRIBING CYRANO'S NOSE

1. E. Rostand, *Cyrano de Bergerac* (Paris: Fasquelle/Le Livre de Poche, 1964 edn) pp. 44–5.
2. See Celia Brackenridge and Diana Woodward, 'Gender Inequalities in Leisure and Sport in Post-War Britain', in James Obelkevich and Peter Catterall, eds, *Understanding Post-War British Society* (London: Routledge, 1994) ch. 15.
3. Richard Holt and Tony Mason, *Sport in Britain, 1945–2000* (Oxford: Blackwell, 2000) pp. 8, 120.
4. John Benson, *The Rise of Consumer Society in Britain, 1880–1980* (London: Longman, 1995) chs 3, 4 and 5. The proportion of real income spent on both shopping and sport actually declined in the long term.
5. Stefan Szymanski and Tim Kuypers, *Winners and Losers* (Harmondsworth: Penguin Books, 2000) p. 1.
6. Figures quoted in Holt and Mason, *Sport in Britain*, p. 166.
7. See, for example, Martin J. Weiner, *English Culture and the Decline of the Industrial Spirit, 1850–1980* (Harmondsworth: Penguin Books, 1985).
8. A. H. Halsey, *Trends in British Society Since 1900: A Guide to the Changing Social Structure of Britain* (London: Macmillan, 1972) pp. 18–19.
9. *Social Trends*, 21 (London: HMSO, 1991) pp. 186–7.
10. See, for example, *New Statesman*, 2 April 2001, pp. 23–4.
11. See *Guardian*, 2 May 2001.
12. See Jean-François Lyotard, *The Postmodern Condition: A Report on Knowledge*, trans. G. Bennington and B. Massumi (Manchester: Manchester University Press, 1984).
13. R. Holt, *Sport and the British: A Modern History*. (Oxford: Oxford University Press, 1990 edn) p. 355.
14. J. Hargreaves, *Sport, Power and Culture: A Social and Historical Analysis of Popular Sports in Britain* (Cambridge: Polity Press, 1986).
15. See, for example, C. M. Parratt, 'Making Leisure Work: Women's Rational Recreation in Late Victorian and Edwardian England', *Journal of Sport History* 26, 3 (1999) 471–87.
16. See Guttmann, *The Erotic in Sports* (New York: Columbia University Press, 1996); Alphonso Lingis, *Foreign Bodies* (New York: Routledge, 1994).
17. J.-M. Brohm, *Sport – A Prison of Measured Time. Essays*, trans. I. Fraser (London: Ink Links, 1978).
18. See D. Harvey, *The Condition of Postmodernity: An Enquiry into the Origins of Cultural Change* (Oxford: Blackwell, 1990) pp. 121–4.

19. See C. Rojek, *Leisure and Culture* (Basingstoke: Macmillan – now Palgrave, 2000) p. 20.

20. See T. S. Eliot, *Notes Towards the Definition of Culture* (London: Faber and Faber, 1948).

21. See G. Orwell, 'Boys' Weeklies', in *The Penguin Essays of George Orwell* (London: Penguin Books, 1984) pp. 84–106; 'Every hobby and pastime – cage-birds, fretwork, carpentering, bees, carrier-pigeons, home conjuring, philately, chess – has at least one paper devoted to it, and generally several.' Also R. McKibbin, 'Work and Hobbies in Britain, 1880–1950', in J. Winter, ed., *The Working Class in Modern British History: Essays in Honour of Henry Pelling* (Cambridge: Cambridge University Press, 1983) p. 142.

22. J. B. Priestley, *English Journey* (Harmondsworth: Penguin Books, 1977 edn) p. 377.

23. In 1990, for example, the Charity Household Survey reported that female participation in a wide range of voluntary activity significantly outnumbered male. *Social Trends*, 20 (London: HMSO, 1990) p. 167.

24. Clifford Geertz, 'Deep Play: Notes on the Balinese Cockfight', in *The Interpretation of Cultures: Selected Essays* (New York: Basic Books, 1973) pp. 412–53.

25. Stuart Hall, 'Notes on Deconstructing "The Popular"', in R. Samuel, ed., *People's History and Socialist Theory* (London: Routledge and Kegan Paul, 1981) pp. 227–40.

26. Howard Jacobson, *The Mighty Walzer* (London: Vintage, 2000) p. 361.

Further Reading

1 GENERAL

This section contains books that are general in that they cover a large part of the period or the topics included in this book, or that they are key texts but do not fit easily into the other sections of further reading.

Bailey, P. *Leisure and Class in Victorian England*. London: Routledge, 1987 edn. Classic pioneering study which marries leisure and social history in masterly fashion.

Bale, J. *Sport and Place: A Geography of Sport in England, Scotland and Wales*. London: C. Hurst & Company, 1982. Important work by the leading geographer of sport in Britain.

Beckles, H. and Stoddart, B., eds. *Liberation Cricket: West Indies Cricket Culture*. Manchester: Manchester University Press, 1995. Contains some brilliant essays; especially good on the theme of sport and identity.

Birley, D. *Land of Sport and Glory: Sport and British Society 1889–1910*. Manchester: Manchester University Press, 1995. Good discussion of some of the key themes in the early part of the century.

Blake, A. *The Body Language: The Meaning of Modern Sport*. London: Lawrence & Wishart, 1996. Interesting contribution which opens up an important avenue into the semiotics of sport.

Bourke, J. *Working-Class Cultures in Britain, 1890–1960: Gender, Class and Ethnicity*. London: Routledge, 1994. Useful overview, though should say more about sport than it does.

Central Statistical Office. *Annual Abstract of Statistics. No. 98, 1961*. London: HMSO, 1961.

——. *Social Trends*, No. 10, 1980; No. 20, 1990; No. 21, 1991. London: HMSO, 1980, 1990, 1991.

Clarke, J. and Critcher, C. *The Devil Makes Work: Leisure in Capitalist Britain*. London: Macmillan, 1984. A refreshingly radical look at the question of leisure, seeking to bring the question into a cultural studies analysis and link it with broader aspects of social relationships.

Collini, S. *English Pasts: Essays in History and Culture*. Oxford: Oxford University Press, 1999. Illuminating read which repays careful attention for those interested in the links between historical and cultural matters; makes you wish he wrote more about sport and leisure.

Cox, R., Jarvie, G. and Vamplew, W. *Encyclopedia of British Sport*. Oxford: ABC-Clio, 2000. Invaluable coverage of a host of sport-related topics.

Cunningham, H. *Leisure in the Industrial Revolution c.1780–c.1880*. London: Croom Helm, 1980. Another classic; helped to define the field of leisure for historians; alert to theory but not a slave to it.

Davies, A. *Leisure, Gender and Poverty: Working Class Culture in Salford and Manchester 1900–1939*. Buckingham: Open University Press, 1992. Imaginative case study using oral history to great effect.

Dunning, E. and Rojek, C. *Sport and Leisure in the Civilizing Process*. Basingstoke: Macmillan – now Palgrave, 1992. Valuable book providing both an excellent overview of sociological approaches to sport and leisure, and interesting contributions from leading practitioners for and against the 'civilizing process'.

Fussell, P. *Wartime: Understanding and Behavior in the Second World War*. Oxford: Oxford University Press, 1989. Little on sport, but excellent on soldiers' leisure and brilliantly written.

Galbraith, J. K. *The Affluent Society*. London: Andre Deutsch, 1977 3rd edn. Seminal study of a new 'problem' for western societies in the 1950s and 1960s.

Green, E., Hebron, S. and Woodward, D. *Women's Leisure, What Leisure?* Basingstoke: Macmillan – now Palgrave, 1990. Important research bringing fresh insights into the relationship between leisure and gender.

Guttmann, A. *From Ritual to Record: The Nature of Modern Sports*. New York: Columbia University Press, 1978. Valuable historical survey with strong sociological leaning.

——. *The Erotic in Sports*. New York: Columbia University Press, 1996. Interesting angle; relies on American examples in the main.

Halsey, A. H., ed. *Trends in British Society Since 1900: A Guide to the Changing Social Structure of Britain*. Basingstoke: Macmillan – now Palgrave, 1992. A mass of interesting statistics, with a series of valuable commentaries of different aspects of society.

Hargreaves, Jennifer, ed. *Sport, Culture and Ideology*. London: Routledge and Kegan Paul, 1982. A book which registered the importance of theory in studying sport. More sociological than historical, but an essential text for anyone studying sport.

Hargreaves, Jennifer. *Sporting Females: Critical Issues in the History and Sociology of Women's Sports*. London: Routledge, 1994. A sociologist's book, with the history a little thin, but still *the* key British text on sport and women.

Hargreaves, John. *Sport, Power and Culture: A Social and Historical Analysis of Popular Sports in Britain*. Cambridge: Polity Press, 1987. Interesting historical study with a powerful, if debatable, argument.

Hayes, N. and Hill, J., eds. *'Millions Like Us'? British Culture in the Second World War*. Liverpool: Liverpool University Press, 1999. Contains useful discussions on various aspects of sport and leisure in wartime.

Hill, J. and Williams, J., eds. *Sport and Identity in the North of England*. Keele: Keele University Press, 1996. One of the first contributions to take the issue of sport and identity outside a 'Celtic' context.

Holt, R. *Sport and the British*. Oxford: Oxford University Press, 1990 edn. Another classic, and will remain so for a long time. Quite simply a brilliant book.

Holt, R., ed. *Sport and the Working Class in Modern Britain*. Manchester: Manchester University Press, 1990. Contains some valuable contributions, with significance beyond the book's title.

Holt, R. and Mason, T. *Sport in Britain, 1945–2000*. Oxford: Blackwell, 2000. An excellent analysis of the major themes in sport; informative and highly readable.

James, C. L. R. *Beyond a Boundary*. London: Stanley Paul, 1969 edn. Regarded as a classic; certainly one of the first books to link sport and politics in a serious way, though parts of it are overly tendentious and, dare one say, pretentious.

Jarvie, G., ed. *Sport, Racism and Ethnicity*. London: Falmer Press, 1991. Valuable study of this still under-explored topic.

Johnson, P., ed. *Twentieth Century Britain: Economic, Social and Cultural Change*. London: Longman, 1994. Useful collection with good chapters on sport and leisure.

Jones, S. G. *Workers At Play: A Social and Economic History of Leisure, 1918–1939*. London: Routledge and Kegan Paul, 1986. Detailed and innovative coverage of the relationship between leisure and the working class.

———. *Sport, Politics and the Working Class: Organised Labour and Sport in Inter-War Britain*. Manchester: Manchester University Press, 1992 edn. Further develops the themes investigated in the above book.

Langhamer, C. *Women's Leisure in England, 1920–60*. Manchester: Manchester University Press, 2000. Important study, using oral testimony.

Llewellyn Smith, H. *The New Survey of London Life and Labour*, Vol. IX *Life and Leisure*. London: P. S. King and Son Ltd, 1935. Fascinating volume with a mass of observation on leisure in 1930s London.

Lowerson, J. *Sport and the English Middle Classes, 1870–1914*. Manchester: Manchester University Press, 1993. Excellent study; the first explicitly to examine middle-class involvement in sport.

Lowerson, J. and Myerscough, J. *Time to Spare in Victorian England*. Brighton: Harvester Press, 1977. Valuable introductory study with a strong south coast emphasis.

MacKenzie, J. M., ed. *Imperialism and Popular Culture*. Manchester: Manchester University Press, 1986. Contains important chapters on leisure.

McKibbin, R. *Classes and Cultures, 1918–1951*. Oxford: Oxford University Press, 1998. Extremely interesting and detailed study of the ways in which cultural life influences class relationships.

Mangan, J. A. *The Games Ethic and Imperialism: Aspects of the Diffusion of an Ideal*. Harmondsworth: Viking, 1986. Pioneering study by a historian who has himself pioneered sport history in Britain.

———. *Athleticism in the Victorian and Edwardian Public School: The Emergence and Consolidation of an Educational Ideology*. Cambridge: Cambridge University Press, 1981. Brilliant and highly-informative study of public school culture and its contribution to the idea of games.

Marwick, A. *British Society Since 1945*. London: Penguin Books, 1991 edn. Absolutely essential accompaniment to any study of post-1945 Britain; extremely informative, and always provocative.

Mason, T., ed. *Sport in Britain: A Social History*. Cambridge: Cambridge University Press, 1989. Excellent collection of influential essays; a major contribution to the social history of sport.

Mason, T. *Sport in Britain*. London: Faber & Faber, 1988. Valuable introductory discussion which opens up key themes.

Mass-Observation. (Madge, C. and Harrison, T.) *Britain*. Harmondsworth: Penguin Books, 1939. Interesting observations on a range of topics.

Office For National Statistics. *Annual Abstract of Statistics*. No. 134, 1998. London: Stationery Office, 1998.

——. *Social Trends*. No. 30, 2000. London: Stationery Office, 2000.

Perkin, H. *The Rise of Professional Society: England Since 1880*. London: Routledge, 1989. Little on sport, more on leisure; but an important study by a historian who helped to put British social history on the academic map.

Polley, M. *Moving the Goalposts: A History of Sport and Society Since 1945*. London: Routledge, 1998. Masterly synthesis within a thematic treatment.

Reynolds, D. *Rich Relations: The American Occupation of Britain, 1942–1945*. London: HarperCollins Publishers, 1995. A *magnum opus* if ever there was one; makes one feel that there might be such a thing as 'definitive' history.

Rojek, C. *Decentring Leisure: Rethinking Leisure Theory*. London: Sage Publications, 1995. Interesting and challenging study by a leading sociologist of leisure.

——. *Leisure and Culture*. Basingstoke: Macmillan – now Palgrave, 2000. Takes the analysis into new areas, and sheds some of the conventional moral hang-ups about 'leisure'.

Shanks, M. *The Stagnant Society*. Harmondsworth: Penguin Books, 1961. Perhaps the characteristic statement of early 1960s academic *ennui* with British society. A clarion call for 'modernization'.

Slater, D. 'Work/Leisure', in Jenks, C., ed. *Core Sociological Dichotomies*. London: Sage Publications, 1998, pp. 391–404. Useful discussion of sociological themes and issues.

Smith, D. and Williams, G. *Fields of Praise: The Official History of the Welsh Rugby Union, 1881–1981*. Cardiff: The University of Wales Press, 1980. Wonderfully passionate and incisive account of Welsh rugby, with one of the best titles of any sport book.

Stoddart, B. 'Cricket and Colonialism in the English-Speaking Caribbean to 1914: Towards a Cultural Analysis', in Mangan, J. A., ed. *Pleasure, Profit, Proselytism: British Culture and Sport at Home and Abroad, 1780–1914*. London: Frank Cass, 1988, pp. 231–57. An excellent example how to conduct a close analysis of a local society; sport, status and race are intertwined in a fascinating way.

Wigglesworth, N. *The Evolution of English Sport*. London: Frank Cass, 1996. Good general history.

Williams, J. *Cricket and England: A Cultural and Social History of the Interwar Years*. London: Frank Cass, 1999. A gem; marvellously original; more cultural history should be like this.

Wilson, E. *Only Halfway to Paradise: Women in Postwar Britain, 1945–68*. London: Tavistock Publications, 1980. Important contribution to women's history, if a little 'Whiggish'.

Wimbush, E. and Talbot, M. *Relative Freedoms – Women and Leisure*. Milton Keynes: Open University Press, 1988. One of the most important studies on women and leisure, with a range of valuable case studies.

Winship, J. *Inside Women's Magazines*. London: Pandora, 1987. Illuminating analysis on representations of gender.

Zweig, F. *The Worker in an Affluent Society: Family Life and Industry*. London: Heinemann, 1961. Some first-hand accounts of working class life in the 1950s.

2 SPORT AND BUSINESS

Benson, J. *The Rise of Consumer Society in Britain, 1880–1980*. London: Longman, 1994. Very important pioneering study of sport and leisure as consumption, with valuable contributions on sport, shopping and tourism.

Chinn, C. *Better Betting with a Decent Feller: Bookmaking, Betting and the British Working Class, 1750–1900*. London: Harvester/Wheatsheaf, 1991. Essential reading, alongside Clapson (see below).

Clapson, M. *A Bit of a Flutter: Popular Gambling and English Society, c.1823–1961*. Manchester: Manchester University Press, 1992.

Collins, T. *Rugby's Great Split: Class, Culture and the Origins of Rugby League Football*. London: Frank Cass, 1998. The first detailed analysis of the class and regional conflicts that brought about the secession of northern clubs from the RFU.

Inglis, S. *The Football Grounds of Britain*. London: CollinsWillow, 1996 edn. Enormously impressive and interesting; a book that deserves far more credit among academic historians than it has received.

King, A. *The End of the Terraces: The Transformation of English Football in the 1990s*. Leicester: Leicester University Press, 1998. Looks at the impact of new entrepreneurs on post-Taylor football.

Korr, C. *West Ham United: The Making of a Football Club*. London: Duckworth, 1986. This is how the social and business history of an individual club should be done; contains some remarkable insights.

Mason, T. *Association Football & English Society, 1863–1915*. Brighton: Harvester Press, 1981 edn. An absolutely seminal book; Mason is to sports history what Bobby Jones was to golf.

Rae, S. *W. G. Grace: A Life*. London: Faber & Faber, 1998. Long, detailed, and excellent.

Russell, D. *Football and the English: A Social History of Association Football in England, 1863–1995*. London: Carnegie Publishing, 1997. The best general history of English football there is.

Szymanski, S. and Kuypers, T. *Winners and Losers*. London: Penguin Books, 2000 edn. Very statistical, and therefore useful, especially on the 1990s.

Tischler, S. *Footballers and Businessmen: The Origins of Professional Soccer in England*. New York: Holmes and Meier, 1981. Important pioneering study of football as business.

Tranter, N. *Sport, Economy and Society in Britain, 1750–1914*. Cambridge: Cambridge University Press, 1998. Excellent short analysis of a key period in sporting changes; part of a high-class series whose aim is to discuss and evaluate the work of historians.

Vamplew, W. *Pay Up and Play the Game: Professional Sport in Britain, 1875–1914*. Cambridge: Cambridge University Press, 1988. Another classic; the 'definitive' study of the commercialization of sport in Britain in this period.

Varley, N. *Golden Boy: A Biography of Wilf Mannion*. London: Aurum Press, 1997. Good player biography, with a strong grasp of the social and economic context of employment in football.

Walvin, J. *The People's Game: A Social History of British Football*. London: Allen Lane, 1975. Pioneering and readable study by a leading social historian, with a 1994 revised edition; now surpassed by Russell (see above).

3 SPORT AND MEDIA

Arlott, J. *Basingstoke Boy: The Autobiography*. London: Fontana, 1992 edn. Curious autobiography which conceals as much as it reveals.

Cadogan, M. and Craig, P. *You're A Brick, Angela! A New Look at Girl's Fiction from 1839–1975*. London: Victor Gollancz, 1976. Useful study, though relatively little on sport.

Carpenter, H. and Prichard, M. *The Oxford Companion to Children in Literature*. Oxford: Oxford University Press, 1984. Valuable general reference.

Cullingford, C. *Children's Literature and its Effects: The Formative Years*. London: Cassell, London, 1998. Useful.

Glanville, B. *Football Memories*. London: Virgin Publishing, 1999. Interesting account of the interesting life of one of Britain's leading sport writers; a little grumpy in places.

——. *People in Sport*. London: Secker & Warburg, 1967. Contains some good examples of 1960s sport.

Hardcastle, M. *Soccer Special*. London: Dean, 1992 edn. Sport stories aimed at youngsters.

Hobson, J. W. and Henry, H. *The Hulton Readership Survey*. London: Hulton Press, 1947. Invaluable detail on newspaper circulation and readership compiled to inform advertisers.

Hornby, N. *Fever Pitch*. London: Gollancz, 1992. The classic piece of 1990s 'new writing' on football; spawned a whole genre.

Kelly, S. F., ed. *A Game of Two Halves*. London: Mandarin, 1993 edn. Valuable collection of pieces on football.

MacDonnell, A. G. *England Their England*. London: Macmillan, 1964 edn. Oft-quoted for its chapter on the village cricket match, but nowadays less often read; a still-lively and amusing account of 1920s England with an almost surrealist ending.

Rader, B. *In Its Own Image: How Television Has Transformed Sports*. London: Collier Macmillan, 1984. Important study by a leading American academic.

Richards, J. *Happiest Days: The Public Schools in English Fiction*. Manchester: Manchester University Press, 1988. Good study from a historian whose main emphasis has been on the cinema.

Seymour-Ure, C. *The British Press and Broadcasting Since 1945*. Oxford: Blackwell, 1991. Useful overview.

Whannel, G. *Fields in Vision: Television, Sport and Cultural Transformation*. London: Routledge, 1992. A key study bringing together detailed observation of broadcasting practice and theoretical insight drawn from cultural studies.

Wolstenholme, K. *Sports Special*. London: Stanley Paul, 1956. Early autobiographical account of television sports broadcasting.

4 CINEMA

Aldgate, A. and Richards, J. *Britain Can Take It: The British Cinema in the Second World War.* Edinburgh: Edinburgh University Press, 1994 edn. Good detail on key films.

Bailey, P. *Popular Culture and Performance in the Victorian City.* Cambridge: Cambridge University Press, 1998. Collection of previously published essays which trace important features of popular culture in the pre-film era.

Barr, C., ed. *All Our Yesterdays: 90 Years of British Cinema.* London: British Film Institute, 1986. Excellent overview.

Dixon, W. W., ed. *Re-Viewing British Cinema, 1900–1992: Essays and Interviews.* Albany: State University of New York Press, 1994. Useful though uneven collection of pieces.

Murphy, R., ed. *The British Cinema Book.* London: British Film Institute, 1997. Covers a wide range and extremely useful.

O'Brien, M. and Eyles, A., eds. *Enter the Dream House: Memories of Cinemas in South London from the Twenties to the Sixties.* London: British Film Institute, 1993. Interesting account of cinema styles and culture.

Pimlott, B. *Harold Wilson.* London: HarperCollins Publishers, 1993 edn. Classic biography which covers Wilson's work on the film industry at the Board of Trade in the 1940s and early 1950s.

Ramsden, J. 'Refocusing the People's War: British War Films of the 1950s', *Journal of Contemporary History*, 1 (1998) 35–63. Stimulating essay on class representations in 1950s war films.

Rattigan, N. 'The Last Gasp of the Middle Class: British War Films of the 1950s', in Dixon, W. W., ed., *Re-Viewing British Cinema, 1900–1992: Essays and Interviews.* Albany: State University of New York Press, 1994. pp. 143–53. Similar to above.

Richards, J. *Stars In Our Eyes: Lancashire Stars of Stage, Screen and Radio.* Preston: Lancashire County Books, 1994. Entertaining piece, very readable, with the added virtue of rescuing the great Frank Randle from the enormous condecension of posterity.

——. *Visions of Yesterday.* London: Routledge and Kegan Paul, 1975. Incisive analysis of historical films in a number of contexts, including that of Britain and its empire.

Richards, J. and Sheridan, D. eds. *Mass-Observation at the Movies.* London: Routledge and Kegan Paul, 1987. Valuable use of MO material.

Stead, P. *Film and the Working Class: The Feature Film in British and American Society.* London: Routledge, 1991 edn. Excellent study, strong on analysis of key films.

5 HOLIDAYS AND TOURISM

Burkart, A. J. and Medlik, S. *Tourism: Past, Present and Future.* London: Heinemann, 1981 edn. Good overview with a wealth of statistics up to the late 1970s.

Hewison, R. *The Heritage Industry: Britain in a Climate of Decline.* London: Methuen, 1987. Perhaps the key study of the rise of the heritage industry, with a powerful and critical thesis.

Inglis, F. *The Delicious History of the Holiday.* London: Routledge, 2000. Interesting mixture of history and cultural studies; displays great erudition.

MacCannell, D. *Empty Meeting Grounds: The Tourist Papers*. London: Routledge, 1992. Useful collection of essays from a leading American theorist of tourism.

Perkin, H. *The Age of the Railway*. London: Panther Books, 1970. Excellent social history of the impact of the railways, with a brilliant chapter on holidays.

Pimlott, J. A. R. *The Englishman's Holiday: A Social History*. Hassocks: Harvester Press, 1976 edn. Written just after the Second World War, and still as interesting as anything done since on this topic.

Poole, R. *The Lancashire Wakes Holidays*. Preston: Lancashire County Books, 1994. Valuable 'local' case study of the transformation of holiday practices.

Ring, J. *How the English Made the Alps*. London: Murray, 2000. Good study of a case of English tourist imperialism.

Urry, J. *The Tourist Gaze: Leisure and Travel in Contemporary Societies*. London: Sage, 1990. Important study by the leading British theorist on tourism; marries sociology and cultural studies in interesting and very helpful ways.

——. *Consuming Places*. London: Routledge, 1995. A collection of essays which covers some of the same ground as above.

Walton, J. K. *The English Seaside Resort: A Social History, 1750–1914*. Leicester: Leicester University Press, 1983. Opening salvo from the country's leading social historian of the seaside.

——. *The British Seaside: Holidays and Resorts in the Twentieth Century*. Manchester: Manchester University Press, 2000. Some two decades after the above Walton brings together in compelling fashion a range of aspects of seaside development; this is the seaside history of the twentieth century *par excellence* with geography, economics, sociology, cultural studies and literature all brought to bear on the subject.

Walton, J. K. and Walvin, J. *Leisure in Britain, 1780–1939*. Manchester: Manchester University Press, 1983. Important collection with heavyweight contributions, especially on tourism.

Walvin, J. *Beside the Seaside: A Social History of the Popular Seaside Holiday*. London: Allen Lane, 1978. More 'popular' in approach than Walton, but an important introductory analysis.

6 RADIO AND TELEVISION

Ang, I. *Watching Dallas: Soap Opera and the Melodramatic Imagination*. (trans. Couling, D.) London: Routledge, 1989. Celebrated analysis of a prime component of contemporary television viewing.

Briggs, A. *The History of Broadcasting in the UK*.

——. Vol. I *The Birth of Broadcasting*. London: Oxford University Press, 1961.

——. Vol. II *The Golden Age of Wireless*. London: Oxford University Press, 1965.

——. Vol. IV *Sound and Vision*. Oxford: Oxford University Press, 1979.

——. Vol. V *Competition, 1955–1974*. Oxford: Oxford University Press, 1995. An extensive history of broadcasting which provides information on virtually everything; inevitably an institutional bias, though, and needs to be set alongside some of those studies which seek to open up the issue of the 'reception' of programmes.

Buscombe, E., ed. *British Television: A Reader*. Oxford: Clarendon Press, 2000. Very valuable and up-to-date collection.

Corner, J., ed. *Popular Television in Britain: Studies in Cultural History*. London: British Film Institute Publishing, 1991. Also very important and authoritative.

Crisell, A. *An Introductory History of British Broadcasting*. London: Routledge, 1997. Good overview of a big topic; excellent starting point.

Jennings, H. and Gill, W. *Broadcasting in Everyday Life: A Survey of the Social Effects of the Coming of Broadcasting*. London: BBC, n.d. [1939]. Interesting early attempt, based on a working-class district of Bristol, to understand the effects of radio; on the whole provides a positive picture.

O'Sullivan, T. 'Television Memories and Culture of Viewing, 1950–65', in Corner, J., ed. *Popular Television in Britain: Studies in Cultural History*. London: British Film Institute, 1991, pp. 159–81. Important because it opens up new ground by considering viewers' reactions to television.

Pegg, M. *Broadcasting and Society, 1918–1939*. London: Croom Helm, 1983. Very good history of a key period.

Report of the Committee on Broadcasting (the Pilkington Report). London: HMSO, 1962 (Cmnd. 1753). Perhaps the most important official enquiry into broadcasting; a very good source for 'elite' attitudes about television.

Scannell, P. and Cardiff, D. *A Social History of British Broadcasting, Vol. I 1922–39: Serving the Nation*. Oxford: Basil Blackwell, 1991. First-rate account which complements Pegg (see above).

Silverstone, R. *Television and Everyday Life*. London: Routledge, 1994. Looks at television's impact on individuals and families; intersting approach, if rather tough going.

Whitehead, K. *The Third Programme: A Literary History*. Oxford: Clarendon Press, 1989. Deals mainly with programme content.

7 YOUTH AND AGE

Abrams, M. *The Teenage Consumer*. London: London Press Exchange, 1959. Classic British account by a market-researcher which helped to confirm the concept of the 'teenager', though his definition includes people in their twenties.

Benson, J. *Prime Time: A History of the Middle Aged in Twentieth-Century Britain*. London: Longman, 1997. Another innovative study from Benson, invaluable on this topic.

Brake, M. *Comparative Youth Culture: The Sociology of Youth Culture and Youth Subcultures in America, Britain and Canada*. London: Routledge and Kegan Paul, 1985. Excellent, detailed and comparative; an invaluable book on this topic.

Cohen, S. *Folk Devils and Moral Panics: The Creation of the Mods and Rockers*. London: MacGibbon and Kee, 1972. Cited by everyone who works on contemporary youth culture; Cohen elaborates his thesis of the media as creators of images of deviance, which then stimulate 'deviants' to emulate them.

Fowler, D. *The First Teenagers: The Lifestyle of Young Wage-Earners in Interwar Britain*. London: Woburn Press, 1995. Very important study, based largely on the Manchester area, which places the emergence of the teenager in the 1930s.

Gorer, G. *Exploring British Character*. London: Cresset Press, 1955. Fascinating descriptions, originally written as newspapers articles, of British attitudes to a range of issues, especially sex; we emerge from this as a very 'proper' lot.

Gosling, R. *Lady Albemarle's Boys*. London: Fabian Society, 1961. Critical reaction from a youth club organizer to the Albemarle Report.

Hendrick, H. *Images of Youth: Age, Class, and the Male Youth Problem, 1880–1920*. Oxford: Clarendon Press, 1990. Important study which investigates the place of male youth in the labour market and 'official' perceptions of young people.

Jephcott, P. *Rising Twenty: Notes on Some Ordinary Girls*. London: Faber & Faber, 1948. This study, together with the slightly earlier one listed immediately below, provides a wealth of first-hand observation on mainly working-class girls; sensitively done, without moral overtone, showing immense understanding for the subjects, their families, and their communities.

———. *Girls Growing Up*. London: Faber & Faber, 1942.

Kelly, J. R., ed. *Activity and Ageing: Staying Involved in Later Life*. London: Sage Publications, 1995. Useful material on this neglected topic.

Leech, K. *Youthquake: The Growth of a Counter-Culture Through Two Decades*. London: Sheldon Press, 1973. Worth reading if only for the brilliant first chapter.

McRobbie, A. *Feminism and Youth Culture: From 'Jackie' to 'Just Seventeen'*. Basingstoke: Macmillan – now Palgrave, 1991. Collection of essays from one of the most perceptive cultural observers of female adolescence.

Ministry of Education. *The Youth Service in England and Wales*. London: HMSO, 1960. (Cmnd.929). The 'Albemarle Report', which sought to orchestrate the various players in the youth service of the late 1950s.

Osgerby, B. *Youth in Britain Since 1945*. Oxford: Blackwell, 1998. One of the most important studies of youth in the second half of the twentieth century.

Pearson, G. *Hooligan: A History of Respectable Fears*. London: Macmillan, 1983. Shows that moral panics did not start with the Teddy Boys.

Springhall, J. *Coming of Age: Adolescence in Britain, 1860–1960*. Dublin: Gill and Macmillan, 1986. Very perceptive study which complements Osgerby (see above).

Thompson, P., Itzin, C. and Abendstern, M. *I Don't Feel Old: The Experience of Later Life*. Oxford: Oxford University Press, 1991. Invaluable; based on oral testimony.

Wellings, K., Field, J., Johnson, A. and Wadsworth, J. (with Bradshaw, S.) *Sexual Behaviour in Britain: The National Survey of Sexual Attitudes and Lifestyle*. Harmondsworth: Penguin Books, 1994. Important source for 1980s/90s sexual attitudes and behaviour.

Willis, P. E. *Learning to Labour: How Working-Class Kids Get Working-Class Jobs*. Farnborough: Saxon House, 1977. Key study of how 'masculinity' is produced and reproduced.

8 CLUBS AND VOLUNTARY ASSOCIATIONS

Bishop, J. and Hoggett, P. *Organizing Around Enthusiasms*. London: Comedia, 1986. Useful account of contemporary voluntary activities.

Clark, P. *British Clubs and Societies, 1580–1800: The Origins of an Associational World*. Oxford: Oxford University Press, 2000. Major book by the leading historian on voluntary association in pre-nineteenth century Britain.

Dennis, N., Henriques, F. and Slaughter, C. *Coal Is Our Life: An Analysis of a Yorkshire Mining Community*. London: Eyre and Spottiswoode, 1956. Celebrated and frequently cited ethnographic study of miners and their families in 'Ashton' (Featherstone).

Frankenberg, R. *Communities in Britain: Social Life in Town and Country*. Harmondsworth: Penguin Books, 1966. Very valuable compilation from one of the leading academics in this field at the time.

Glass, R. *Newcomers: The West Indians in London*. London: Centre for Urban Studies/George Allen and Unwin, 1960. Early study of immigrant communities; Glass was a veteran social observer who had been working in the field since before the Second World War.

Harrison, T. *Britain Revisited*. London: Victor Gollancz, 1961. Rather eccentric study from one of the founders of Mass Observation.

Hill, J. *Nelson: Politics, Economy, Community*. Edinburgh: Keele University Press, 1997. Case study of a cotton town which attempts to show how 'civic identity' is created.

Holt, R. *Stanmore Golf Club, 1893–1993: A Social History*. Stanmore: Stanmore Golf Club, 1993. Classy case study of a golf club in the London suburbs; contains far more than the title might suggest.

Jackson, B. *Working Class Community: Some General Notions Raised by a Series of Studies in Northern England*. London: Routledge and Kegan Paul, 1968. Very valuable observations from a writer who knew the region intimately.

McKibbin, R. 'Work and Hobbies in Britain, 1880–1950', in Winter, J., ed. *The Working Class in Modern British History: Essays in Honour of Henry Pelling*. Cambridge: Cambridge University Press, 1983, pp. 127–46. Important study, mainly male-centred, of a perceived problem of early twentieth-century social and cultural history.

Mass-Observation. *The Pub and the People: A Worktown Study*. London: Victor Gollancz, 1943. In spite of MO's reputation for taking a romantic view of British popular society, this study, conducted just before the outbreak of the war, is immensely informative about the function of pubs in Bolton, Lancs.

Meller, H. *Leisure and the Changing City, 1870–1914*. London: Routledge and Kegan Paul, 1976. An important historical monograph on the provision of leisure and the activities of city elites in Bristol.

Stacey, M. *Tradition and Change: A Study of Banbury*. Oxford: Oxford University Press, 1960. Classic sociological study of a town and its associational life; immensely influential.

Willmott, P. and Young, M. *Family and Class in a London Suburb*. London: Routledge and Kegan Paul, 1960. Like Stacey (see above), Willmott and Young conducted pioneering sociological studies into communities, their transformation, and their reconstruction; an invaluable guide to the 'state of Britain' in the 1950s.

Young, M. and Willmott, P. *Family and Kinship in East London*. London: Routledge and Kegan Paul, 1957.

9 STATE: NATIONAL AND LOCAL

Allison, L., ed. *The Changing Politics of Sport*. Manchester: Manchester University Press, 1993. Valuable collection of essays by leading commentators on various aspects of sport and politics.

Central Committee of Physical Recreation. *Sport and the Community* (the Wolfenden Report). London: CCPR, 1960. Key document for what was happening to British sport at the end of the 1950s.

Coghlan, J. F. with Webb, I. M. *Sport and British Politics since 1960*. London: Falmer Press, 1990. Extremely informative and at times passionate account of the development of the Sports Council by a former Deputy Director.

Department of the Environment. *Sport and Recreation*. London: HMSO, 1975. Important White Paper published at a difficult time for the economy and urban relations.

Department of National Heritage. *Sport: Raising the Game*. London: Department of National Heritage, 1995. Policy statement setting out government plans to encourage sport with the help of funds from the National Lottery; interesting, rather moralistic foreword from the Prime Minister of the time, John Major.

Henry, I. *The Politics of Leisure Policy*. Basingstoke: Macmillan – now Palgrave, 1993. Valuable discussion of national and municipal policy, mainly relating to the later part of the twentieth century.

Houlihan, B. *The Government and Politics of Sport*. London: Routledge, 1991. Key text by the leading writer in this field; essential for this topic.

Howell, D. *Made in Birmingham: The Memoirs of Denis Howell*. London: MacDonald, Queen Anne Press, 1990. Howell was the first 'minister of sport', and this detailed and slightly dull autobiography covers some important developments such as the creation of the Sports Council and the D'Oliveira affair.

Labour Party. *Leisure for Living*. London: Labour Party, 1959. Labour was very upbeat about solving the 'problem' of leisure in 1959.

D'Oliveira, B. (with Murphy, P.) *Time to Declare: An Autobiography*. London: J. M. Dent & Sons, 1980. Contains intersting personal slant on the D'Oliveira affair.

Sugden, J. and Bairner, A. *Sport, Sectarianism and Society in a Divided Ireland*. Leicester: Leicester University Press, 1993. Excellent analysis of a unique situation; shows why there are so many leisure centres in Belfast.

Torkildsen, G. *Leisure and Recreation Management*. London: E. & F. N. Spon, 1992 edn. Worthwhile account; a book for the leisure management specialist.

Index